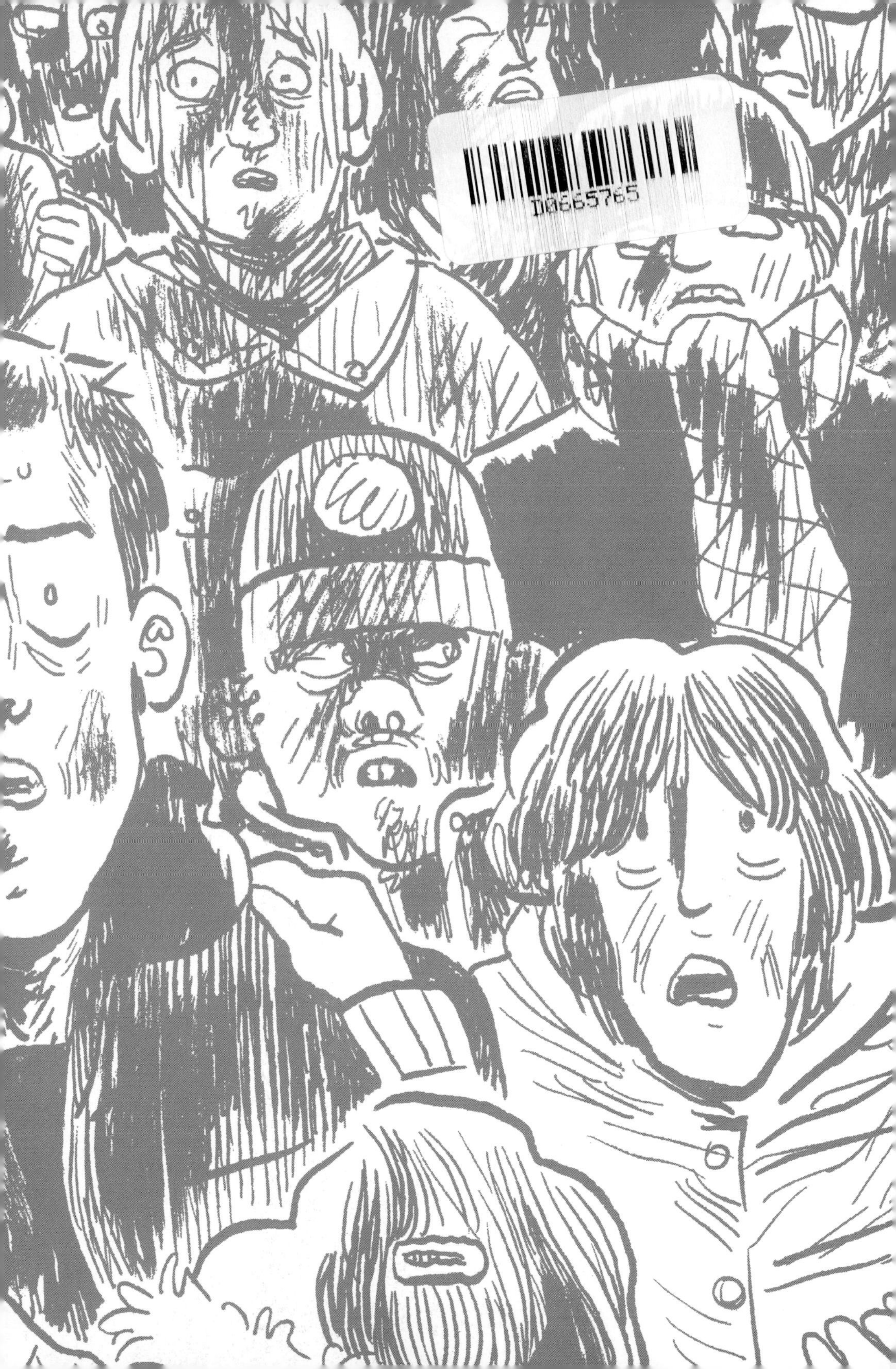

ALSO BY MIKE DAWSON:

FREDDIE & ME: A COMING-OF-AGE BOHEMIAN RHAPSODY
ACE-FACE: THE MOD WITH THE METAL ARMS
TROOP 142
ANGIE BONGIOLATTI

Art Direction by Tom Kaczynski

Design by Mike Dawson and Jordan Shiveley

Uncivilized Books
P.O. Box 6534
Minneapolis, MN 55406
USA
uncivilizedbooks.com

First Edition, April 2016

10 9 8 7 6 5 4 3 2 1

ISBN 978-1-941250-11-2

DISTRIBUTED TO THE TRADE BY:
Consortium Book Sales & Distribution, LLC.
34 Thirteenth Avenue NE, Suite 101
Minneapolis, MN 55413-1007
cbsd.com, Orders: (800) 283-3572

Printed in USA

RULES
FOR DATING MY
DAUGHTER

THE MODERN FATHER'S GUIDE
TO **GOOD** PARENTING

BY MIKE DAWSON

UNCIVILIZED BOOKS

AM I GOOD?

JANUARY 2014

I WAS AT DINNER WITH A FRIEND IN KENTUCKY WHO REMARKED AT ONE POINT OF HER STATE SENATOR, **RAND PAUL**:

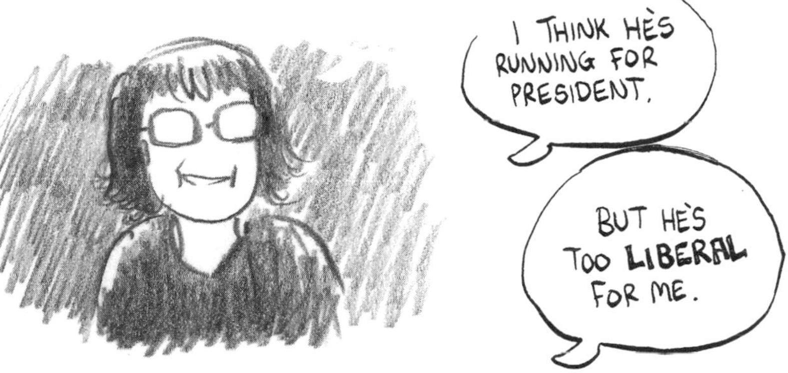
I THINK HE'S RUNNING FOR PRESIDENT.
BUT HE'S TOO **LIBERAL** FOR ME.

LATER THE SUBJECT OF THAT **DUCK DYNASTY** GUY CAME UP - HE'D BEEN IN THE NEWS A LOT-

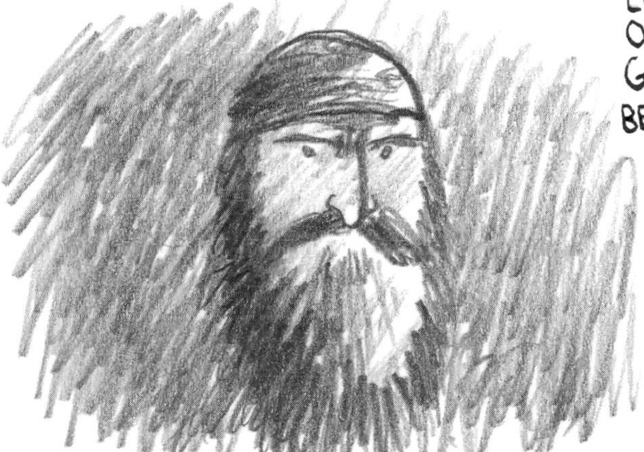

PERHAPS KNOWING THAT I DISAGREED **POLITICALLY** WITH THE THINGS THIS GUY HAD SAID, MY FRIEND SAID "BUT, HE'S A **GOOD** PERSON."

AND I THOUGHT, WHY?

BECAUSE HE
BELIEVES IN GOD?
BECAUSE HE GOES
TO CHURCH?

DOESN'T SAYING AND
THINKING **RACIST**,
HOMOPHOBIC, AND
MISOGYNIST THINGS
MAKE A PERSON
NOT-GOOD?

I DON'T GO TO
CHURCH, I DON'T
THINK I BELIEVE
IN GOD... DOES
THAT MAKE ME
LESS-GOOD?

I LIKE TO THINK I'M GOOD.

I HAVE "GOOD POLITICS".

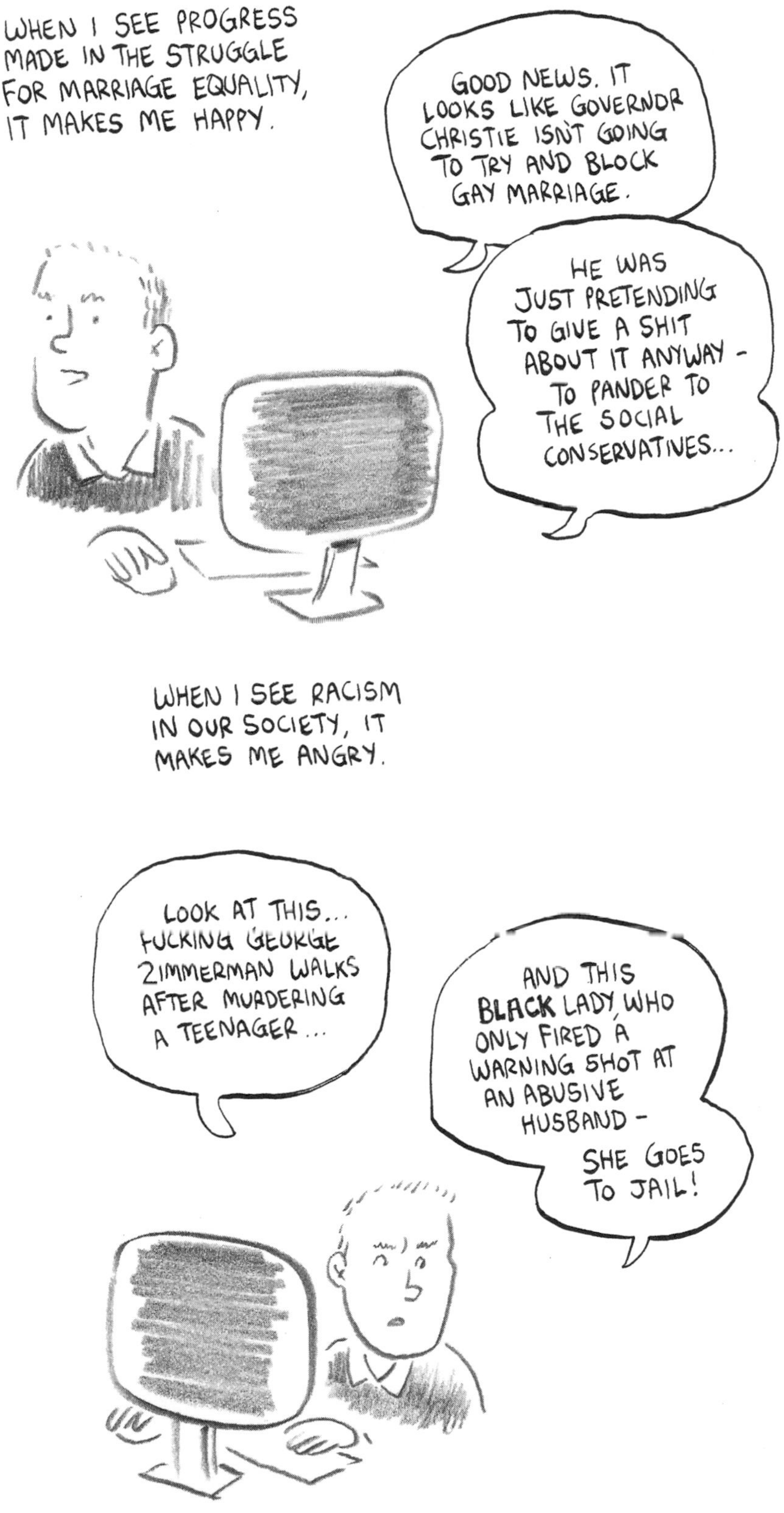
WHEN I SEE PROGRESS MADE IN THE STRUGGLE FOR MARRIAGE EQUALITY, IT MAKES ME HAPPY.
GOOD NEWS. IT LOOKS LIKE GOVERNOR CHRISTIE ISN'T GOING TO TRY AND BLOCK GAY MARRIAGE.
HE WAS JUST PRETENDING TO GIVE A SHIT ABOUT IT ANYWAY - TO PANDER TO THE SOCIAL CONSERVATIVES...
WHEN I SEE RACISM IN OUR SOCIETY, IT MAKES ME ANGRY.
LOOK AT THIS... FUCKING GEORGE ZIMMERMAN WALKS AFTER MURDERING A TEENAGER...
AND THIS BLACK LADY, WHO ONLY FIRED A WARNING SHOT AT AN ABUSIVE HUSBAND -
SHE GOES TO JAIL!

BUT,

I'LL CONFESS, I'M MAYBE NOT AS **CHARITABLE** AS I COULD BE.

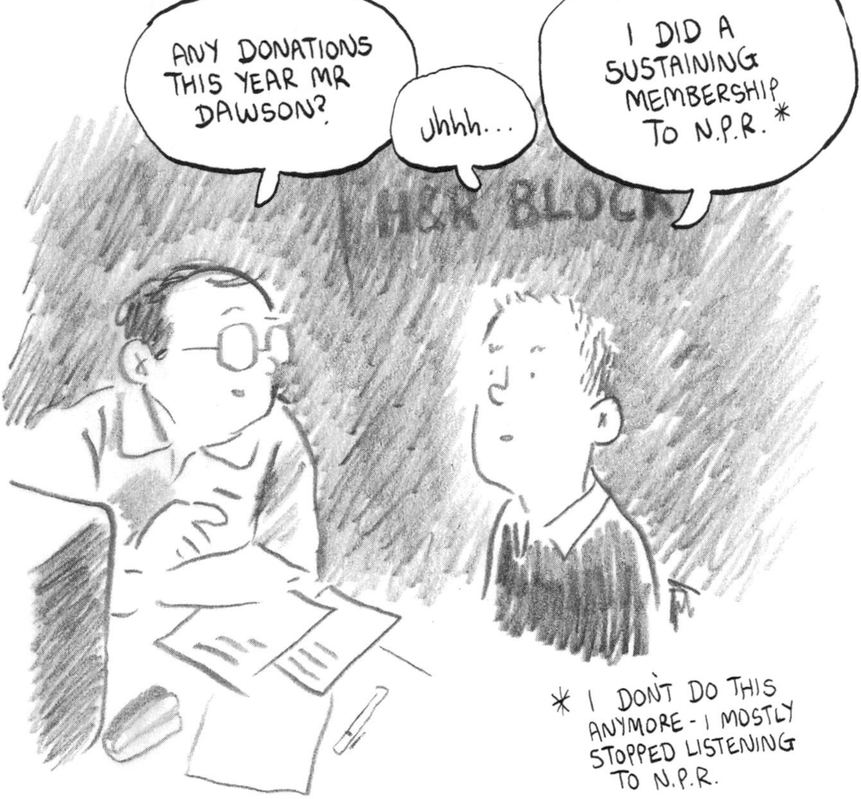
ANY DONATIONS THIS YEAR MR DAWSON?
Uhhh...
I DID A SUSTAINING MEMBERSHIP TO N.P.R. *
H&R BLOCK

* I DON'T DO THIS ANYMORE - I MOSTLY STOPPED LISTENING TO N.P.R.

TEN YEARS LIVING IN NEW YORK CITY HAD THE SHAMEFUL EFFECT OF HARDENING ME TO THE SIGHT OF THE HOMELESS.

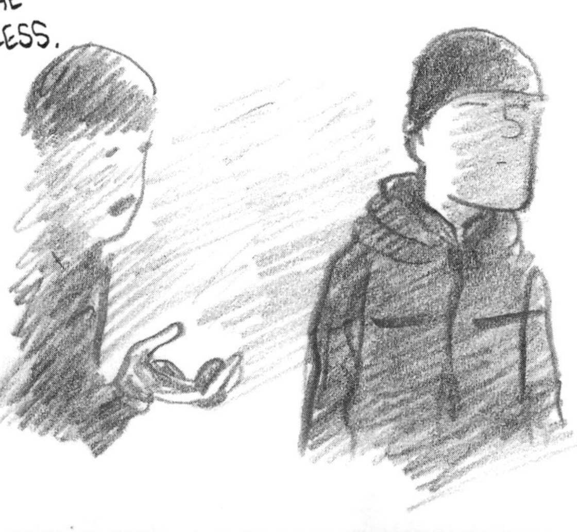

I'M VERY MUCH IN FAVOR OF MORE GUN CONTROL—

ESPECIALLY SINCE WHAT HAPPENED IN NEWTOWN—

BUT ON THE ONE YEAR ANNIVERSARY OF THE TRAGEDY, I GOT A CALL FROM A POLITICAL GROUP TRYING TO RAISE FUNDS TO SUPPORT GUN-CONTROL LEGISLATION...

HELLO, AS YOU KNOW THIS IS THE ONE-YEAR ANNIVERSARY OF THE SHOOTING IN NEWTOWN—

AND I HUNG UP.

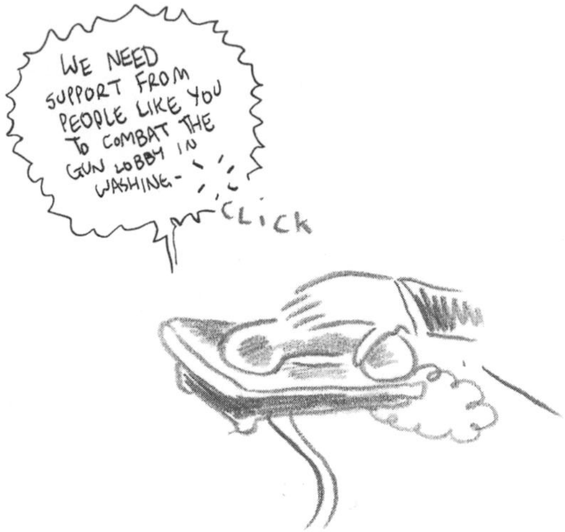
WE NEED SUPPORT FROM PEOPLE LIKE YOU TO COMBAT THE GUN LOBBY IN WASHING-
CLICK

I CAN JUSTIFY IT TO MYSELF - I CAN POINT OUT THAT THE GUN LOBBY IS TOO POWERFUL, THAT ABSOLUTELY ZERO THINGS WOULD CHANGE FROM ME GIVING MONEY TO A POLITICAL GROUP, THAT THERE ISN'T ANY POINT IN TRYING.*...

* THIS IS ALL TRUE

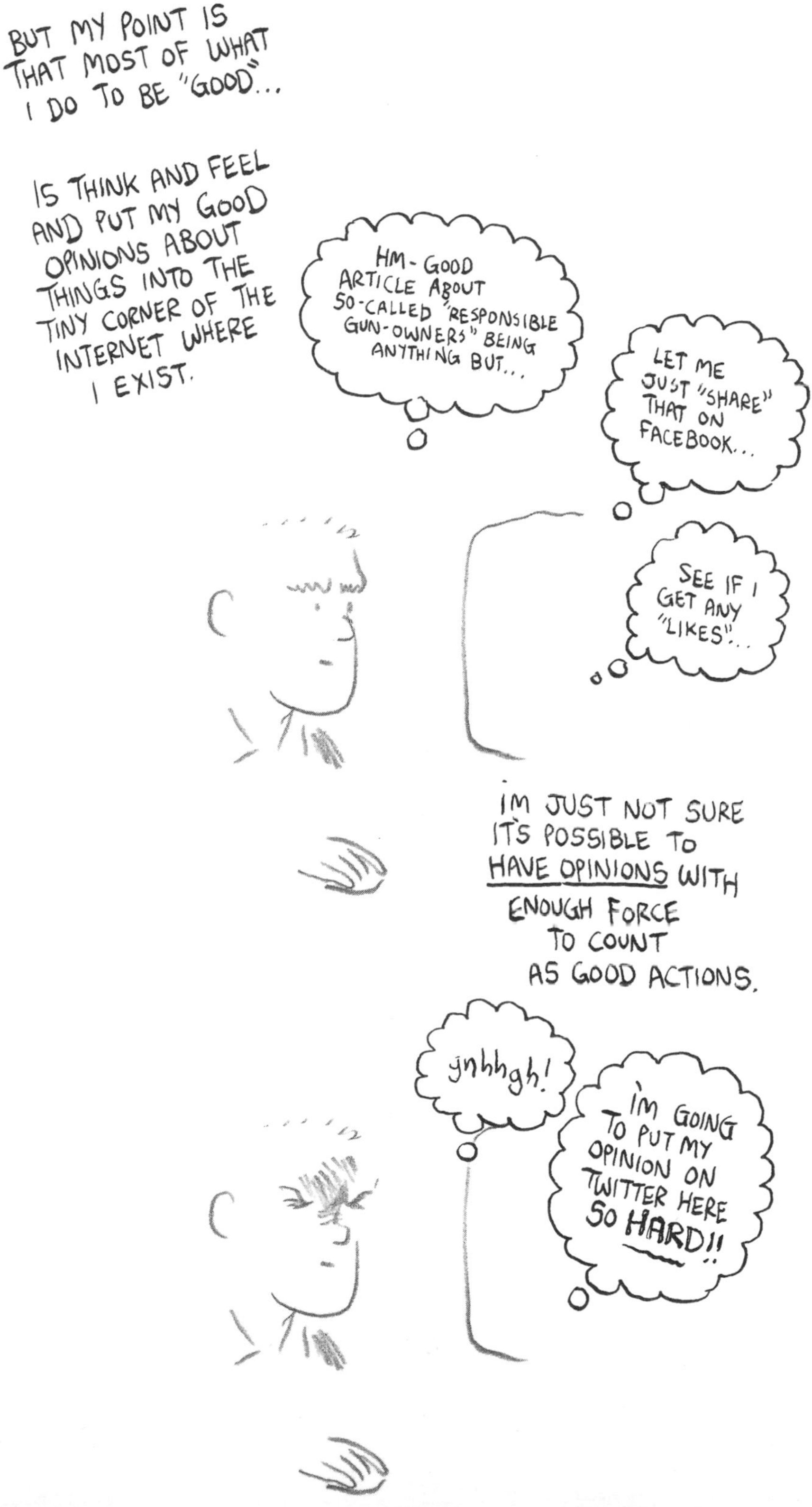
BUT MY POINT IS THAT MOST OF WHAT I DO TO BE "GOOD"...
IS THINK AND FEEL AND PUT MY GOOD OPINIONS ABOUT THINGS INTO THE TINY CORNER OF THE INTERNET WHERE I EXIST.
HM - GOOD ARTICLE ABOUT SO-CALLED "RESPONSIBLE GUN-OWNERS" BEING ANYTHING BUT...
LET ME JUST "SHARE" THAT ON FACEBOOK...
SEE IF I GET ANY "LIKES"...
I'M JUST NOT SURE IT'S POSSIBLE TO HAVE OPINIONS WITH ENOUGH FORCE TO COUNT AS GOOD ACTIONS.
ynhhgh!
I'M GOING TO PUT MY OPINION ON TWITTER HERE SO HARD!!

I'M REALIZING, THAT UNLESS
I WANT TO ACCEPT THAT
THERE'S REALLY NOTHING
CONCRETE THAT MAKES ME
ANY BETTER THAN SOME
BACKWARDS THINKING
BIGOT —

I'VE GOT TO DO
BETTER THAN JUST
HAVING BETTER
OPINIONS.

"GOOD POLITICS"
ARE A START.

BUT REALLY, THEY'RE
JUST THE **LEAST**
I CAN DO.

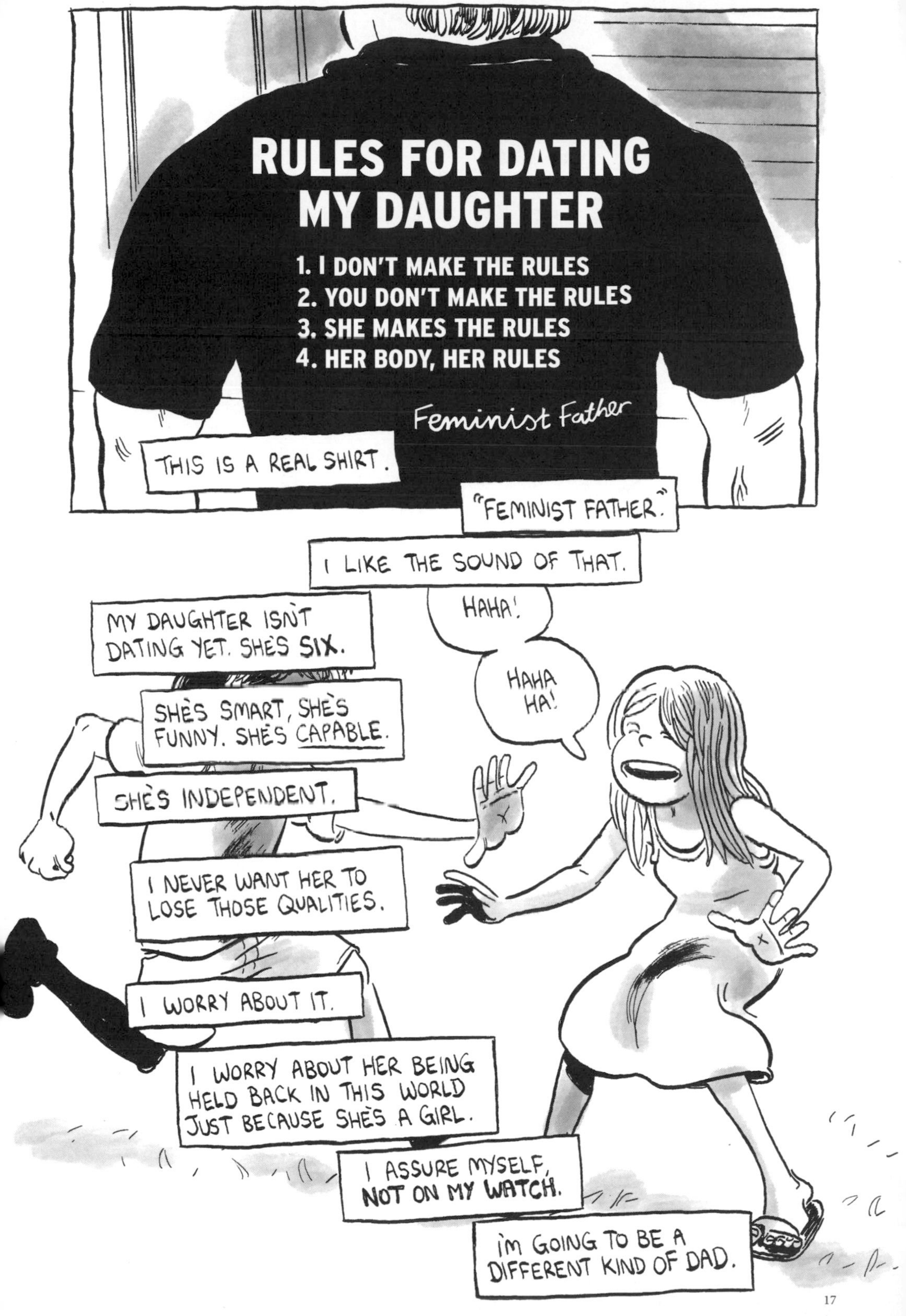
RULES FOR DATING MY DAUGHTER
1. I DON'T MAKE THE RULES
2. YOU DON'T MAKE THE RULES
3. SHE MAKES THE RULES
4. HER BODY, HER RULES
Feminist Father
THIS IS A REAL SHIRT.
"FEMINIST FATHER."
I LIKE THE SOUND OF THAT.
HAHA!
HAHA HA!
MY DAUGHTER ISN'T DATING YET. SHE'S SIX.
SHE'S SMART, SHE'S FUNNY. SHE'S CAPABLE.
SHE'S INDEPENDENT.
I NEVER WANT HER TO LOSE THOSE QUALITIES.
I WORRY ABOUT IT.
I WORRY ABOUT HER BEING HELD BACK IN THIS WORLD JUST BECAUSE SHE'S A GIRL.
I ASSURE MYSELF, NOT ON MY WATCH.
I'M GOING TO BE A DIFFERENT KIND OF DAD.

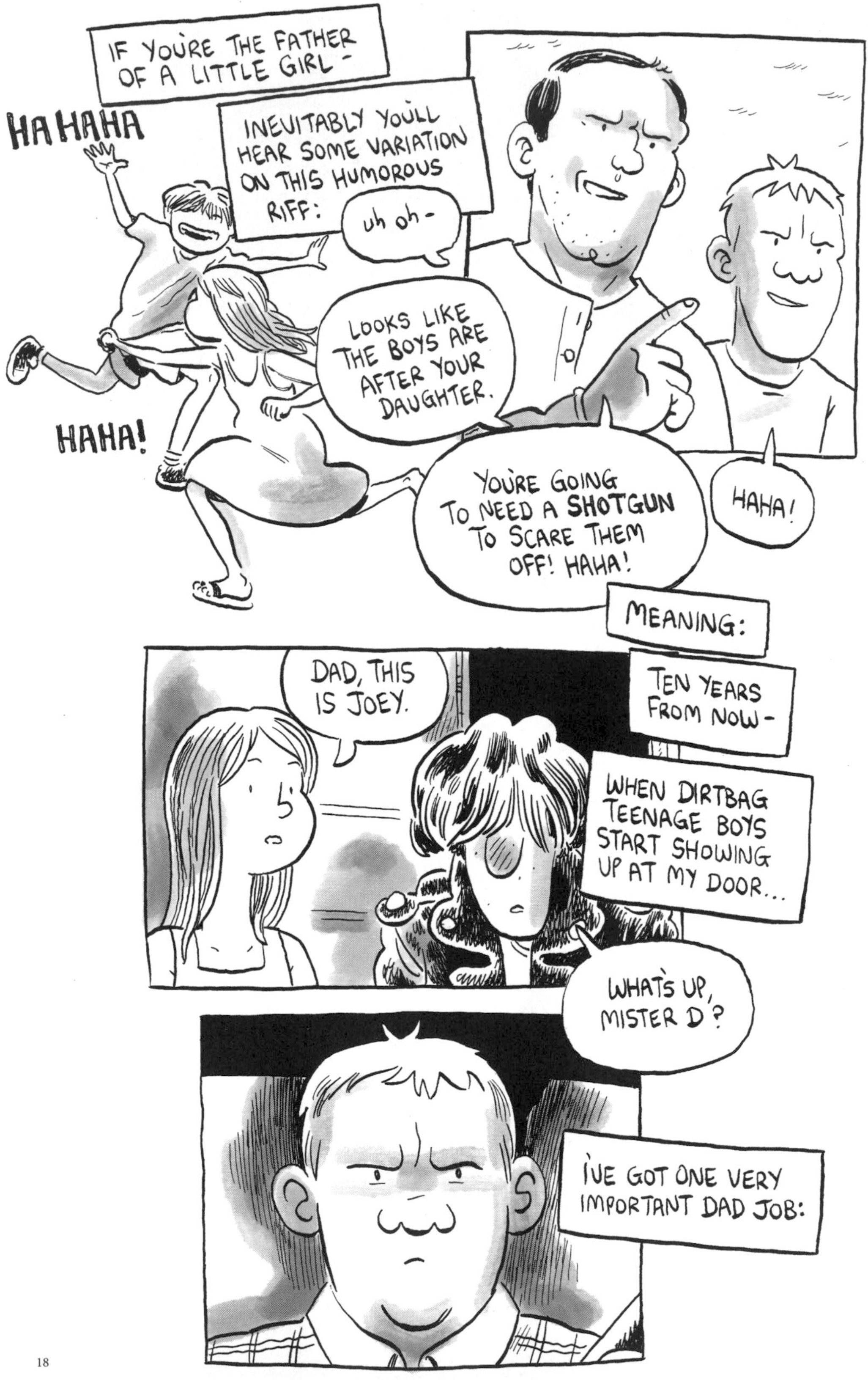
IF YOU'RE THE FATHER OF A LITTLE GIRL -
INEVITABLY YOU'LL HEAR SOME VARIATION ON THIS HUMOROUS RIFF:
HAHAHA
HAHA!
uh oh -
LOOKS LIKE THE BOYS ARE AFTER YOUR DAUGHTER.
YOU'RE GOING TO NEED A **SHOTGUN** TO SCARE THEM OFF! HAHA!
HAHA!
MEANING:
TEN YEARS FROM NOW -
WHEN DIRTBAG TEENAGE BOYS START SHOWING UP AT MY DOOR...
DAD, THIS IS JOEY.
WHAT'S UP, MISTER D?
I'VE GOT ONE VERY IMPORTANT DAD JOB:

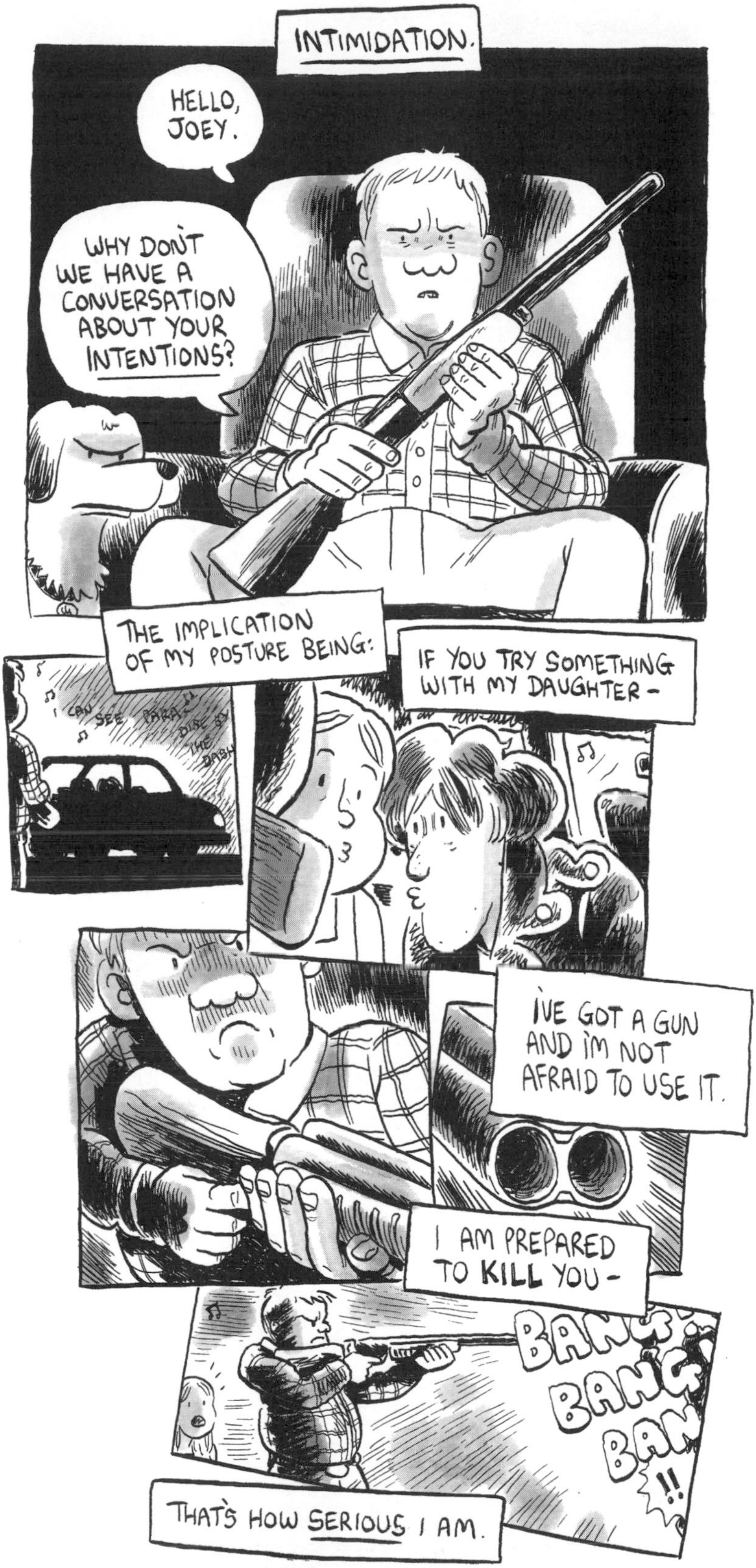
INTIMIDATION.
HELLO, JOEY.
WHY DON'T WE HAVE A CONVERSATION ABOUT YOUR INTENTIONS?
THE IMPLICATION OF MY POSTURE BEING:
I CAN SEE PARA- DISE BY THE DASH
IF YOU TRY SOMETHING WITH MY DAUGHTER -
I'VE GOT A GUN AND I'M NOT AFRAID TO USE IT.
I AM PREPARED TO KILL YOU -
BANG
BANG
BAN
!!
THAT'S HOW SERIOUS I AM.

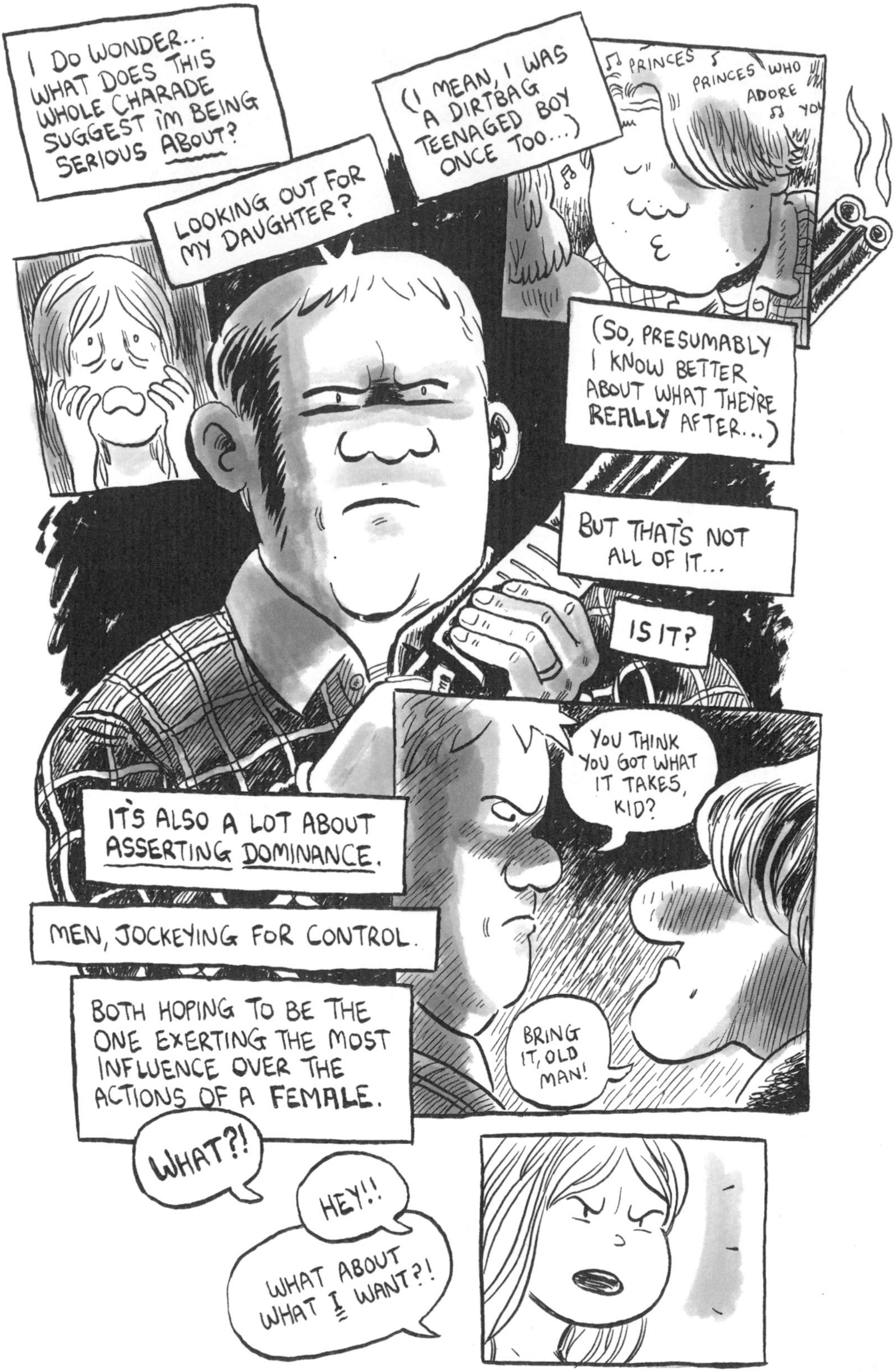
I DO WONDER... WHAT DOES THIS WHOLE CHARADE SUGGEST I'M BEING SERIOUS ABOUT?
LOOKING OUT FOR MY DAUGHTER?
(I MEAN, I WAS A DIRTBAG TEENAGED BOY ONCE TOO...)
PRINCES PRINCES WHO ADORE YOU
(SO, PRESUMABLY I KNOW BETTER ABOUT WHAT THEY'RE REALLY AFTER...)
BUT THAT'S NOT ALL OF IT...
IS IT?
YOU THINK YOU GOT WHAT IT TAKES, KID?
IT'S ALSO A LOT ABOUT ASSERTING DOMINANCE.
MEN, JOCKEYING FOR CONTROL.
BOTH HOPING TO BE THE ONE EXERTING THE MOST INFLUENCE OVER THE ACTIONS OF A FEMALE.
BRING IT, OLD MAN!
WHAT?!
HEY!!
WHAT ABOUT WHAT I WANT?!

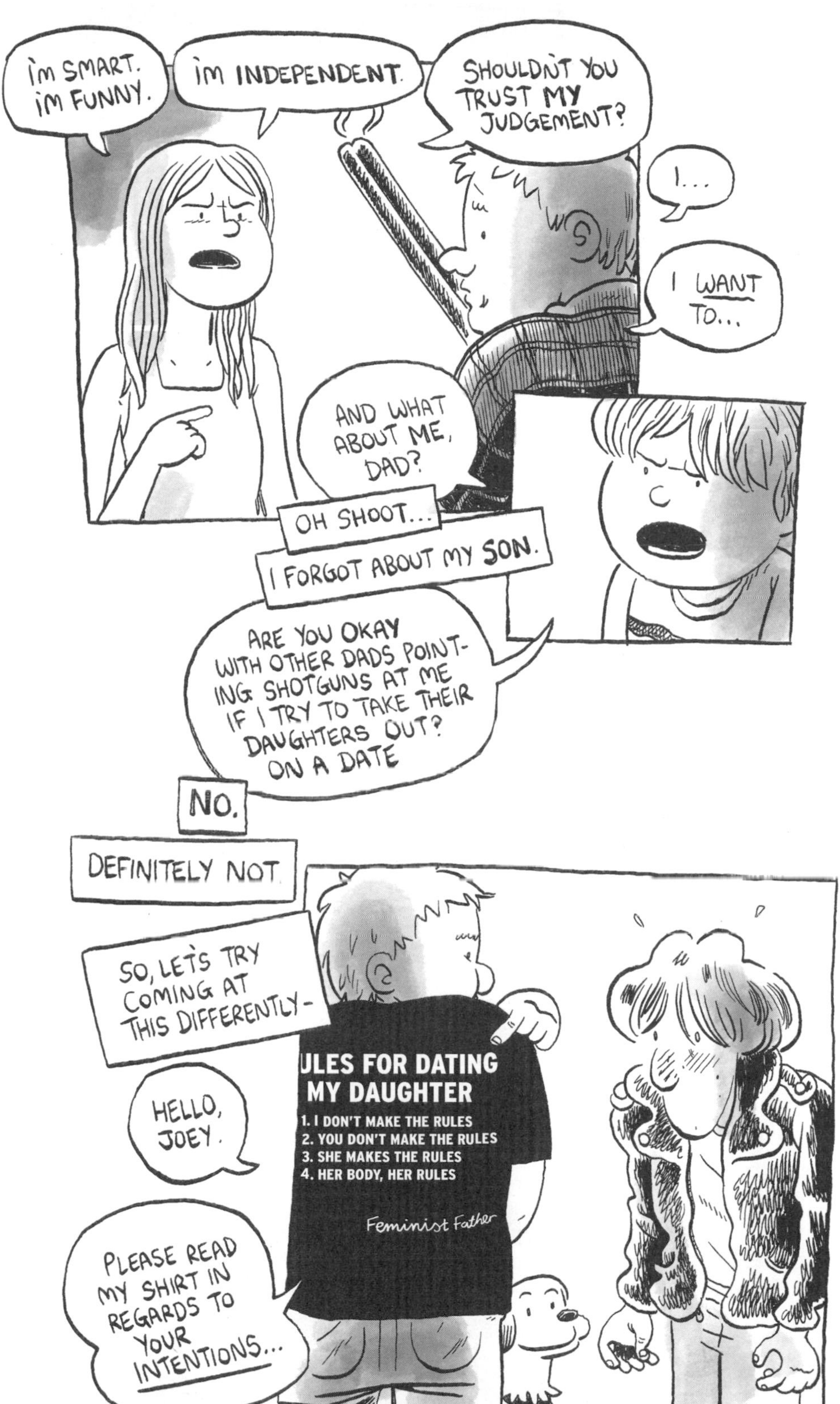
I'M SMART. I'M FUNNY.
I'M INDEPENDENT.
SHOULDN'T YOU TRUST MY JUDGEMENT?
I...
I WANT TO...
AND WHAT ABOUT ME, DAD?
OH SHOOT...
I FORGOT ABOUT MY SON.
ARE YOU OKAY WITH OTHER DADS POINT-ING SHOTGUNS AT ME IF I TRY TO TAKE THEIR DAUGHTERS OUT? ON A DATE
NO.
DEFINITELY NOT.
SO, LET'S TRY COMING AT THIS DIFFERENTLY-
HELLO, JOEY.
ULES FOR DATING MY DAUGHTER
1. I DON'T MAKE THE RULES
2. YOU DON'T MAKE THE RULES
3. SHE MAKES THE RULES
4. HER BODY, HER RULES
Feminist Father
PLEASE READ MY SHIRT IN REGARDS TO YOUR INTENTIONS...

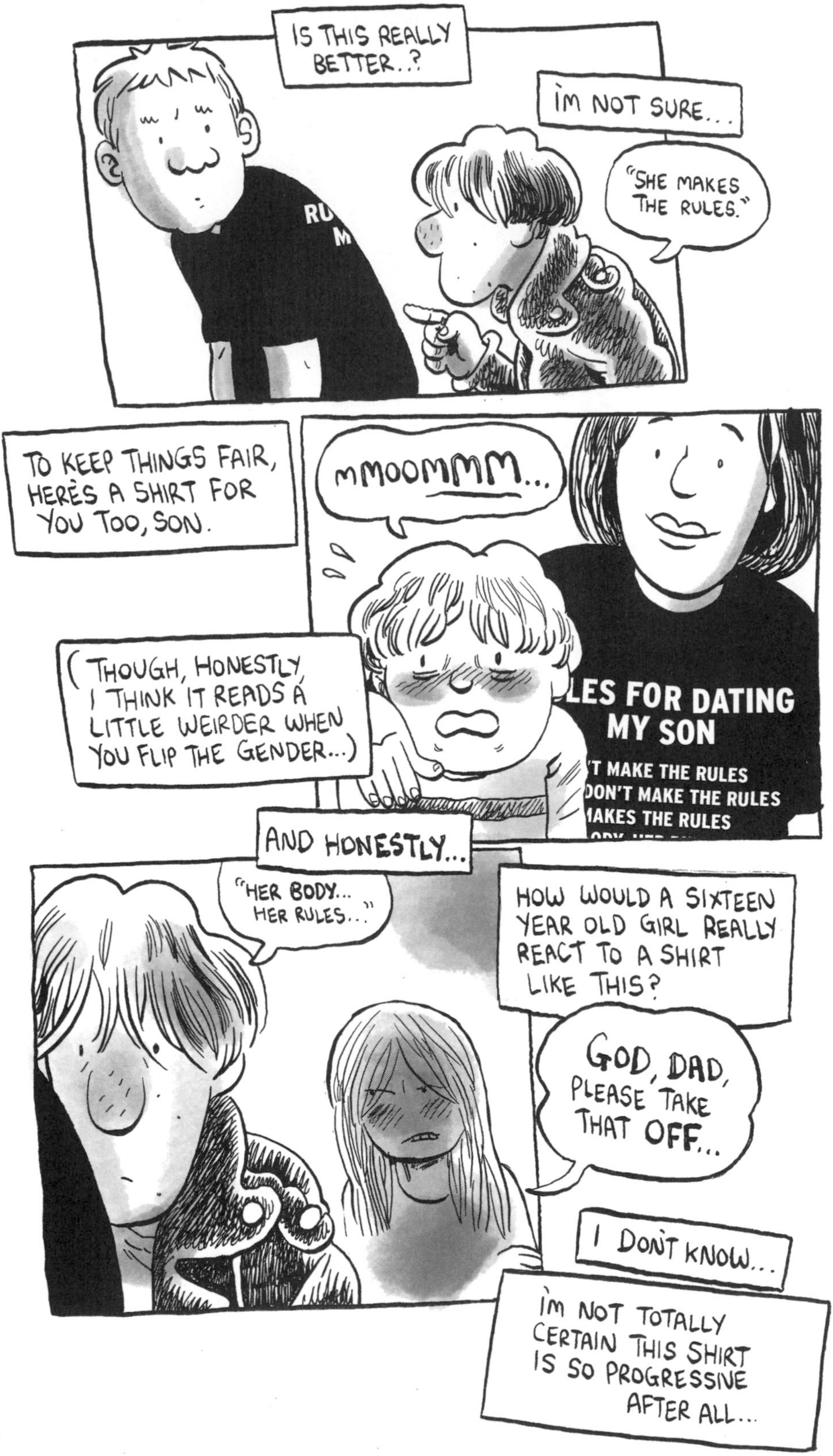
IS THIS REALLY BETTER..?
I'M NOT SURE...
"SHE MAKES THE RULES."
TO KEEP THINGS FAIR, HERE'S A SHIRT FOR YOU TOO, SON.
MMOOMMM...
LES FOR DATING
MY SON
T MAKE THE RULES
DON'T MAKE THE RULES
AKES THE RULES
(THOUGH, HONESTLY, I THINK IT READS A LITTLE WEIRDER WHEN YOU FLIP THE GENDER...)
AND HONESTLY...
"HER BODY... HER RULES..."
HOW WOULD A SIXTEEN YEAR OLD GIRL REALLY REACT TO A SHIRT LIKE THIS?
GOD, DAD, PLEASE TAKE THAT OFF...
I DON'T KNOW...
I'M NOT TOTALLY CERTAIN THIS SHIRT IS SO PROGRESSIVE AFTER ALL...

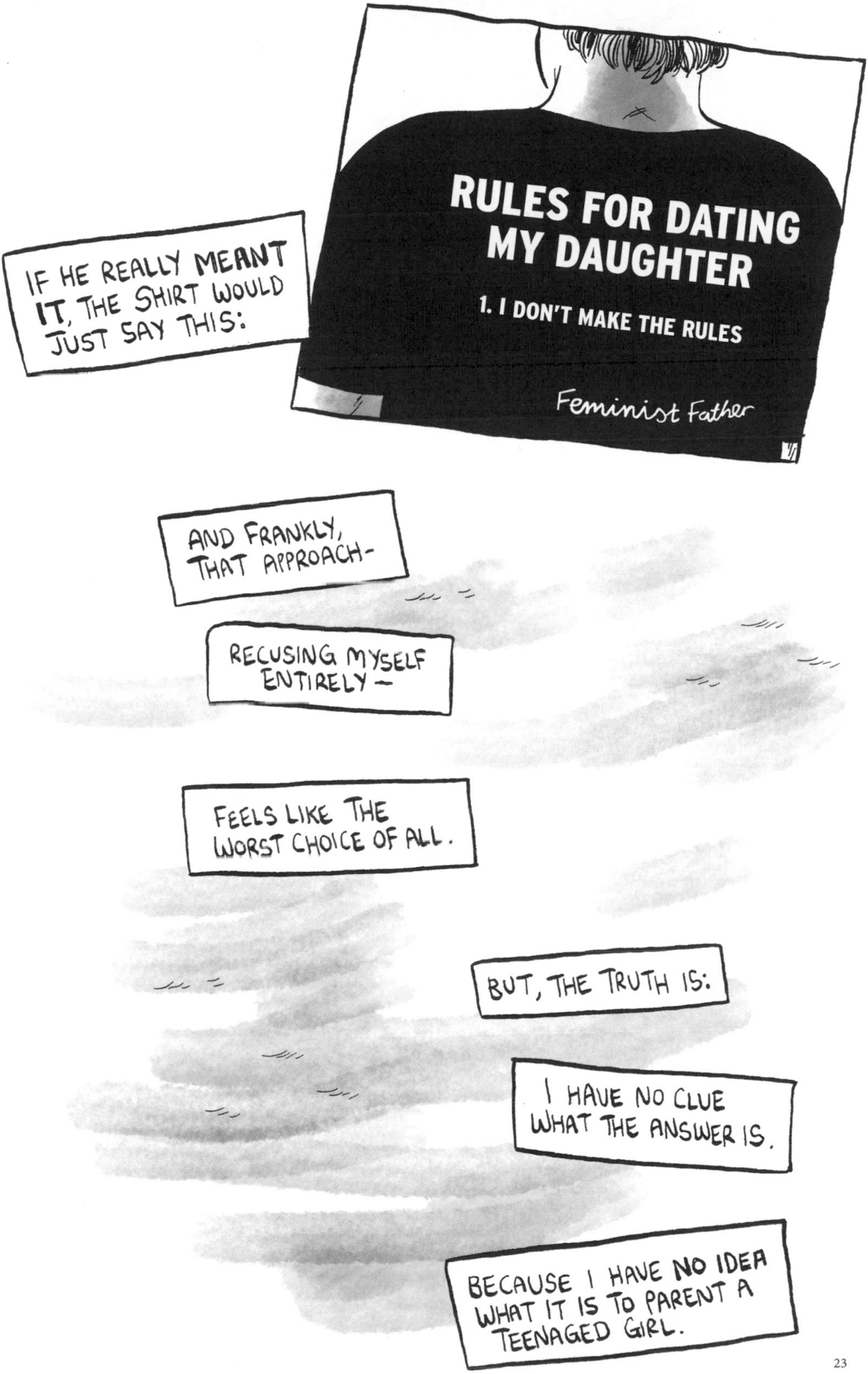
IF HE REALLY MEANT IT, THE SHIRT WOULD JUST SAY THIS:
RULES FOR DATING MY DAUGHTER
1. I DON'T MAKE THE RULES
Feminist Father
AND FRANKLY, THAT APPROACH-
RECUSING MYSELF ENTIRELY —
FEELS LIKE THE WORST CHOICE OF ALL.
BUT, THE TRUTH IS:
I HAVE NO CLUE WHAT THE ANSWER IS.
BECAUSE I HAVE NO IDEA WHAT IT IS TO PARENT A TEENAGED GIRL.

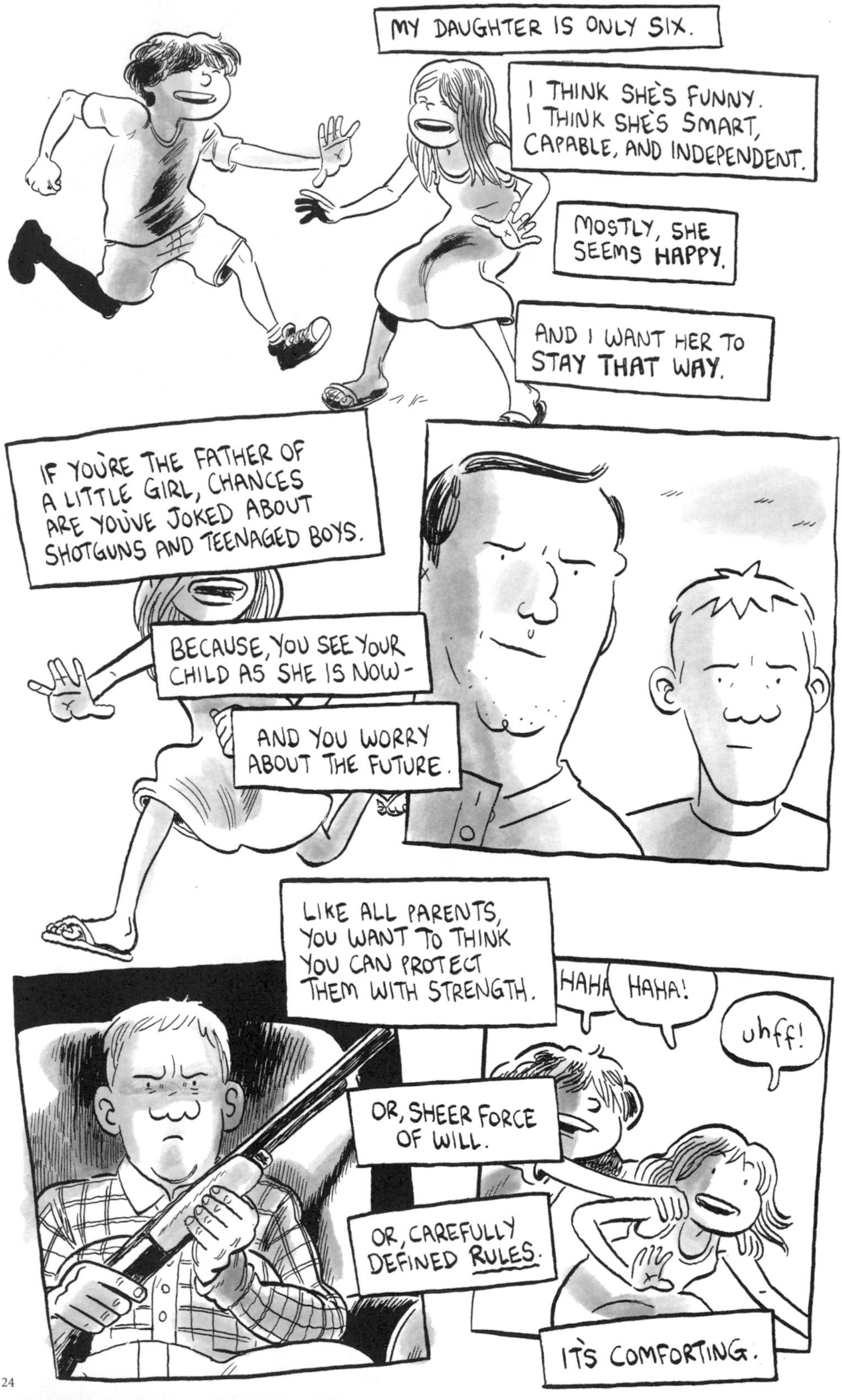
MY DAUGHTER IS ONLY SIX.
I THINK SHE'S FUNNY. I THINK SHE'S SMART, CAPABLE, AND INDEPENDENT.
MOSTLY, SHE SEEMS HAPPY.
AND I WANT HER TO STAY THAT WAY.
IF YOU'RE THE FATHER OF A LITTLE GIRL, CHANCES ARE YOU'VE JOKED ABOUT SHOTGUNS AND TEENAGED BOYS.
BECAUSE, YOU SEE YOUR CHILD AS SHE IS NOW-
AND YOU WORRY ABOUT THE FUTURE.
LIKE ALL PARENTS, YOU WANT TO THINK YOU CAN PROTECT THEM WITH STRENGTH.
OR, SHEER FORCE OF WILL.
OR, CAREFULLY DEFINED RULES.
HAHA
HAHA!
uhff!
IT'S COMFORTING.

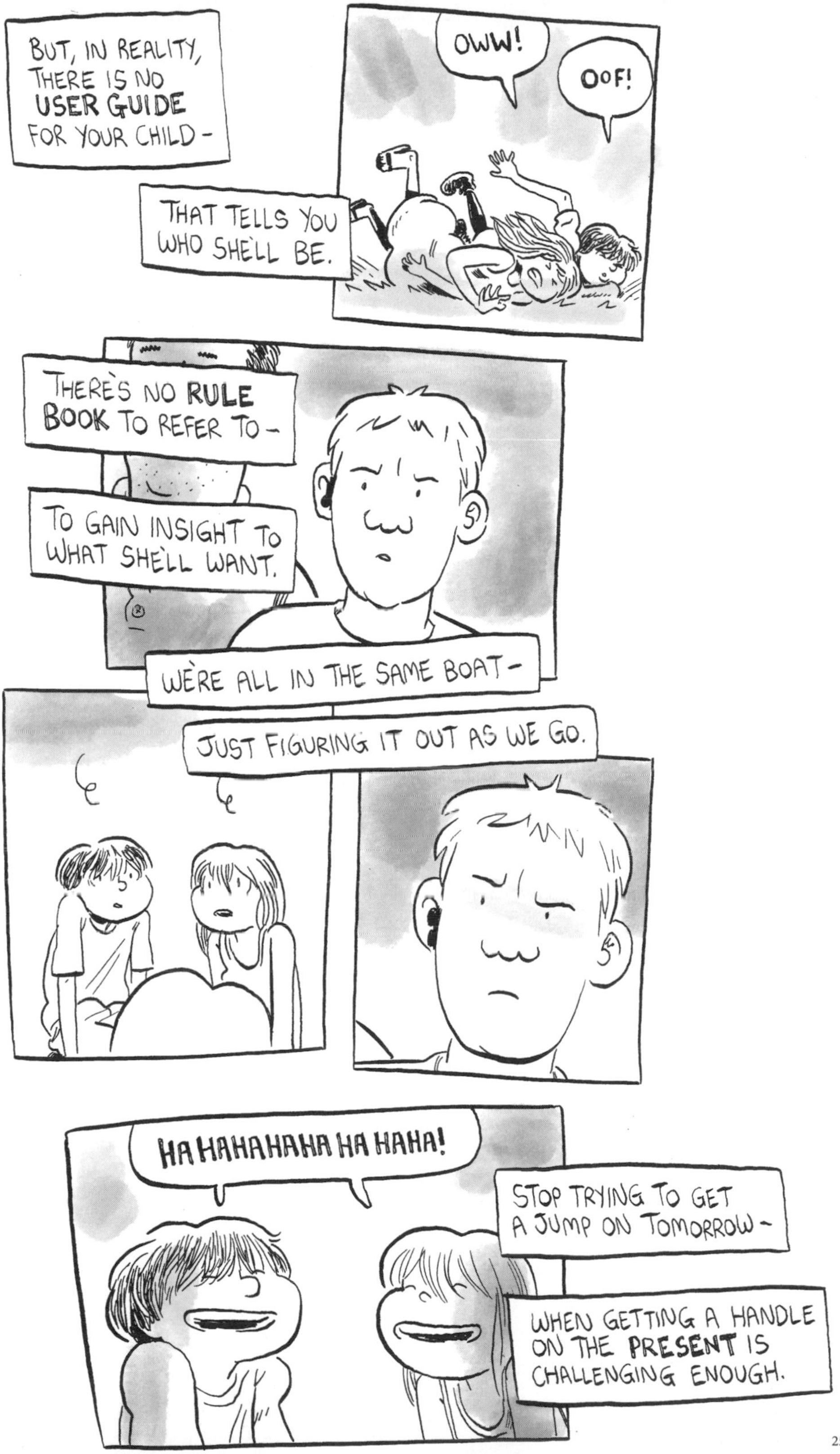
BUT, IN REALITY, THERE IS NO **USER GUIDE** FOR YOUR CHILD -
OWW!
OOF!
THAT TELLS YOU WHO SHE'LL BE.
THERE'S NO **RULE BOOK** TO REFER TO -
TO GAIN INSIGHT TO WHAT SHE'LL WANT.
WE'RE ALL IN THE SAME BOAT -
JUST FIGURING IT OUT AS WE GO.
HA HAHAHAHAHA HA HAHA!
STOP TRYING TO GET A JUMP ON TOMORROW -
WHEN GETTING A HANDLE ON THE **PRESENT** IS CHALLENGING ENOUGH.

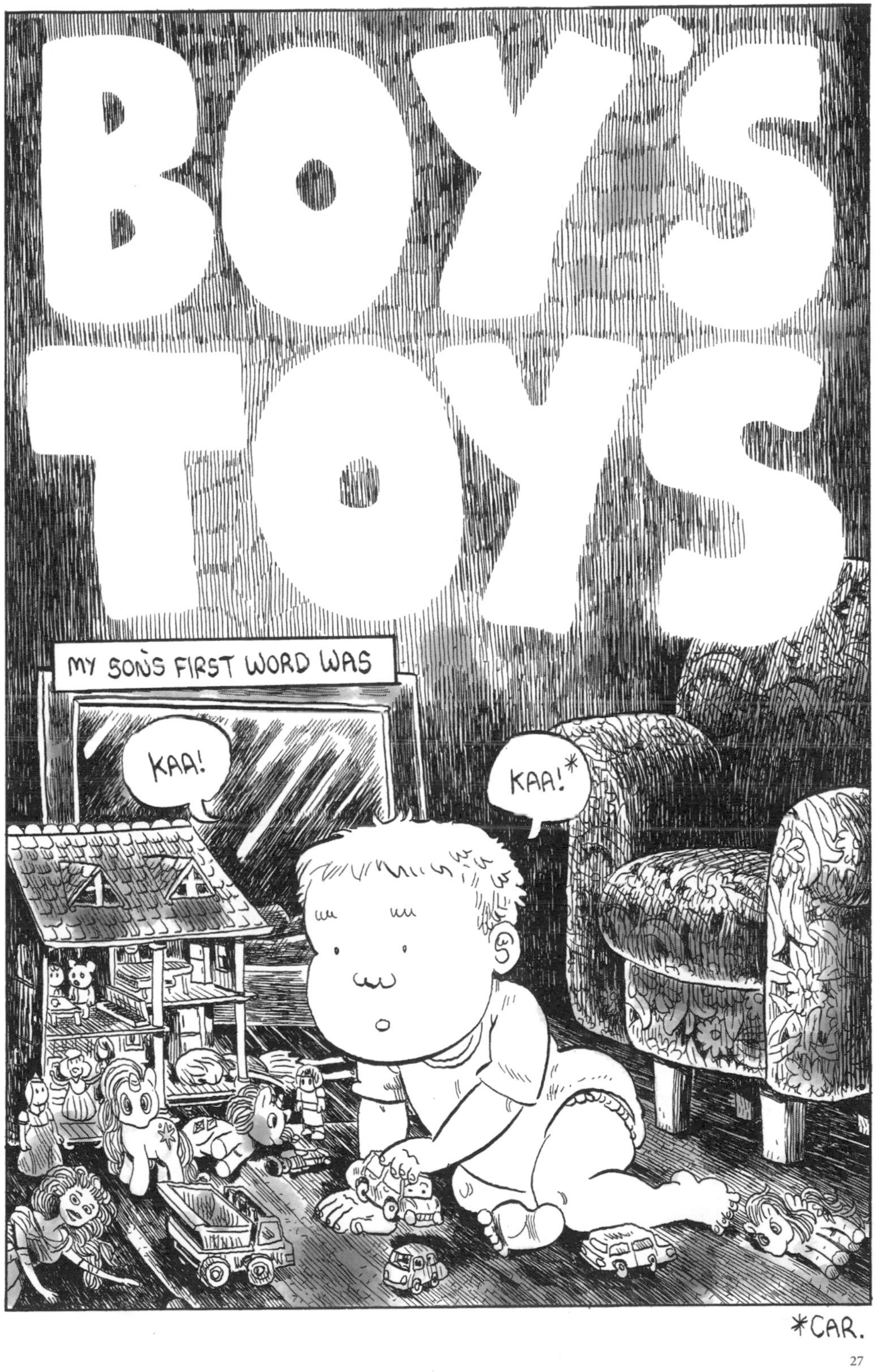
BOY'S TOYS
MY SON'S FIRST WORD WAS
KAA!
KAA!*

*CAR.

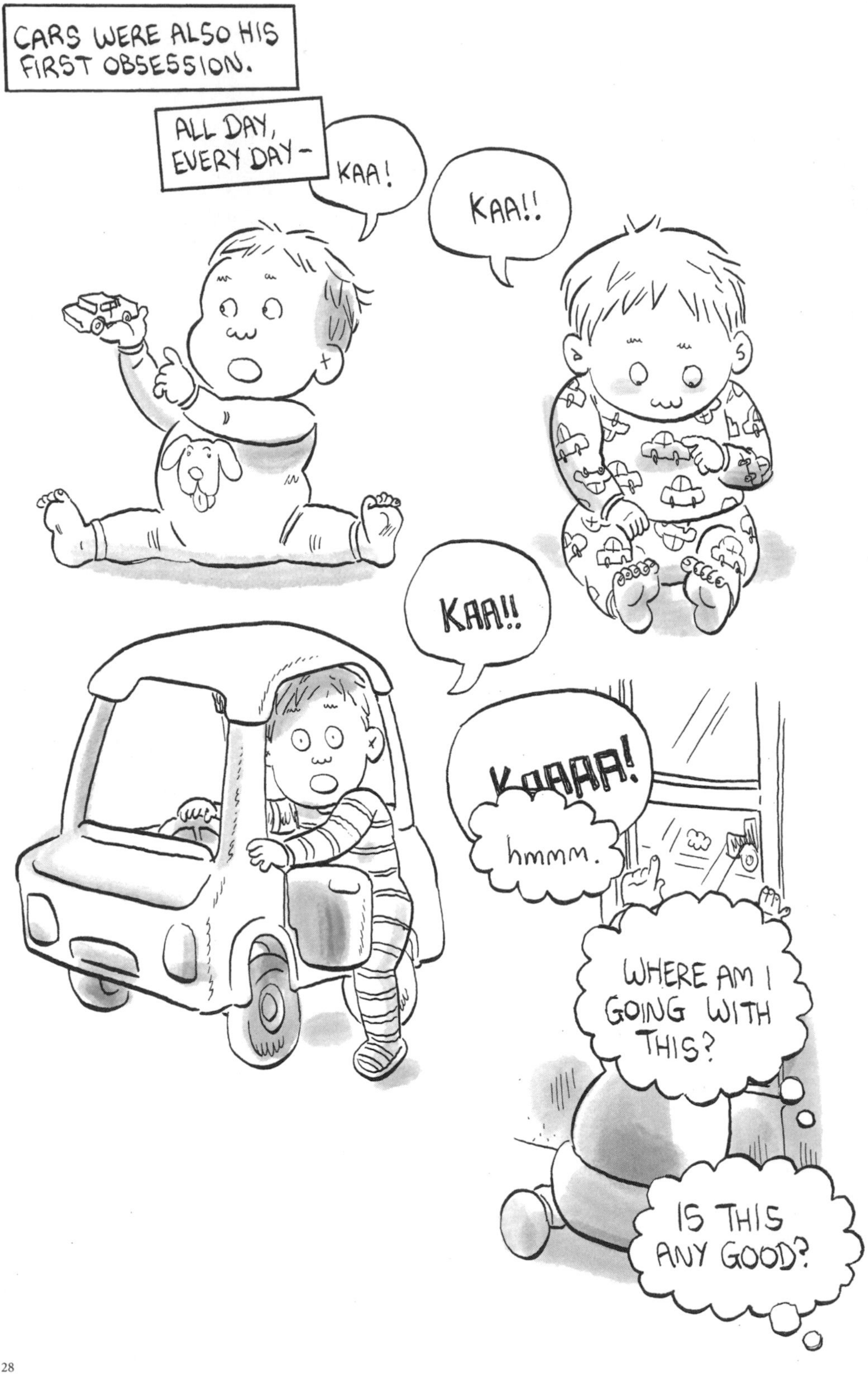
CARS WERE ALSO HIS FIRST OBSESSION.
ALL DAY, EVERY DAY -
KAA!
KAA!!
KAA!!
KAAAA!
hmmm.
WHERE AM I GOING WITH THIS?
IS THIS ANY GOOD?

MONDAY MARCH 10TH 2014: MONDAY MORNINGS ARE BUSY. I'M UP AROUND 7AM, AND I NEED TO GET MY SON OVER TO MY PARENT'S HOUSE AND MY DAUGHTER TO SCHOOL. THE CLEANING LADY COMES ON MONDAYS AND I TRY TO GET THE KIDS OUT OF THE HOUSE BY THE TIME SHE ARRIVES.

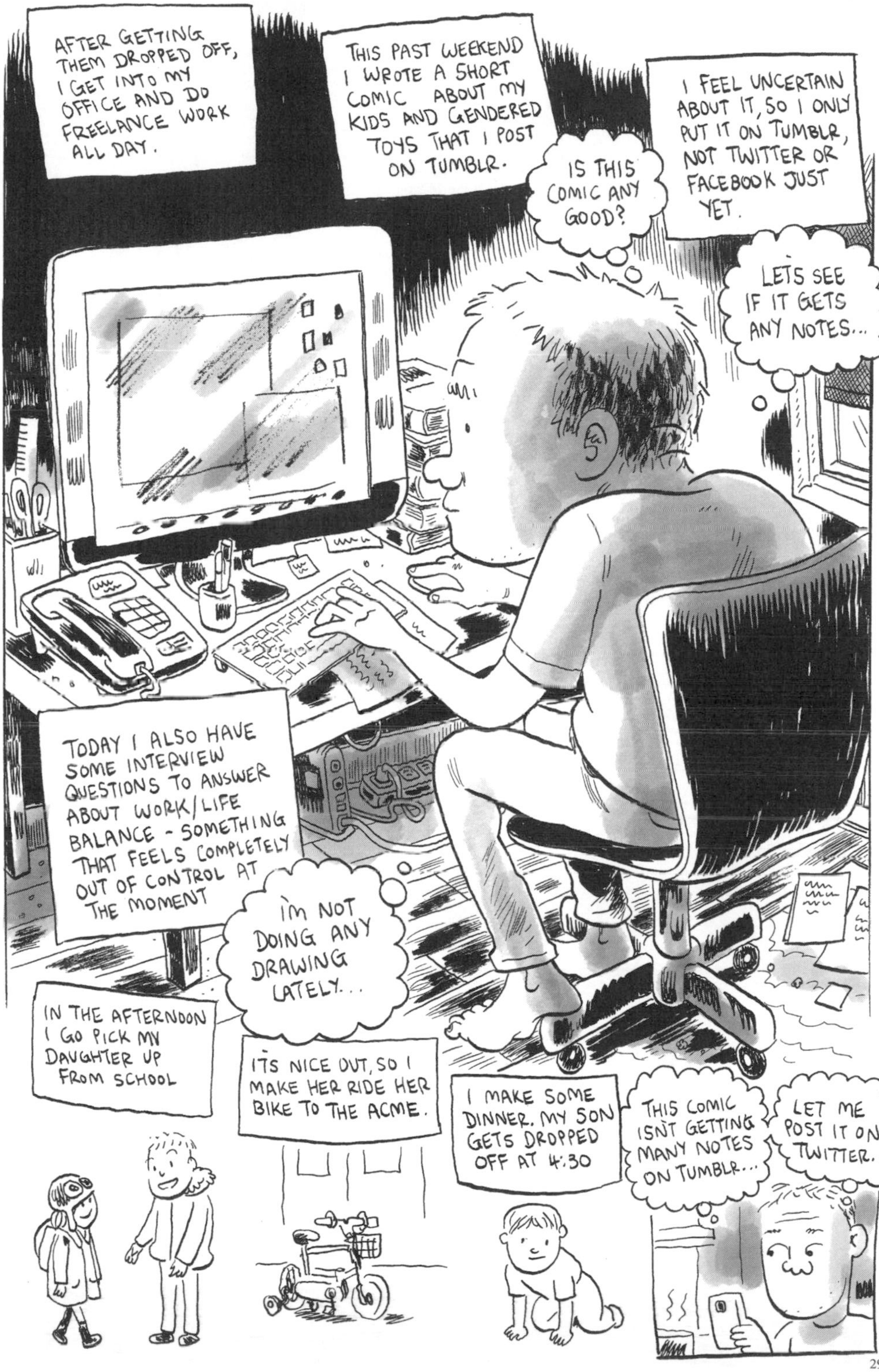
AFTER GETTING THEM DROPPED OFF, I GET INTO MY OFFICE AND DO FREELANCE WORK ALL DAY.
THIS PAST WEEKEND I WROTE A SHORT COMIC ABOUT MY KIDS AND GENDERED TOYS THAT I POST ON TUMBLR.
IS THIS COMIC ANY GOOD?
I FEEL UNCERTAIN ABOUT IT, SO I ONLY PUT IT ON TUMBLR, NOT TWITTER OR FACEBOOK JUST YET.
LETS SEE IF IT GETS ANY NOTES...
TODAY I ALSO HAVE SOME INTERVIEW QUESTIONS TO ANSWER ABOUT WORK/LIFE BALANCE - SOMETHING THAT FEELS COMPLETELY OUT OF CONTROL AT THE MOMENT
I'M NOT DOING ANY DRAWING LATELY...
IN THE AFTERNOON I GO PICK MY DAUGHTER UP FROM SCHOOL
ITS NICE OUT, SO I MAKE HER RIDE HER BIKE TO THE ACME.
I MAKE SOME DINNER. MY SON GETS DROPPED OFF AT 4:30
THIS COMIC ISN'T GETTING MANY NOTES ON TUMBLR...
LET ME POST IT ON TWITTER...

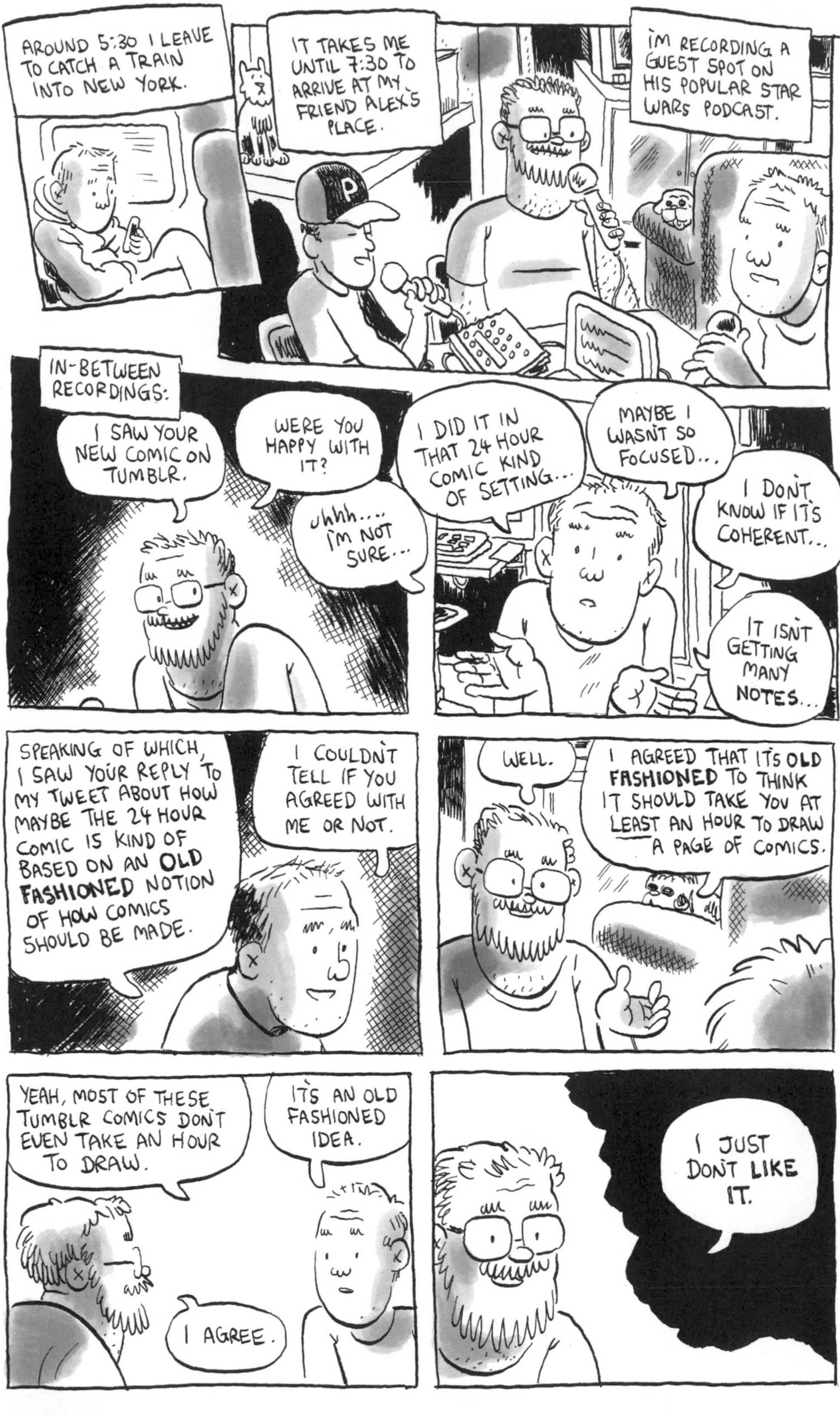
AROUND 5:30 I LEAVE TO CATCH A TRAIN INTO NEW YORK.
IT TAKES ME UNTIL 7:30 TO ARRIVE AT MY FRIEND ALEX'S PLACE.
I'M RECORDING A GUEST SPOT ON HIS POPULAR STAR WARS PODCAST.
IN-BETWEEN RECORDINGS:
I SAW YOUR NEW COMIC ON TUMBLR.
WERE YOU HAPPY WITH IT?
UHHH.... I'M NOT SURE...
I DID IT IN THAT 24 HOUR COMIC KIND OF SETTING...
MAYBE I WASN'T SO FOCUSED...
I DON'T KNOW IF IT'S COHERENT...
IT ISN'T GETTING MANY **NOTES**...
SPEAKING OF WHICH, I SAW YOUR REPLY TO MY TWEET ABOUT HOW MAYBE THE 24 HOUR COMIC IS KIND OF BASED ON AN **OLD FASHIONED** NOTION OF HOW COMICS SHOULD BE MADE.
I COULDN'T TELL IF YOU AGREED WITH ME OR NOT.
WELL.
I AGREED THAT IT'S **OLD FASHIONED** TO THINK IT SHOULD TAKE YOU AT LEAST AN HOUR TO DRAW A PAGE OF COMICS.
YEAH, MOST OF THESE TUMBLR COMICS DON'T EVEN TAKE AN HOUR TO DRAW.
I AGREE.
IT'S AN OLD FASHIONED IDEA.
I JUST DON'T **LIKE** IT.

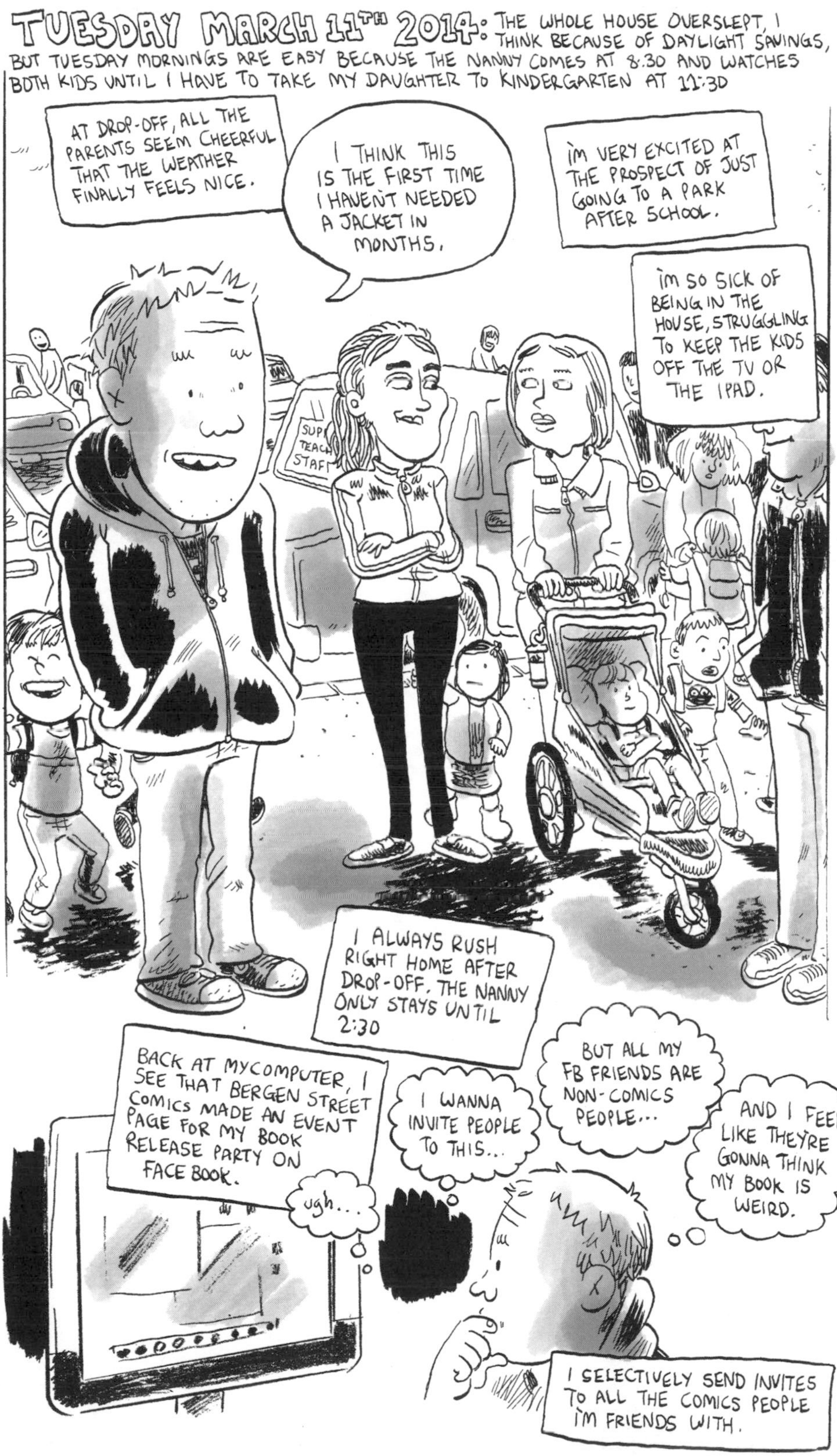
TUESDAY MARCH 11TH 2014: THE WHOLE HOUSE OVERSLEPT, I THINK BECAUSE OF DAYLIGHT SAVINGS, BUT TUESDAY MORNINGS ARE EASY BECAUSE THE NANNY COMES AT 8:30 AND WATCHES BOTH KIDS UNTIL I HAVE TO TAKE MY DAUGHTER TO KINDERGARTEN AT 11:30
AT DROP-OFF, ALL THE PARENTS SEEM CHEERFUL THAT THE WEATHER FINALLY FEELS NICE.
I THINK THIS IS THE FIRST TIME I HAVEN'T NEEDED A JACKET IN MONTHS.
I'M VERY EXCITED AT THE PROSPECT OF JUST GOING TO A PARK AFTER SCHOOL.
I'M SO SICK OF BEING IN THE HOUSE, STRUGGLING TO KEEP THE KIDS OFF THE TV OR THE IPAD.
I ALWAYS RUSH RIGHT HOME AFTER DROP-OFF. THE NANNY ONLY STAYS UNTIL 2:30
BACK AT MYCOMPUTER, I SEE THAT BERGEN STREET COMICS MADE AN EVENT PAGE FOR MY BOOK RELEASE PARTY ON FACE BOOK.
ugh...
I WANNA INVITE PEOPLE TO THIS...
BUT ALL MY FB FRIENDS ARE NON-COMICS PEOPLE...
AND I FEEL LIKE THEY'RE GONNA THINK MY BOOK IS WEIRD.
I SELECTIVELY SEND INVITES TO ALL THE COMICS PEOPLE I'M FRIENDS WITH.

WE SPEND AN HOUR AT THE PLAYPARK AFTER SCHOOL, BUT HAVE TO GO HOME EARLY BECAUSE OF A **BATHROOM EMERGENCY**. IT'S SO NICE OUT, THOUGH, I INSIST ON GOING RIGHT BACK OUT.

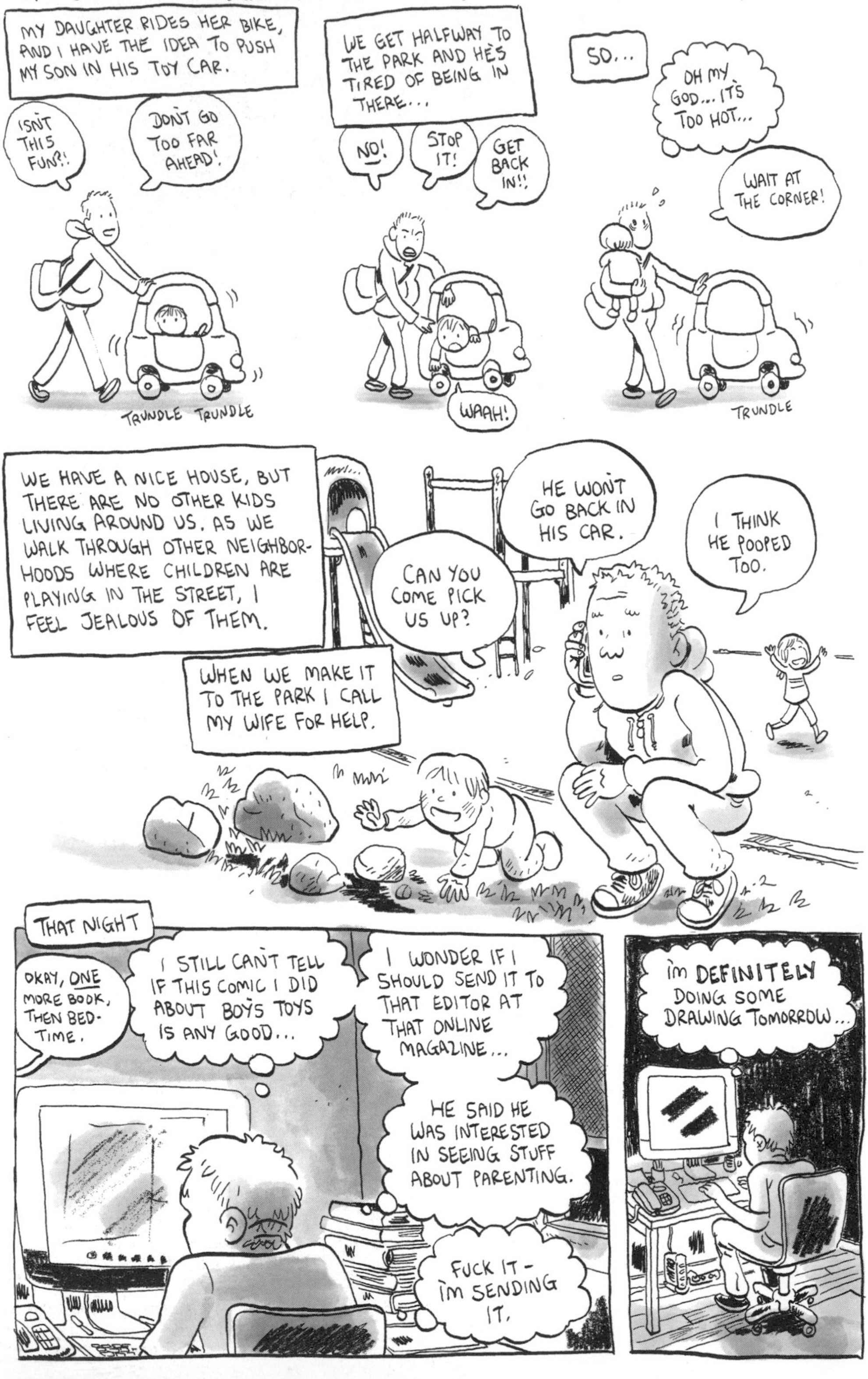

MY DAUGHTER RIDES HER BIKE, AND I HAVE THE IDEA TO PUSH MY SON IN HIS TOY CAR.
ISN'T THIS FUN?!
DON'T GO TOO FAR AHEAD!
TRUNDLE TRUNDLE
WE GET HALFWAY TO THE PARK AND HE'S TIRED OF BEING IN THERE...
NO!
STOP IT!
GET BACK IN!!
WAAH!
SO...
OH MY GOD... IT'S TOO HOT...
WAIT AT THE CORNER!
TRUNDLE
WE HAVE A NICE HOUSE, BUT THERE ARE NO OTHER KIDS LIVING AROUND US. AS WE WALK THROUGH OTHER NEIGHBORHOODS WHERE CHILDREN ARE PLAYING IN THE STREET, I FEEL JEALOUS OF THEM.
WHEN WE MAKE IT TO THE PARK I CALL MY WIFE FOR HELP.
CAN YOU COME PICK US UP?
HE WON'T GO BACK IN HIS CAR.
I THINK HE POOPED TOO.
THAT NIGHT
OKAY, ONE MORE BOOK, THEN BED-TIME.
I STILL CAN'T TELL IF THIS COMIC I DID ABOUT BOYS TOYS IS ANY GOOD...
I WONDER IF I SHOULD SEND IT TO THAT EDITOR AT THAT ONLINE MAGAZINE...
HE SAID HE WAS INTERESTED IN SEEING STUFF ABOUT PARENTING.
FUCK IT - I'M SENDING IT.
I'M DEFINITELY DOING SOME DRAWING TOMORROW...

WEDNESDAY MARCH 12TH 2014: THE NANNY CALLS IN SICK...

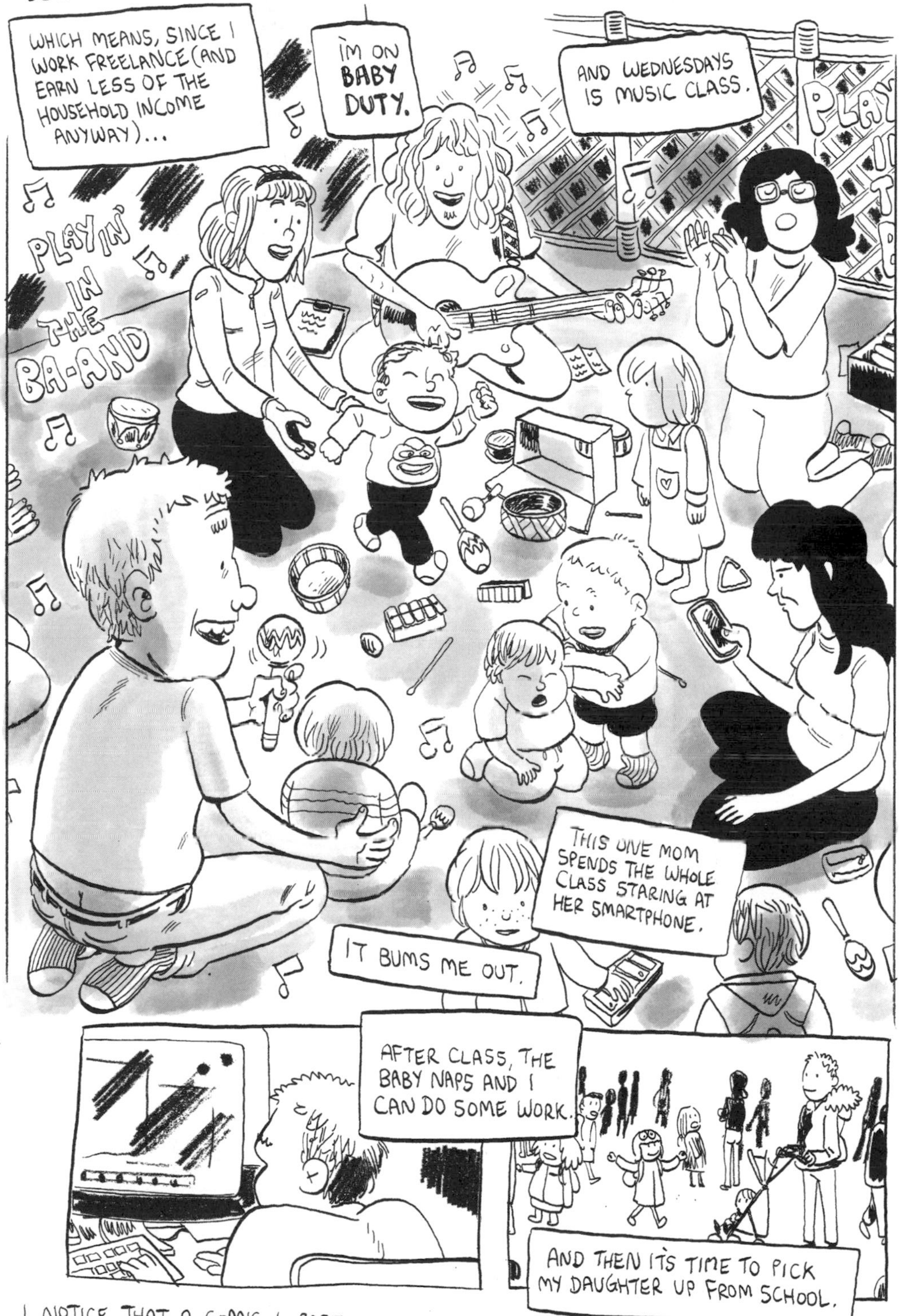
WHICH MEANS, SINCE I WORK FREELANCE (AND EARN LESS OF THE HOUSEHOLD INCOME ANYWAY)...
I'M ON BABY DUTY.
AND WEDNESDAYS IS MUSIC CLASS.
PLAYIN' IN THE BA-AND
THIS ONE MOM SPENDS THE WHOLE CLASS STARING AT HER SMARTPHONE.
IT BUMS ME OUT.
AFTER CLASS, THE BABY NAPS AND I CAN DO SOME WORK.
AND THEN IT'S TIME TO PICK MY DAUGHTER UP FROM SCHOOL.

I NOTICE THAT A COMIC I POSTED ON TUMBLR EARLIER IN THE WEEK, THAT DIDN'T SEEM TO GET MUCH NOTICE, HAS ACTUALLY STARTED TO GET PASSED AROUND A BIT.

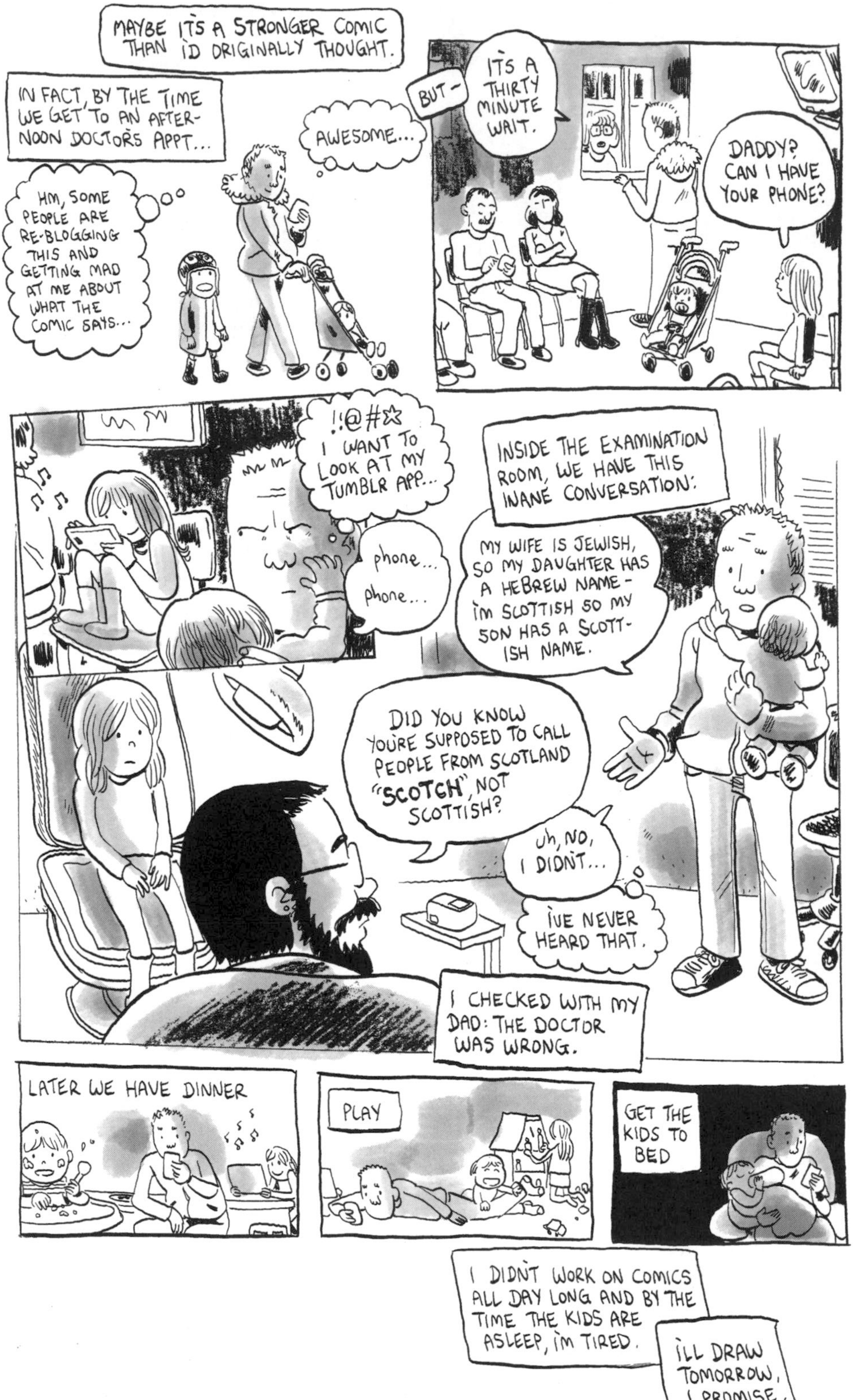
MAYBE IT'S A STRONGER COMIC THAN I'D ORIGINALLY THOUGHT.
IN FACT, BY THE TIME WE GET TO AN AFTER-NOON DOCTOR'S APPT...
HM, SOME PEOPLE ARE RE-BLOGGING THIS AND GETTING MAD AT ME ABOUT WHAT THE COMIC SAYS...
AWESOME...
BUT—
IT'S A THIRTY MINUTE WAIT.
DADDY? CAN I HAVE YOUR PHONE?
!!@#☆ I WANT TO LOOK AT MY TUMBLR APP...
phone...
phone...
INSIDE THE EXAMINATION ROOM, WE HAVE THIS INANE CONVERSATION:
MY WIFE IS JEWISH, SO MY DAUGHTER HAS A HEBREW NAME - I'M SCOTTISH SO MY SON HAS A SCOTT-ISH NAME.
DID YOU KNOW YOU'RE SUPPOSED TO CALL PEOPLE FROM SCOTLAND "SCOTCH", NOT SCOTTISH?
UH, NO, I DIDN'T...
I'VE NEVER HEARD THAT.
I CHECKED WITH MY DAD: THE DOCTOR WAS WRONG.
LATER WE HAVE DINNER
PLAY
GET THE KIDS TO BED
I DIDN'T WORK ON COMICS ALL DAY LONG AND BY THE TIME THE KIDS ARE ASLEEP, I'M TIRED.
I'LL DRAW TOMORROW, I PROMISE.

THURSDAY MARCH 13TH 2014: THE NANNY IS SICK, AGAIN, PART 2, THE SEQUEL

I'M ON KID DUTY AGAIN ALL MORNING, WHICH IS MORE CHALLENGING ON THURSDAYS BECAUSE MY DAUGHTER DOESN'T GO TO SCHOOL UNTIL 11:30 – BUT WE MAKE PANCAKES, DRAW DRAWINGS, PLAY WITH TOYS, AND WATCH SOME OF DISNEY'S **FROZEN**. I WISH WE COULD GO OUTSIDE. I NEVER USED TO CARE ABOUT THE WEATHER SO MUCH BEFORE I HAD CHILDREN.

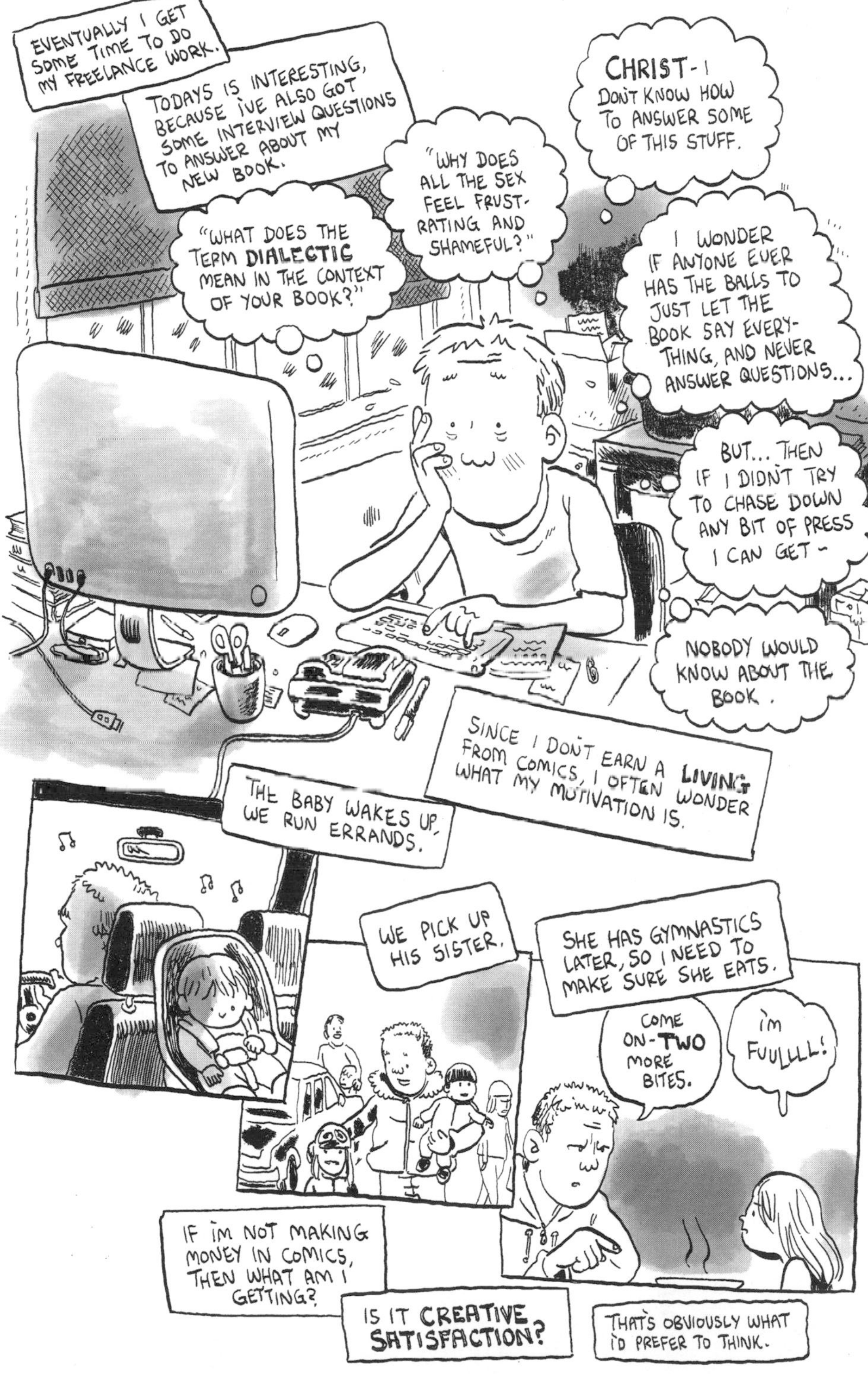

EVENTUALLY I GET SOME TIME TO DO MY FREELANCE WORK.
TODAYS IS INTERESTING, BECAUSE I'VE ALSO GOT SOME INTERVIEW QUESTIONS TO ANSWER ABOUT MY NEW BOOK.
"WHAT DOES THE TERM **DIALECTIC** MEAN IN THE CONTEXT OF YOUR BOOK?"
"WHY DOES ALL THE SEX FEEL FRUSTRATING AND SHAMEFUL?"
CHRIST - I DON'T KNOW HOW TO ANSWER SOME OF THIS STUFF.
I WONDER IF ANYONE EVER HAS THE BALLS TO JUST LET THE BOOK SAY EVERYTHING, AND NEVER ANSWER QUESTIONS...
BUT... THEN IF I DIDN'T TRY TO CHASE DOWN ANY BIT OF PRESS I CAN GET -
NOBODY WOULD KNOW ABOUT THE BOOK.
SINCE I DON'T EARN A **LIVING** FROM COMICS, I OFTEN WONDER WHAT MY MOTIVATION IS.
THE BABY WAKES UP. WE RUN ERRANDS.
WE PICK UP HIS SISTER.
SHE HAS GYMNASTICS LATER, SO I NEED TO MAKE SURE SHE EATS.
COME ON - **TWO** MORE BITES.
I'M FUULLLL!
IF I'M NOT MAKING MONEY IN COMICS, THEN WHAT AM I GETTING?
IS IT **CREATIVE SATISFACTION?**
THAT'S OBVIOUSLY WHAT I'D PREFER TO THINK.

WHILE MY DAUGHTER IS AT GYMNASTICS I GO TO THE LIBRARY WITH THE BOY.

I LIKE STAYING AND WATCHING HER LESSON IF IT'S JUST ME, BUT HAVING THE BABY THERE IS A NIGHTMARE.

I'M SPECIFICALLY LOOKING FOR A **SHORT** BOOK FOR ME TO READ.

I'VE BEEN SO BRAIN-DEAD LATELY, I HAVEN'T GOTTEN TO THE END OF A BOOK IN MONTHS.

THE GREAT GATSBY

AFTER GYMNASTICS IT'S DINNERTIME THEN BATH-TIME THEN BEDTIME.

OCCASIONALLY ROUTINES LIKE OURS CAN FEEL REPETITIVE, UNEVENTFUL...

BUT SOMETIMES I'LL TAKE A STEP BACK AND IT'LL STRIKE ME—

HOW **LUCKY** I AM TO SPEND ALL MY TIME WITH THESE PEOPLE I LOVE.

I SPEND HALF MY TIME BORED AND THE OTHER HALF TERRIFIED THAT THINGS WOULD EVER CHANGE.

IF IT'S CREATIVE SATISFACTION,

WHY DO I CARE ABOUT "PRESS" AND SALES?

HOW MANY PAGES LEFT IN THIS CHAPTER..?

CAMUS THE STRANGER

hmmm... NEW TUMBLR NOTES...

THAT EDITOR NEVER EMAILED ME BACK...

WHAT ABOUT TWITT

CAMUS THE STRANGER

FRIDAY MARCH 14TH 2014: WE ALL OVERSLEEP, BUT THE NANNY IS BACK IN ACTION AND MY WIFE HANDLES GETTING MY DAUGHTER OFF TO SCHOOL, SO I FINALLY MANAGE TO START MY WORK EARLY.

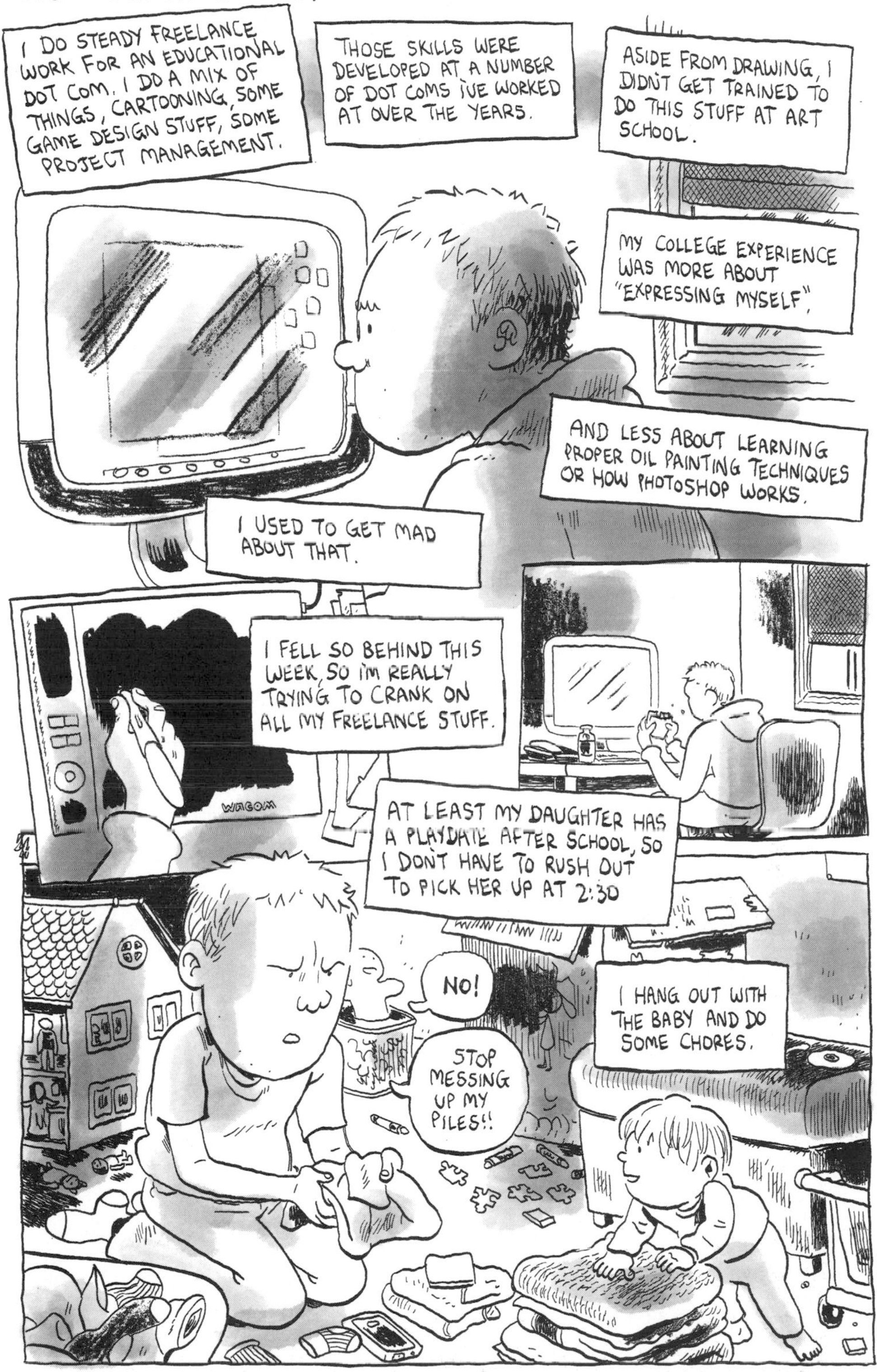

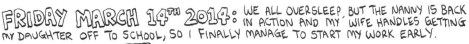

I DO STEADY FREELANCE WORK FOR AN EDUCATIONAL DOT COM. I DO A MIX OF THINGS, CARTOONING, SOME GAME DESIGN STUFF, SOME PROJECT MANAGEMENT.
THOSE SKILLS WERE DEVELOPED AT A NUMBER OF DOT COMS I'VE WORKED AT OVER THE YEARS.
ASIDE FROM DRAWING, I DIDN'T GET TRAINED TO DO THIS STUFF AT ART SCHOOL.
MY COLLEGE EXPERIENCE WAS MORE ABOUT "EXPRESSING MYSELF",
AND LESS ABOUT LEARNING PROPER OIL PAINTING TECHNIQUES OR HOW PHOTOSHOP WORKS.
I USED TO GET MAD ABOUT THAT.
I FELL SO BEHIND THIS WEEK, SO I'M REALLY TRYING TO CRANK ON ALL MY FREELANCE STUFF.
WACOM
AT LEAST MY DAUGHTER HAS A PLAYDATE AFTER SCHOOL, SO I DON'T HAVE TO RUSH OUT TO PICK HER UP AT 2:30
NO!
STOP MESSING UP MY PILES!!
I HANG OUT WITH THE BABY AND DO SOME CHORES.

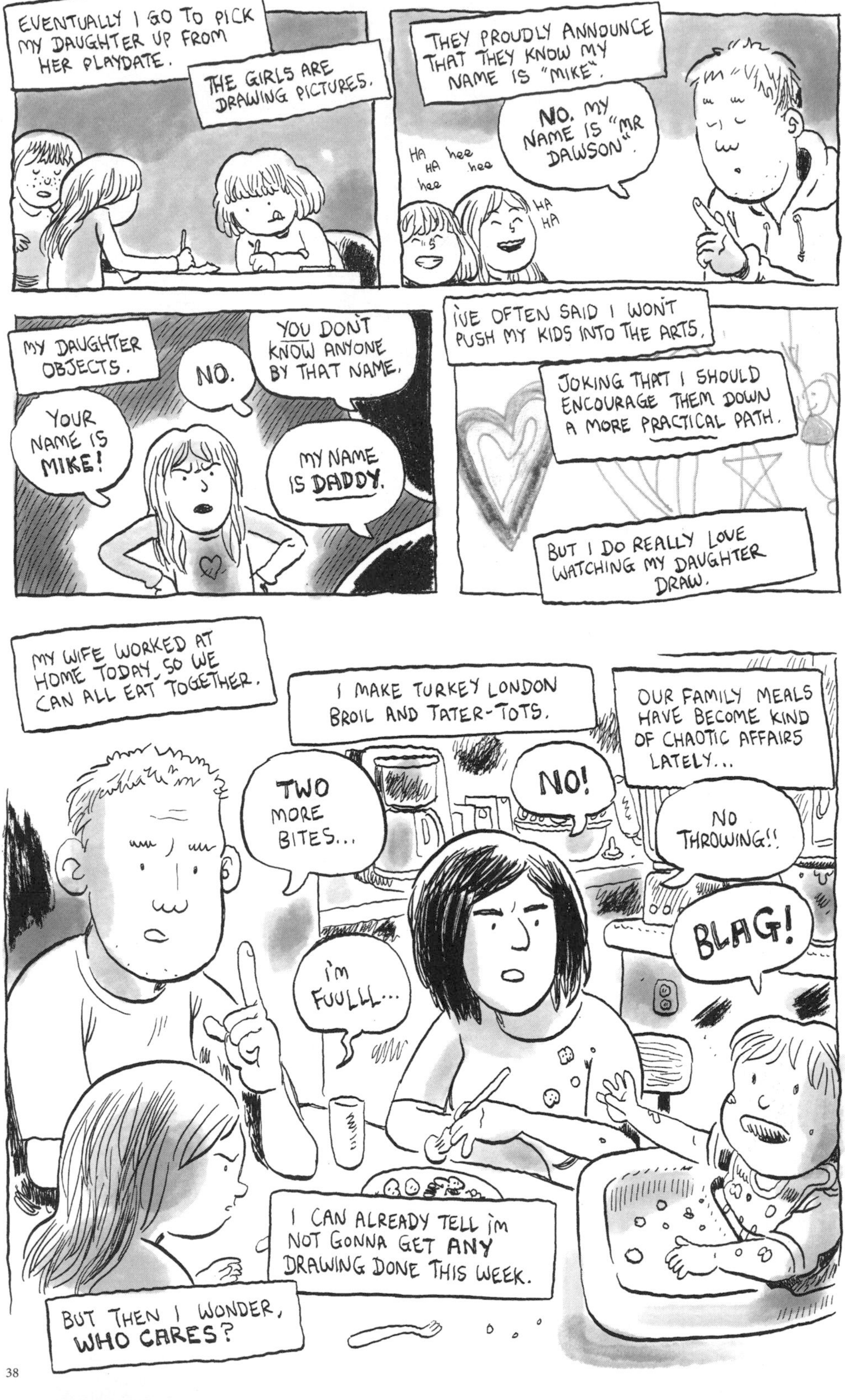
EVENTUALLY I GO TO PICK MY DAUGHTER UP FROM HER PLAYDATE.
THE GIRLS ARE DRAWING PICTURES.
THEY PROUDLY ANNOUNCE THAT THEY KNOW MY NAME IS "MIKE".
HA HA hee hee hee
NO. MY NAME IS "MR DAWSON".
HA HA
MY DAUGHTER OBJECTS.
NO.
YOU DON'T KNOW ANYONE BY THAT NAME.
YOUR NAME IS MIKE!
MY NAME IS DADDY.
I'VE OFTEN SAID I WON'T PUSH MY KIDS INTO THE ARTS,
JOKING THAT I SHOULD ENCOURAGE THEM DOWN A MORE PRACTICAL PATH.
BUT I DO REALLY LOVE WATCHING MY DAUGHTER DRAW.
MY WIFE WORKED AT HOME TODAY, SO WE CAN ALL EAT TOGETHER.
I MAKE TURKEY LONDON BROIL AND TATER-TOTS.
OUR FAMILY MEALS HAVE BECOME KIND OF CHAOTIC AFFAIRS LATELY...
TWO MORE BITES...
NO!
NO THROWING!!
BLAG!
I'M FUULLL...
I CAN ALREADY TELL I'M NOT GONNA GET ANY DRAWING DONE THIS WEEK.
BUT THEN I WONDER, WHO CARES?

IT'S NOT LIKE I'LL NEVER DRAW AGAIN.

MAYBE I JUST DON'T HAVE ANYTHING I WANT TO DRAW RIGHT NOW.

WHEN DID THIS DRAW **SOMETHING EVERY DAY** COMPULSION TAKE OVER?

WHEN DID WE DECIDE THAT WAS SO **HEROIC?**

WHEN I THINK ABOUT MY **WORK/LIFE BALANCE,** I FEEL LIKE MOST OF MY ENERGY GOES INTO TRYING TO SQUEEZE MORE **WORK** INTO AN ALREADY BUSY **LIFE.**

MAYBE FOR A WHILE I SHOULD TRY AND DO THE OPPOSITE OF THAT.

MAYBE IT'S ALL THE **LIFE** PART THAT CAN MAKE MY **WORK** BETTER.

I DUNNO...
WE'LL SEE.

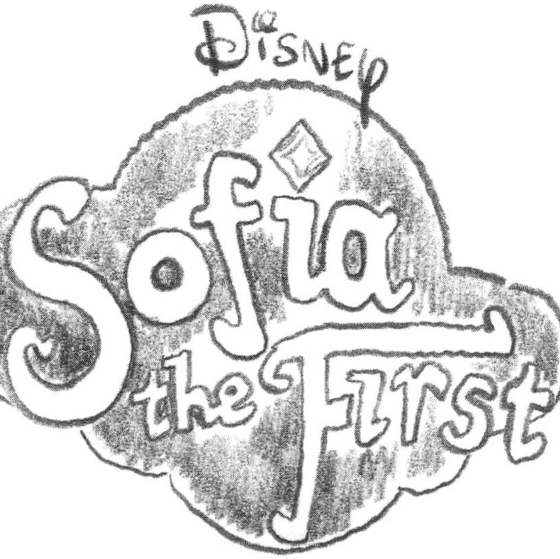
Disney
Sofia
the First

SOFIA THE FIRST IS A SHOW THAT AIRS ON THE DISNEY JUNIOR CHANNEL. IT'S ABOUT A LITTLE GIRL, SOFIA, WHO LIVES AS A COMMONER IN A KINGDOM CALLED ENCHANCIA, UNTIL HER MOTHER MARRIES THE KING AND THEY BECOME ROYALTY.

THE KING HAS TWO CHILDREN OF HIS OWN,
AMBER AND JAMES. THE PREMISE OF THE
SHOW IS THAT SINCE SOFIA BECAME ROYALTY
OVERNIGHT, SHE HAS TO LEARN HOW TO BE
A PRINCESS.

THE TWIST, OF COURSE, BEING THAT SOFIA
FREQUENTLY LEARNS THAT THE QUALITIES THAT
MAKE HER A "TRUE" PRINCESS ARE THINGS
LIKE KINDNESS, LOYALTY, AND GENEROSITY.

SOFIA AND HER MOTHER ARE NOW FABULOUSY
WEALTHY. THE ROYAL CHILDREN'S EVERY NEEDS
ARE ATTENDED TO BY THEIR SERVANT BAILEYWICK.
IN ONE EPISODE BAILEYWICK'S BROTHER CONVINCES
HIM TO TAKE A DAY OFF FOR HIS BIRTHDAY, BUT
BAILEYWICK NEVER MANAGES TO LEAVE THE
CASTLE GROUNDS BECAUSE THE KIDS KEEP NEEDING
HIS HELP, WHICH HE HAPPILY PROVIDES.

SOFIA HAS TWO "COMMONER" FRIENDS FROM
HER LIFE IN THE VILLAGE. STORIES WITH
THEM USUALLY REVOLVE AROUND SOFIA
LEARNING SHE MUST REMAIN DOWN TO
EARTH WITH HER NON-ROYAL FRIENDS, AND
TREAT THEM WITH RESPECT.

IN 1939, GEORGE ORWELL WROTE AN ESSAY ABOUT THE WORKS OF CHARLES DICKENS. HE SAID OF DICKEN'S POLITICS:

"DICKEN'S CRITICISM OF SOCIETY IS ALMOST EXCLUSIVELY MORAL.

—

THERE IS NO CLEAR SIGN HE WANTS THE EXISTING ORDER OVERTHROWN... FOR IN REALITY HIS TARGET IS NOT SO MUCH SOCIETY AS HUMAN NATURE.

IT WOULD BE DIFFICULT TO POINT ANYWHERE IN HIS BOOKS TO A PASSAGE SUGGESTING THAT THE ECONOMIC SYSTEM IS WRONG AS A SYSTEM.

—

[DICKEN'S BOOK HARD TIMES] WHOLE MORAL IS THAT CAPITALISTS OUGHT TO BE KIND, NOT THAT WORKERS OUGHT TO BE REBELLIOUS.

—

HIS WHOLE "MESSAGE" IS... IF MEN WOULD BEHAVE DECENTLY THE WORLD WOULD BE DECENT.

DISNEY'S CONCEPT OF PROGRESSIVISM IS ALL ABOUT THE RULING CLASS BEING <u>KIND</u> AND BENEVOLENT. THE EXISTENCE OF A RULING CLASS (AND THEREFORE LOWER CLASSES) IS NEVER CALLED INTO QUESTION.

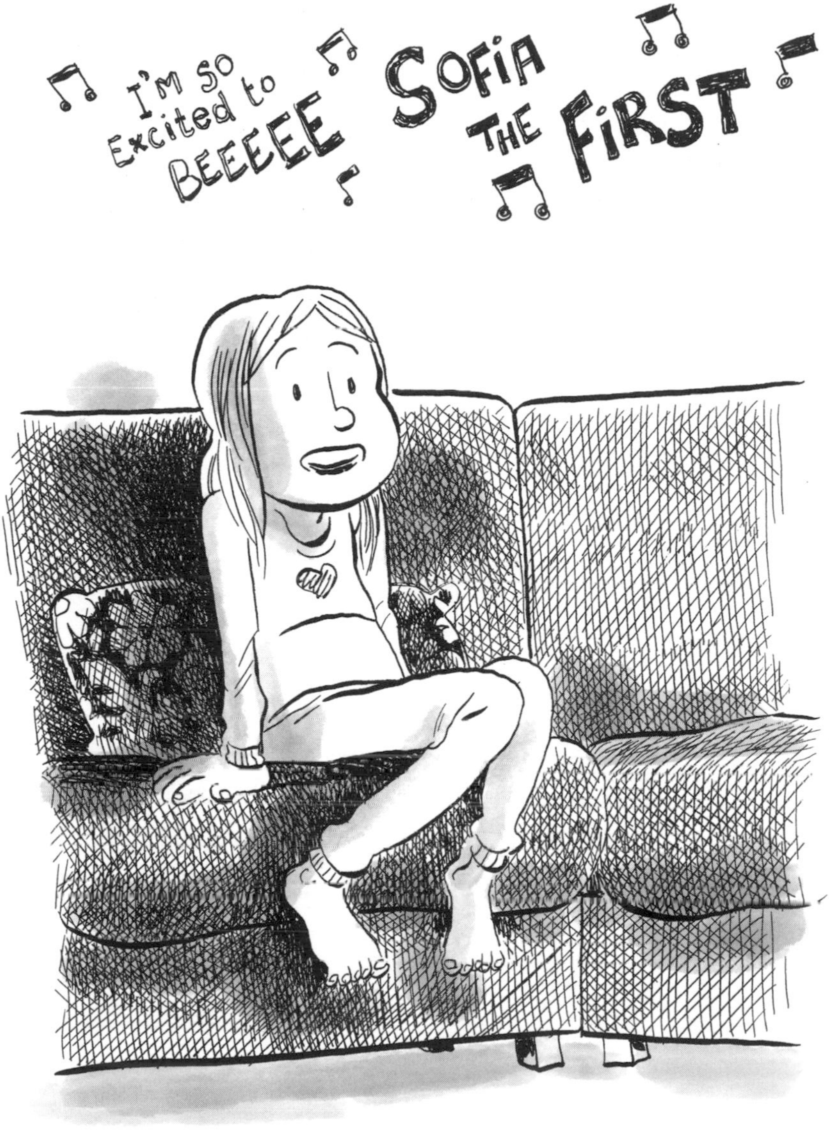
I'M SO Excited to BEEEEE SOFIA THE FIRST

LATELY MY DAUGHTER HAS BEEN TALKING A LOT ABOUT HOW SHE WANTS TO BE A PRINCESS WHEN SHE GROWS UP. SHE WANTS TO LIVE IN A BIG CASTLE WITH A FANCY STAIRCASE AND WEAR BEAUTIFUL DRESSES ALL DAY LONG.

MY PARENTAL DILEMMA NOW IS WHETHER I SHOULD EXPLAIN HOW UNLIKELY IT IS THAT WILL HAPPEN, OR SHOULD I ENCOURAGE HER ASPIRATIONS, AND FOCUS ON MAKING SURE THAT WHEN SHE **DOES** ASCEND TO THE RULING CLASS, SHE TREATS HER SUBJECTS WITH KINDNESS, BENEVOLENCY, AND RESPECT?

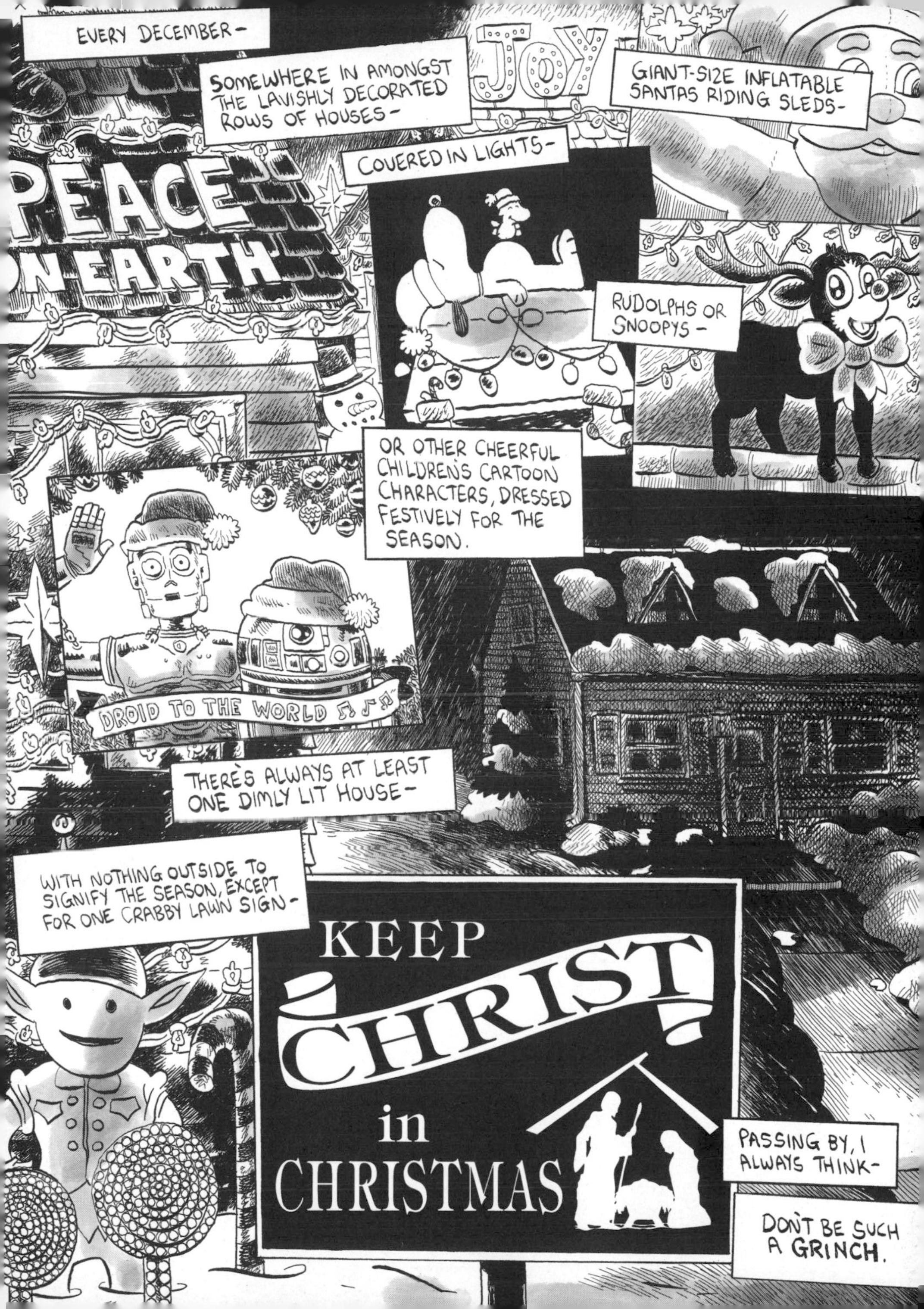
EVERY DECEMBER-
SOMEWHERE IN AMONGST THE LAVISHLY DECORATED ROWS OF HOUSES-
JOY
GIANT-SIZE INFLATABLE SANTAS RIDING SLEDS-
PEACE ON EARTH
COVERED IN LIGHTS-
RUDOLPHS OR SNOOPYS-
OR OTHER CHEERFUL CHILDREN'S CARTOON CHARACTERS, DRESSED FESTIVELY FOR THE SEASON.
DROID TO THE WORLD
THERE'S ALWAYS AT LEAST ONE DIMLY LIT HOUSE-
WITH NOTHING OUTSIDE TO SIGNIFY THE SEASON, EXCEPT FOR ONE CRABBY LAWN SIGN-
KEEP CHRIST in CHRISTMAS
PASSING BY, I ALWAYS THINK-
DON'T BE SUCH A GRINCH.

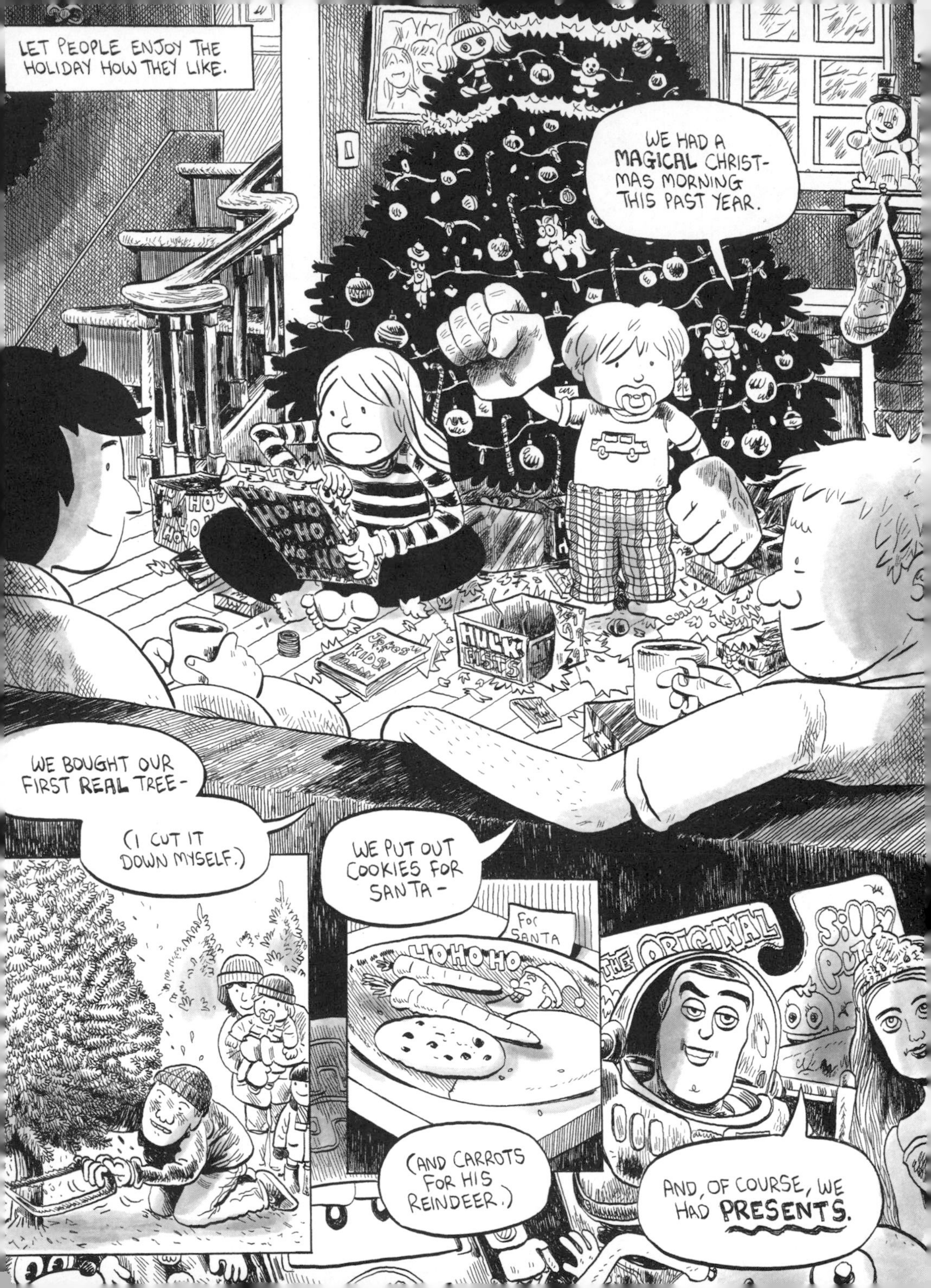
LET PEOPLE ENJOY THE HOLIDAY HOW THEY LIKE.
WE HAD A MAGICAL CHRISTMAS MORNING THIS PAST YEAR.
HO HO HO
HULK FISTS
WE BOUGHT OUR FIRST REAL TREE-
(I CUT IT DOWN MYSELF.)
WE PUT OUT COOKIES FOR SANTA-
FOR SANTA
HOHOHO
(AND CARROTS FOR HIS REINDEER.)
THE ORIGINAL
AND, OF COURSE, WE HAD PRESENTS.

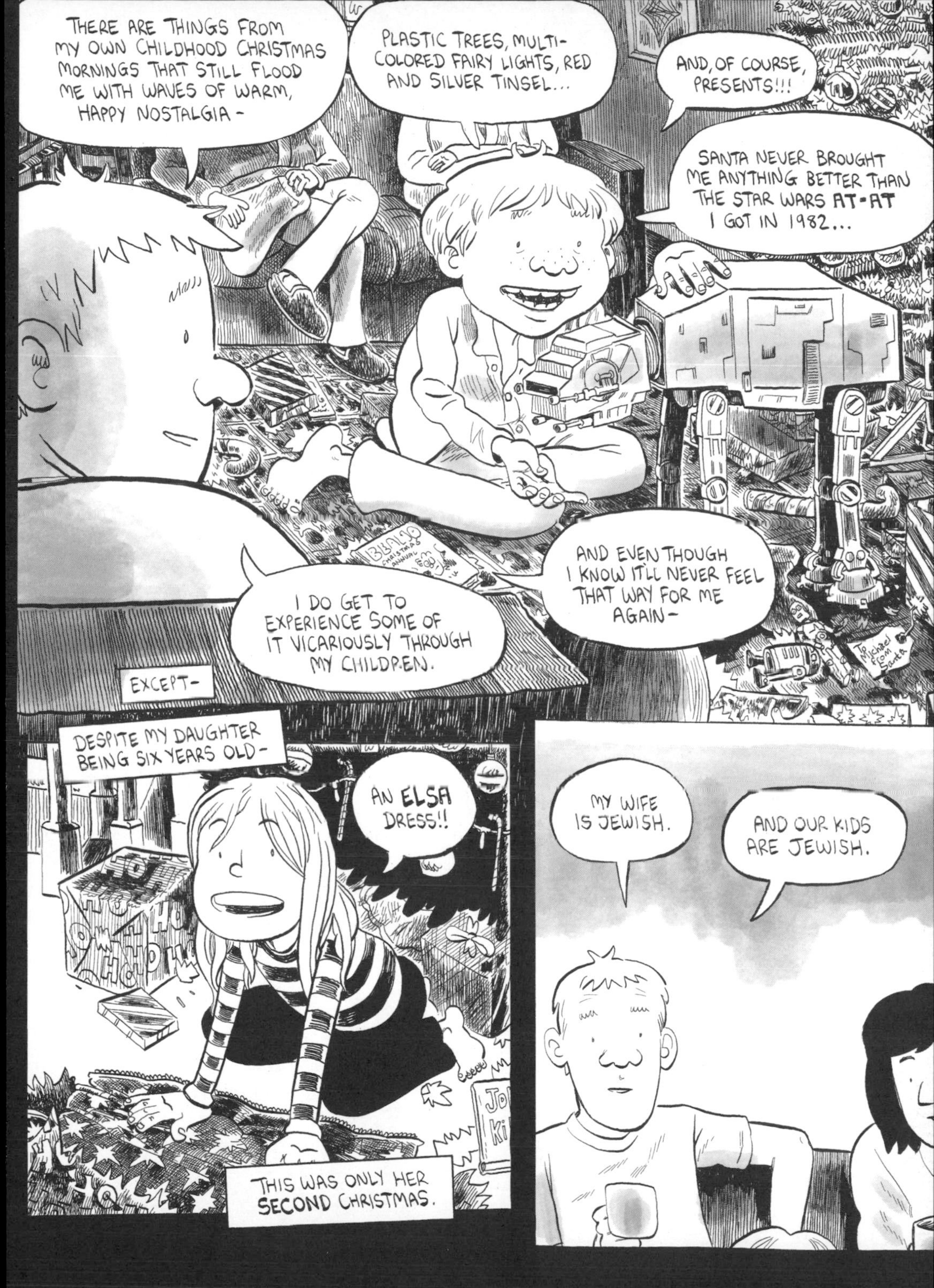
THERE ARE THINGS FROM MY OWN CHILDHOOD CHRISTMAS MORNINGS THAT STILL FLOOD ME WITH WAVES OF WARM, HAPPY NOSTALGIA -
PLASTIC TREES, MULTI-COLORED FAIRY LIGHTS, RED AND SILVER TINSEL...
AND, OF COURSE, PRESENTS!!!
SANTA NEVER BROUGHT ME ANYTHING BETTER THAN THE STAR WARS AT-AT I GOT IN 1982...
AND EVEN THOUGH I KNOW IT'LL NEVER FEEL THAT WAY FOR ME AGAIN -
I DO GET TO EXPERIENCE SOME OF IT VICARIOUSLY THROUGH MY CHILDREN.
EXCEPT -
DESPITE MY DAUGHTER BEING SIX YEARS OLD -
AN ELSA DRESS!!
THIS WAS ONLY HER SECOND CHRISTMAS.
MY WIFE IS JEWISH.
AND OUR KIDS ARE JEWISH.

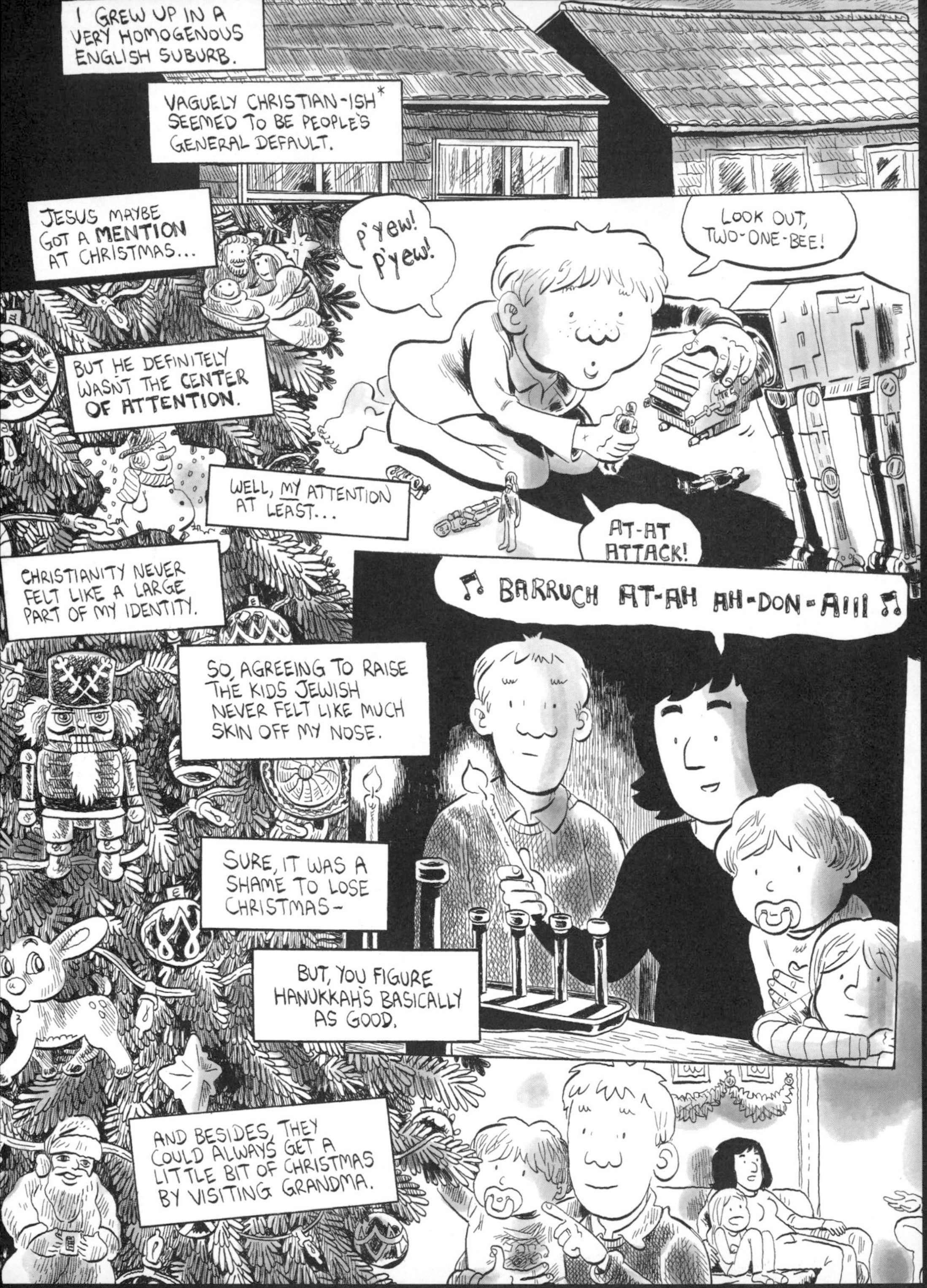
I GREW UP IN A VERY HOMOGENOUS ENGLISH SUBURB.
VAGUELY CHRISTIAN-ISH* SEEMED TO BE PEOPLE'S GENERAL DEFAULT.
JESUS MAYBE GOT A MENTION AT CHRISTMAS...
P'YEW! P'YEW!
LOOK OUT, TWO-ONE-BEE!
BUT HE DEFINITELY WASN'T THE CENTER OF ATTENTION.
WELL, MY ATTENTION AT LEAST...
AT-AT ATTACK!
CHRISTIANITY NEVER FELT LIKE A LARGE PART OF MY IDENTITY.
♫ BARRUCH AT-AH AH-DON-AIII ♫
SO, AGREEING TO RAISE THE KIDS JEWISH NEVER FELT LIKE MUCH SKIN OFF MY NOSE.
SURE, IT WAS A SHAME TO LOSE CHRISTMAS-
BUT, YOU FIGURE HANUKKAH'S BASICALLY AS GOOD.
AND BESIDES, THEY COULD ALWAYS GET A LITTLE BIT OF CHRISTMAS BY VISITING GRANDMA.

* "VAGUELY CHRISTIAN-ISH" IS ALSO MY IMPRESSION OF THE CHURCH OF ENGLAND.

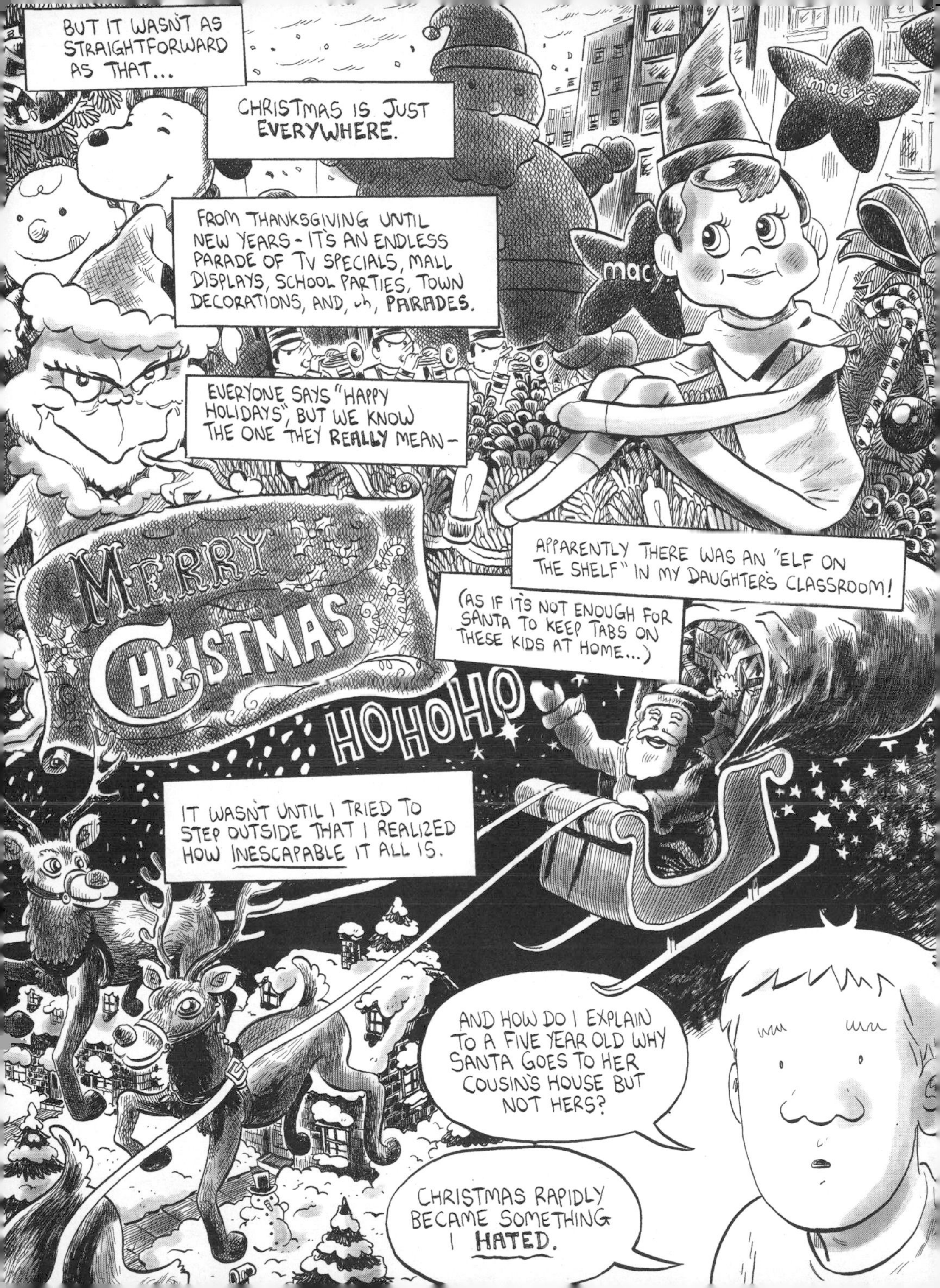
BUT IT WASN'T AS STRAIGHTFORWARD AS THAT...
CHRISTMAS IS JUST EVERYWHERE.
macy's
FROM THANKSGIVING UNTIL NEW YEARS - IT'S AN ENDLESS PARADE OF TV SPECIALS, MALL DISPLAYS, SCHOOL PARTIES, TOWN DECORATIONS, AND, uh, PARADES.
EVERYONE SAYS "HAPPY HOLIDAYS", BUT WE KNOW THE ONE THEY REALLY MEAN-
MERRY CHRISTMAS
APPARENTLY THERE WAS AN "ELF ON THE SHELF" IN MY DAUGHTER'S CLASSROOM!
(AS IF IT'S NOT ENOUGH FOR SANTA TO KEEP TABS ON THESE KIDS AT HOME...)
HOHOHO
IT WASN'T UNTIL I TRIED TO STEP OUTSIDE THAT I REALIZED HOW INESCAPABLE IT ALL IS.
AND HOW DO I EXPLAIN TO A FIVE YEAR OLD WHY SANTA GOES TO HER COUSIN'S HOUSE BUT NOT HERS?
CHRISTMAS RAPIDLY BECAME SOMETHING I HATED.

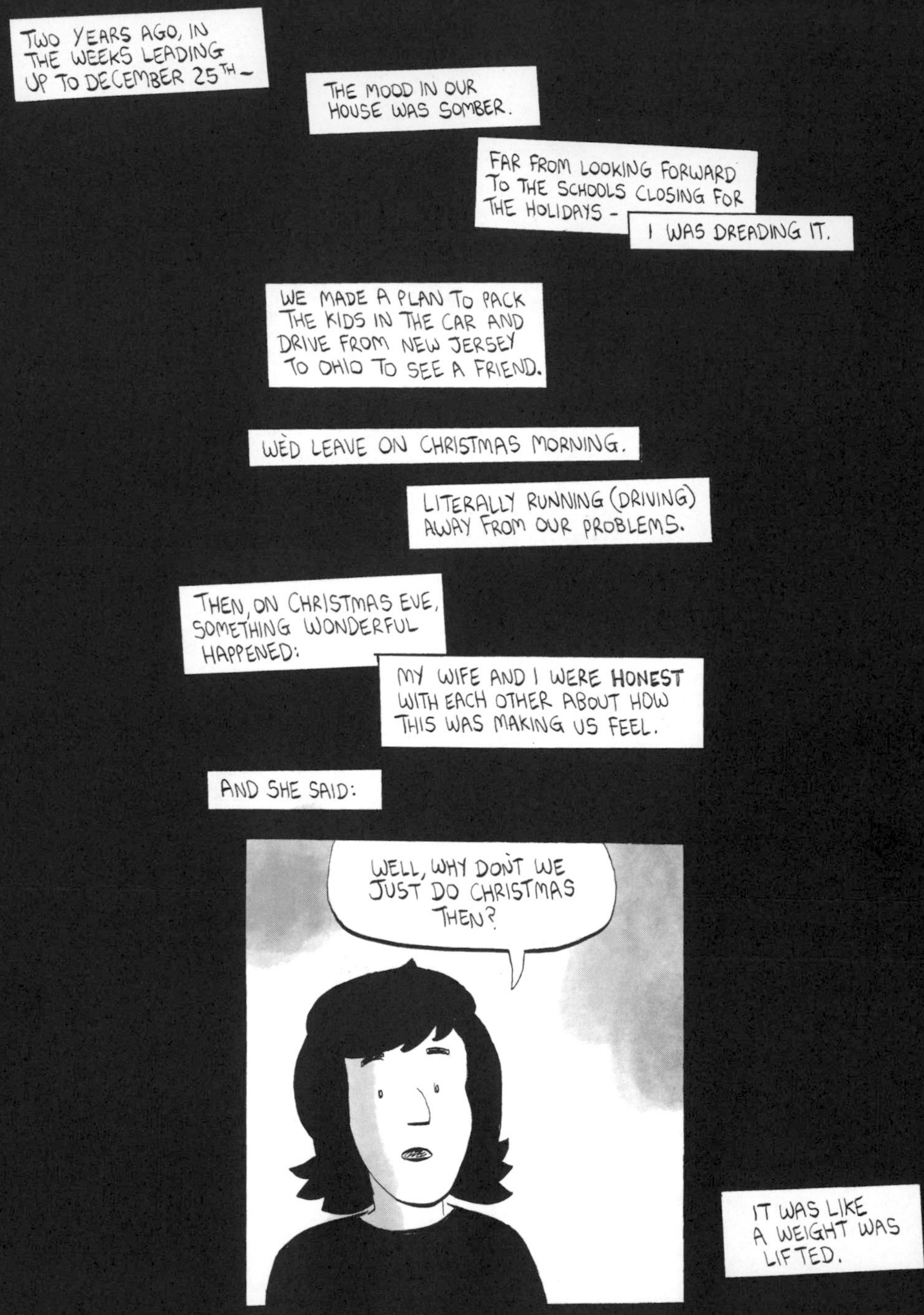
TWO YEARS AGO, IN THE WEEKS LEADING UP TO DECEMBER 25TH –
THE MOOD IN OUR HOUSE WAS SOMBER.
FAR FROM LOOKING FORWARD TO THE SCHOOLS CLOSING FOR THE HOLIDAYS –
I WAS DREADING IT.
WE MADE A PLAN TO PACK THE KIDS IN THE CAR AND DRIVE FROM NEW JERSEY TO OHIO TO SEE A FRIEND.
WE'D LEAVE ON CHRISTMAS MORNING.
LITERALLY RUNNING (DRIVING) AWAY FROM OUR PROBLEMS.
THEN, ON CHRISTMAS EVE, SOMETHING WONDERFUL HAPPENED:
MY WIFE AND I WERE **HONEST** WITH EACH OTHER ABOUT HOW THIS WAS MAKING US FEEL.
AND SHE SAID:
WELL, WHY DON'T WE JUST DO CHRISTMAS THEN?
IT WAS LIKE A WEIGHT WAS LIFTED.

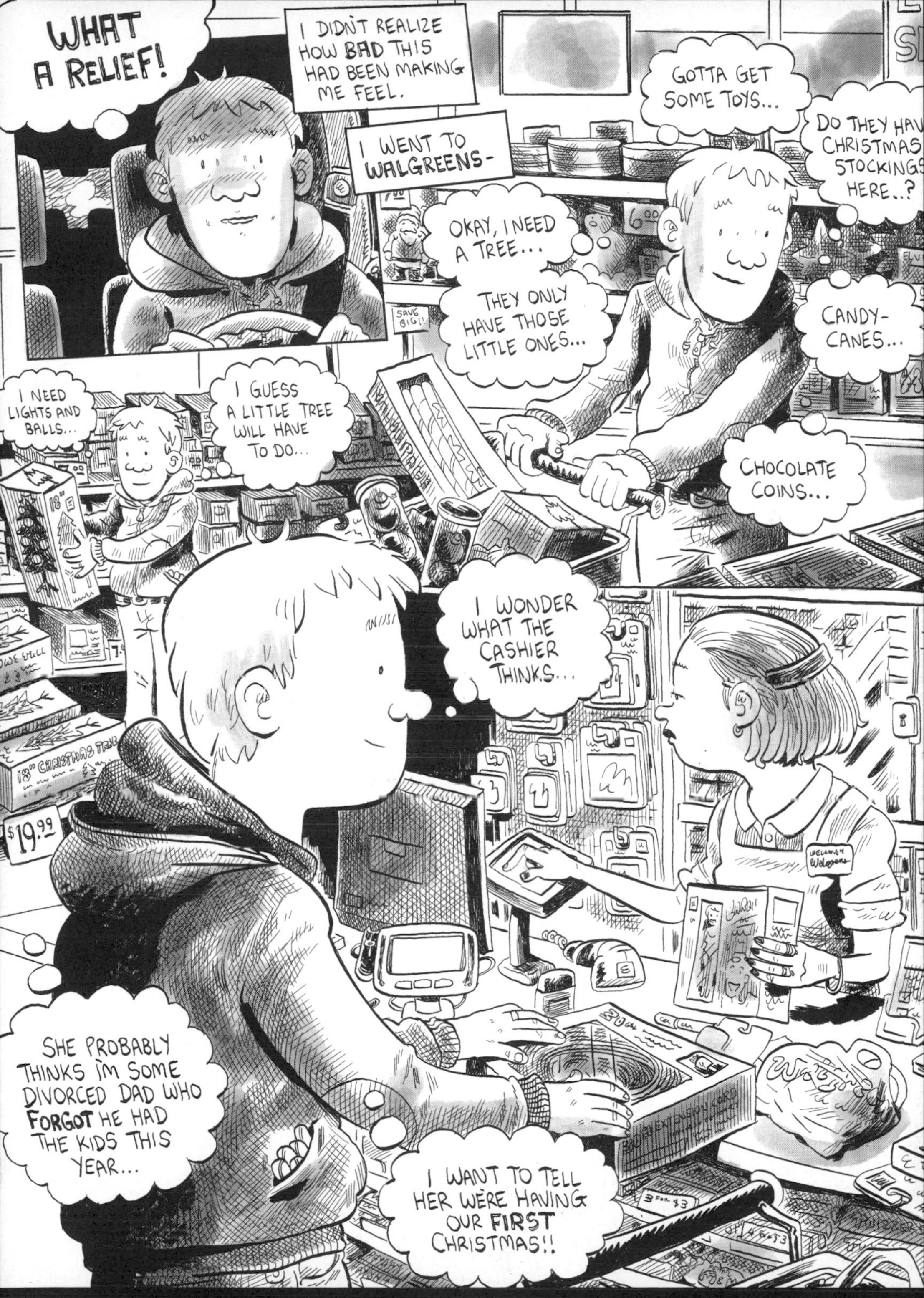
WHAT A RELIEF!
I DIDN'T REALIZE HOW BAD THIS HAD BEEN MAKING ME FEEL.
I WENT TO WALGREENS-
GOTTA GET SOME TOYS...
DO THEY HAVE CHRISTMAS STOCKINGS HERE..?
OKAY, I NEED A TREE...
THEY ONLY HAVE THOSE LITTLE ONES...
CANDY-CANES...
CHOCOLATE COINS...
I NEED LIGHTS AND BALLS...
I GUESS A LITTLE TREE WILL HAVE TO DO...
I WONDER WHAT THE CASHIER THINKS...
SHE PROBABLY THINKS I'M SOME DIVORCED DAD WHO FORGOT HE HAD THE KIDS THIS YEAR...
I WANT TO TELL HER WE'RE HAVING OUR FIRST CHRISTMAS!!

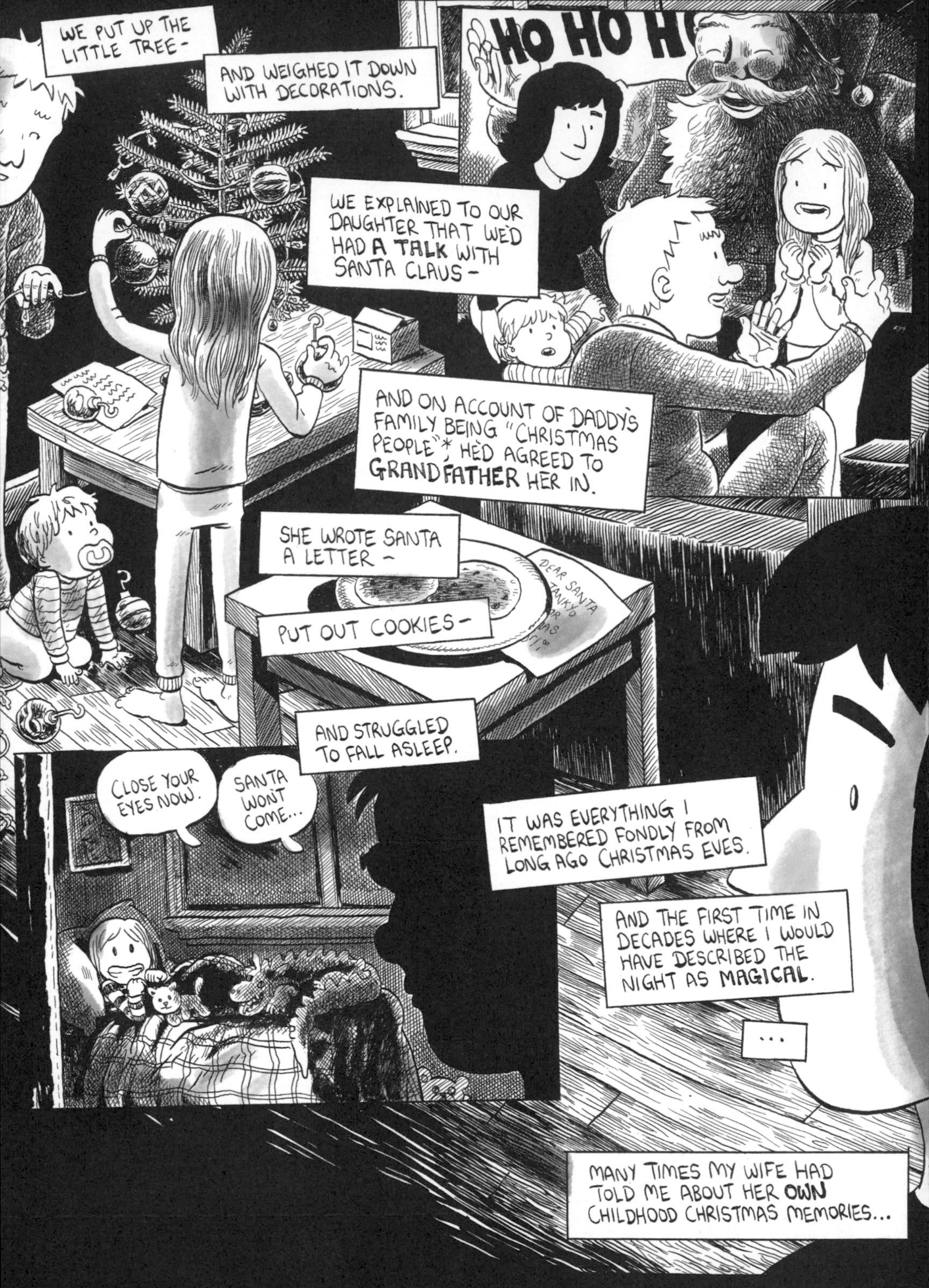
WE PUT UP THE LITTLE TREE -
AND WEIGHED IT DOWN WITH DECORATIONS.
HO HO HO
WE EXPLAINED TO OUR DAUGHTER THAT WE'D HAD A TALK WITH SANTA CLAUS -
AND ON ACCOUNT OF DADDY'S FAMILY BEING "CHRISTMAS PEOPLE"*, HE'D AGREED TO GRANDFATHER HER IN.
SHE WROTE SANTA A LETTER -
DEAR SANTA
PUT OUT COOKIES -
AND STRUGGLED TO FALL ASLEEP.
CLOSE YOUR EYES NOW.
SANTA WON'T COME...
IT WAS EVERYTHING I REMEMBERED FONDLY FROM LONG AGO CHRISTMAS EVES.
AND THE FIRST TIME IN DECADES WHERE I WOULD HAVE DESCRIBED THE NIGHT AS MAGICAL.
...
MANY TIMES MY WIFE HAD TOLD ME ABOUT HER OWN CHILDHOOD CHRISTMAS MEMORIES...
* CHRISTIAN

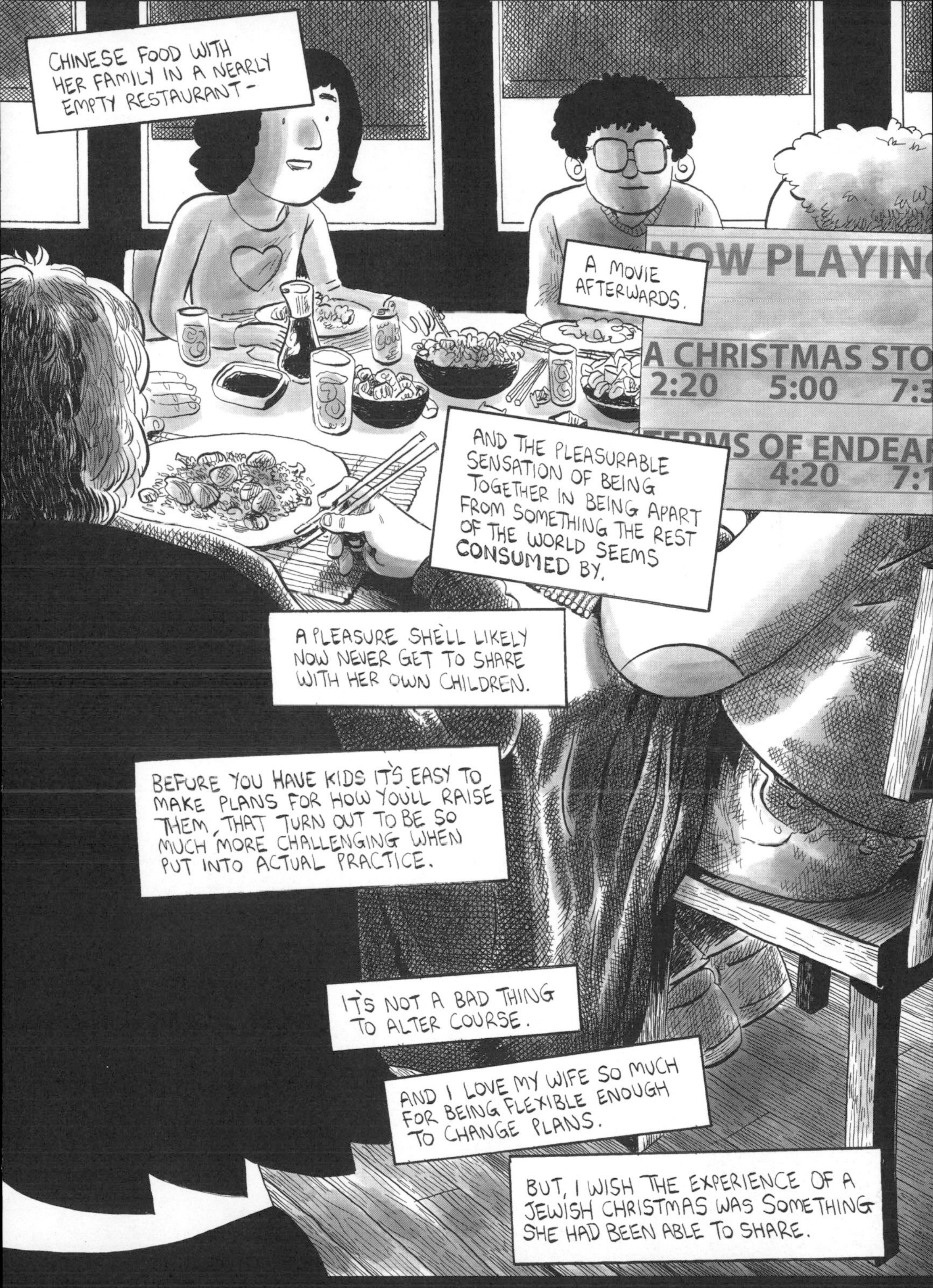
CHINESE FOOD WITH HER FAMILY IN A NEARLY EMPTY RESTAURANT-
A MOVIE AFTERWARDS.
NOW PLAYING
A CHRISTMAS STO
2:20 5:00 7:3
TERMS OF ENDEAR
4:20 7:1
AND THE PLEASURABLE SENSATION OF BEING TOGETHER IN BEING APART FROM SOMETHING THE REST OF THE WORLD SEEMS CONSUMED BY.
A PLEASURE SHE'LL LIKELY NOW NEVER GET TO SHARE WITH HER OWN CHILDREN.
BEFORE YOU HAVE KIDS IT'S EASY TO MAKE PLANS FOR HOW YOU'LL RAISE THEM, THAT TURN OUT TO BE SO MUCH MORE CHALLENGING WHEN PUT INTO ACTUAL PRACTICE.
IT'S NOT A BAD THING TO ALTER COURSE.
AND I LOVE MY WIFE SO MUCH FOR BEING FLEXIBLE ENOUGH TO CHANGE PLANS.
BUT, I WISH THE EXPERIENCE OF A JEWISH CHRISTMAS WAS SOMETHING SHE HAD BEEN ABLE TO SHARE.

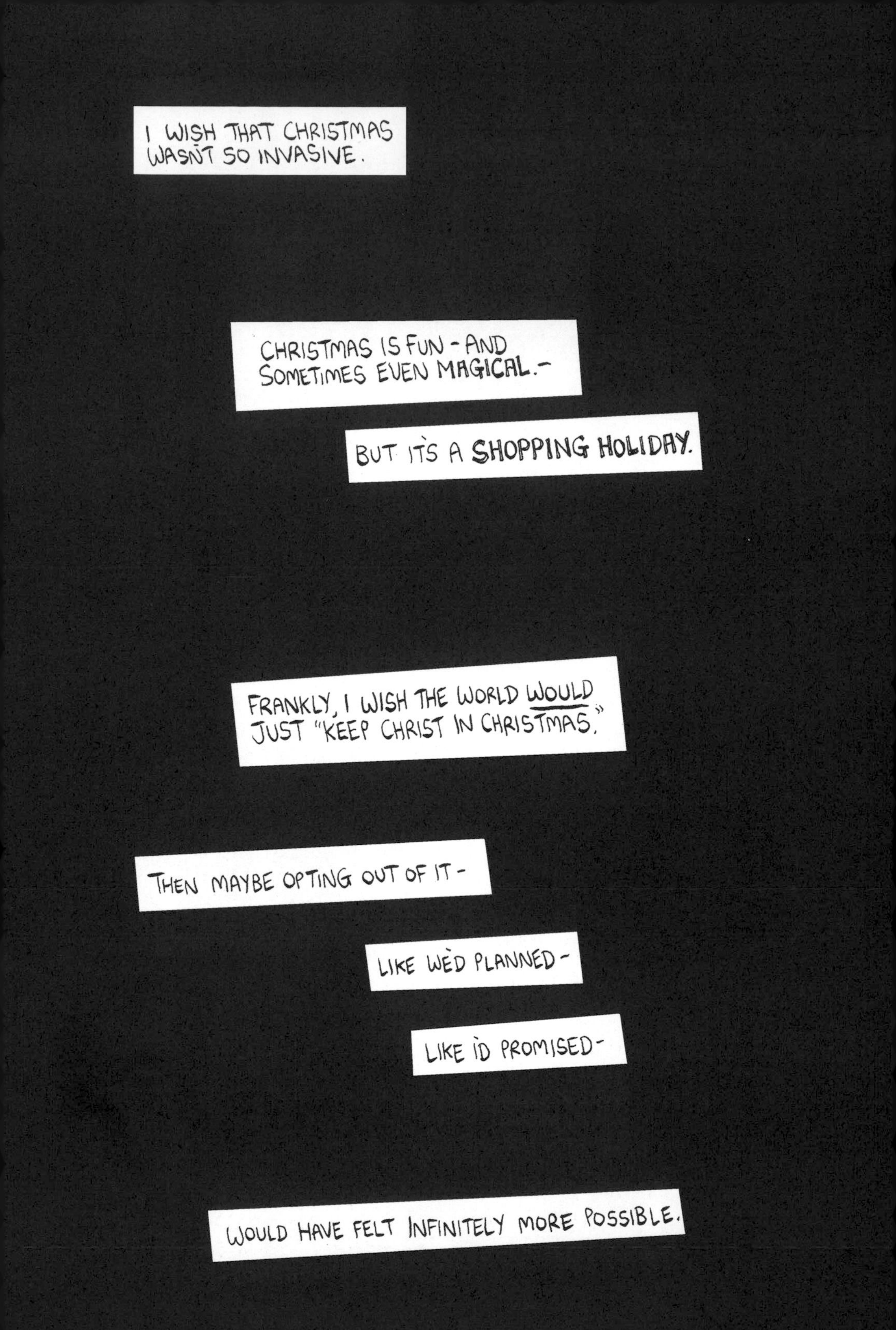
I WISH THAT CHRISTMAS WASN'T SO INVASIVE.
CHRISTMAS IS FUN - AND SOMETIMES EVEN MAGICAL.-
BUT IT'S A SHOPPING HOLIDAY.
FRANKLY, I WISH THE WORLD WOULD JUST "KEEP CHRIST IN CHRISTMAS."
THEN MAYBE OPTING OUT OF IT -
LIKE WE'D PLANNED -
LIKE I'D PROMISED -
WOULD HAVE FELT INFINITELY MORE POSSIBLE.

MONDAY DECEMBER 1ST, 2014: IT'S THE FIRST DAY BACK TO NORMAL AFTER THE THANKSGIVING BREAK. MY DAUGHTER GOES TO SCHOOL, MY SON GOES TO SPEND THE DAY WITH MY PARENTS, AND MY WIFE AND I RESUME WORKING.

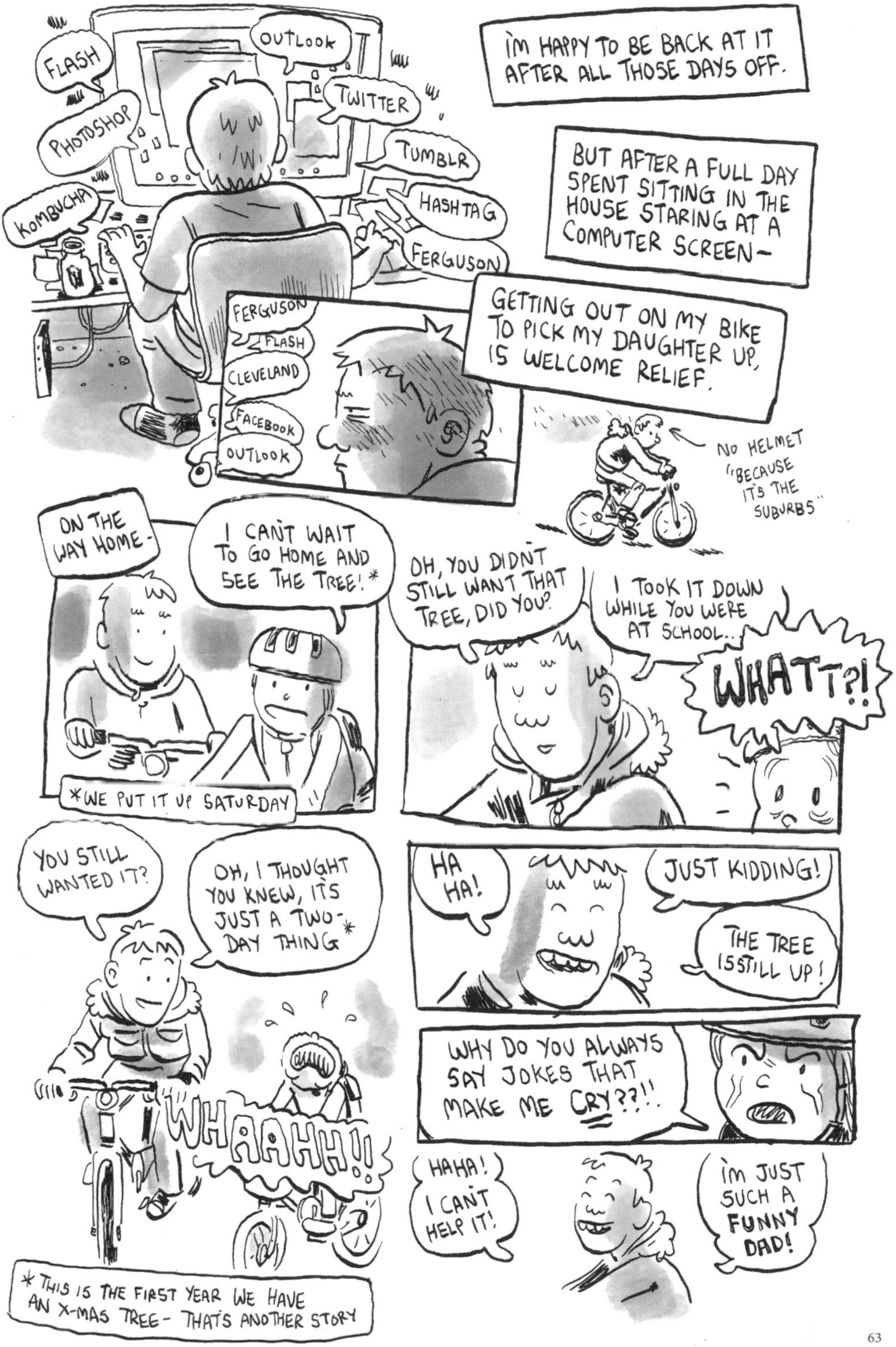
FLASH
OUTLOOK
TWITTER
PHOTOSHOP
TUMBLR
KOMBUCHA
HASHTAG
FERGUSON
I'M HAPPY TO BE BACK AT IT AFTER ALL THOSE DAYS OFF.
BUT AFTER A FULL DAY SPENT SITTING IN THE HOUSE STARING AT A COMPUTER SCREEN–
FERGUSON
FLASH
CLEVELAND
FACEBOOK
OUTLOOK
GETTING OUT ON MY BIKE TO PICK MY DAUGHTER UP, IS WELCOME RELIEF.
NO HELMET "BECAUSE IT'S THE SUBURBS"
ON THE WAY HOME–
I CAN'T WAIT TO GO HOME AND SEE THE TREE! *
*WE PUT IT UP SATURDAY
OH, YOU DIDN'T STILL WANT THAT TREE, DID YOU?
I TOOK IT DOWN WHILE YOU WERE AT SCHOOL...
WHATT?!
YOU STILL WANTED IT?
OH, I THOUGHT YOU KNEW, IT'S JUST A TWO-DAY THING *
WHAAHH!!
HA HA!
JUST KIDDING!
THE TREE IS STILL UP!
WHY DO YOU ALWAYS SAY JOKES THAT MAKE ME CRY??!!
HAHA! I CAN'T HELP IT!
I'M JUST SUCH A FUNNY DAD!
* THIS IS THE FIRST YEAR WE HAVE AN X-MAS TREE– THAT'S ANOTHER STORY

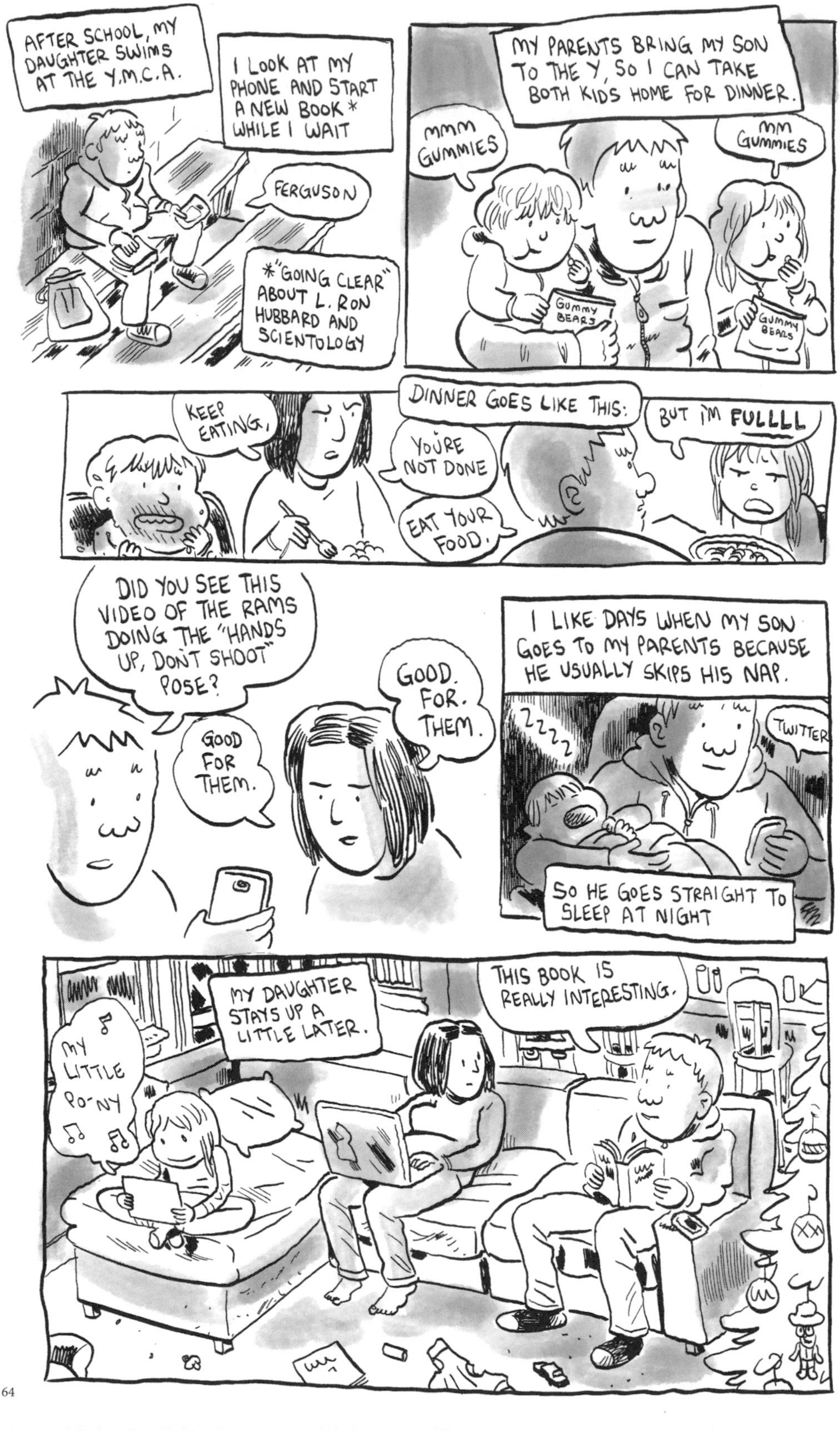
AFTER SCHOOL, MY DAUGHTER SWIMS AT THE Y.M.C.A.
I LOOK AT MY PHONE AND START A NEW BOOK * WHILE I WAIT
FERGUSON
*"GOING CLEAR" ABOUT L. RON HUBBARD AND SCIENTOLOGY
MY PARENTS BRING MY SON TO THE Y, SO I CAN TAKE BOTH KIDS HOME FOR DINNER.
MMM GUMMIES
MM GUMMIES
GUMMY BEARS
GUMMY BEARS
DINNER GOES LIKE THIS:
KEEP EATING.
YOU'RE NOT DONE
EAT YOUR FOOD.
BUT I'M **FULLLL**
DID YOU SEE THIS VIDEO OF THE RAMS DOING THE "HANDS UP, DON'T SHOOT" POSE?
GOOD FOR THEM.
GOOD. FOR. THEM.
I LIKE DAYS WHEN MY SON GOES TO MY PARENTS BECAUSE HE USUALLY SKIPS HIS NAP.
ZZZZ
TWITTER
SO HE GOES STRAIGHT TO SLEEP AT NIGHT
MY DAUGHTER STAYS UP A LITTLE LATER.
MY LITTLE PO-NY
THIS BOOK IS REALLY INTERESTING.

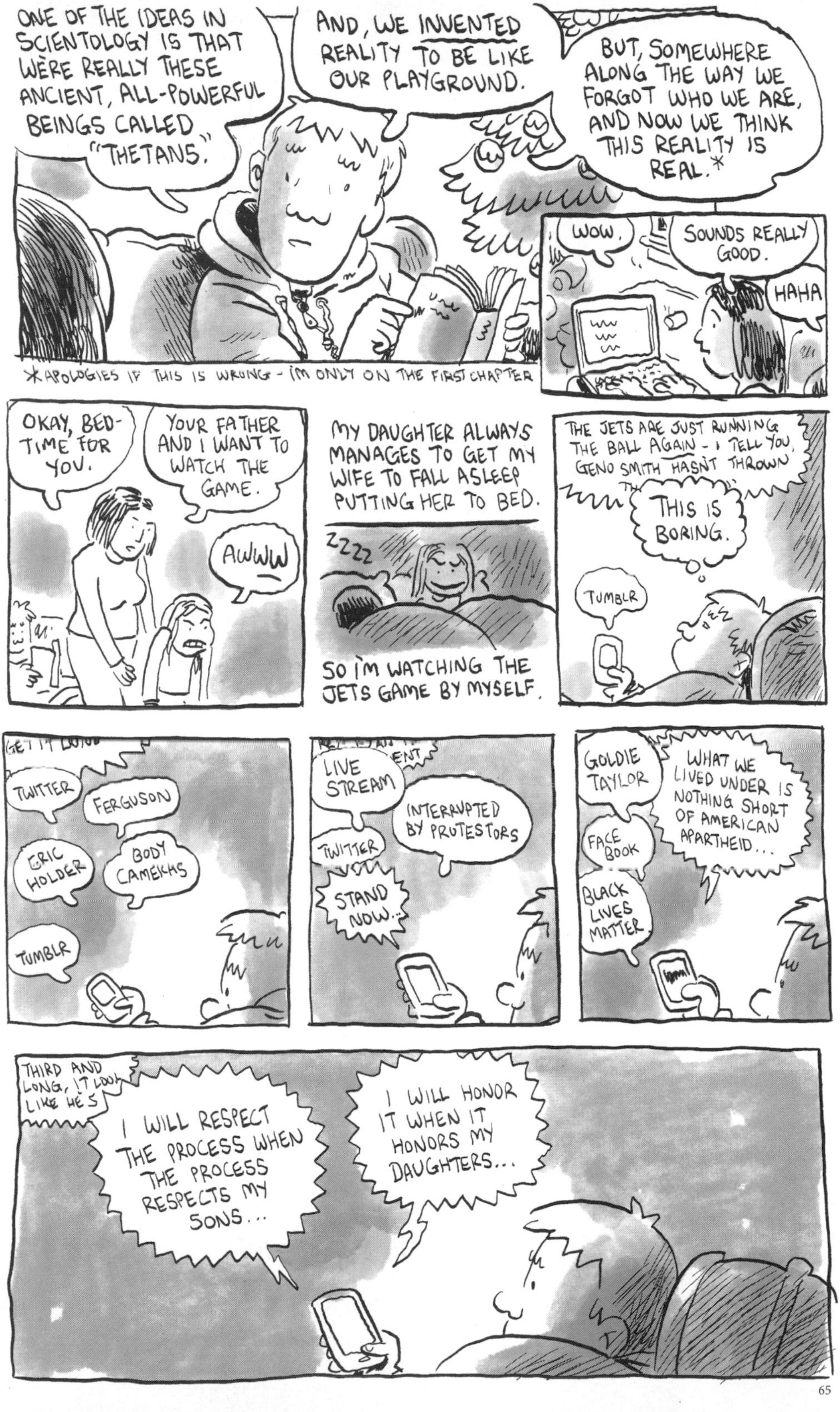
ONE OF THE IDEAS IN SCIENTOLOGY IS THAT WE'RE REALLY THESE ANCIENT, ALL-POWERFUL BEINGS CALLED "THETANS."
AND, WE INVENTED REALITY TO BE LIKE OUR PLAYGROUND.
BUT, SOMEWHERE ALONG THE WAY WE FORGOT WHO WE ARE, AND NOW WE THINK THIS REALITY IS REAL.*
*APOLOGIES IF THIS IS WRONG - I'M ONLY ON THE FIRST CHAPTER
WOW.
SOUNDS REALLY GOOD.
HAHA
OKAY, BED-TIME FOR YOU.
YOUR FATHER AND I WANT TO WATCH THE GAME.
AWWW
MY DAUGHTER ALWAYS MANAGES TO GET MY WIFE TO FALL ASLEEP PUTTING HER TO BED.
ZZZZ
SO I'M WATCHING THE JETS GAME BY MYSELF.
THE JETS ARE JUST RUNNING THE BALL AGAIN - I TELL YOU, GENO SMITH HASN'T THROWN
THIS IS BORING.
TUMBLR
TWITTER
FERGUSON
ERIC HOLDER
BODY CAMERAS
TUMBLR
LIVE STREAM
INTERRUPTED BY PROTESTORS
TWITTER
STAND NOW...
GOLDIE TAYLOR
FACE BOOK
BLACK LIVES MATTER
WHAT WE LIVED UNDER IS NOTHING SHORT OF AMERICAN APARTHEID...
THIRD AND LONG, IT LOOK LIKE HE'S
I WILL RESPECT THE PROCESS WHEN THE PROCESS RESPECTS MY SONS...
I WILL HONOR IT WHEN IT HONORS MY DAUGHTERS...

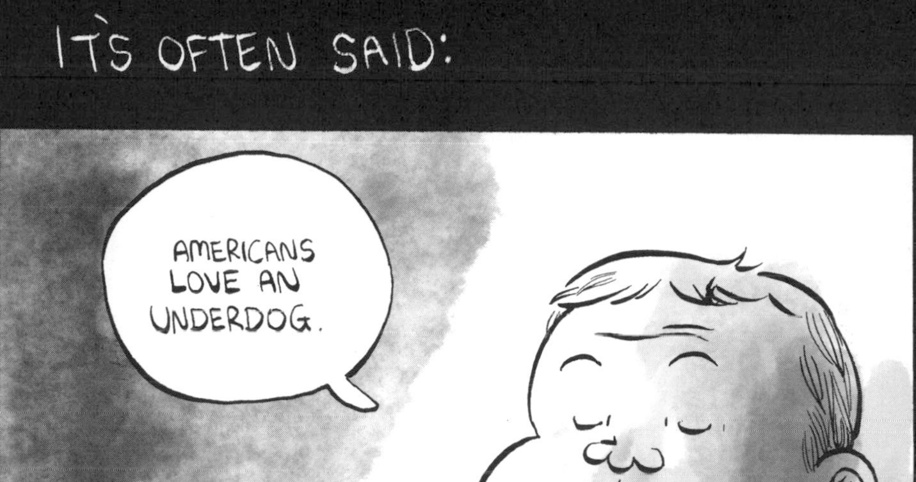
IT'S OFTEN SAID:
AMERICANS LOVE AN UNDERDOG.
BUT, WHEREVER YOU LOOK,
IT'S A DIFFERENT STORY.

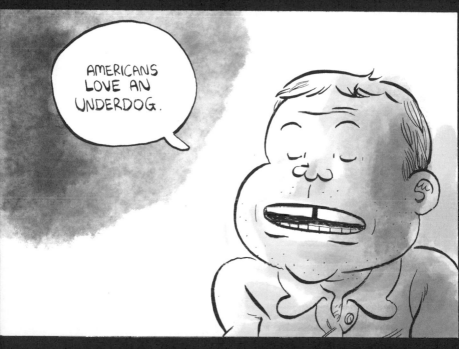

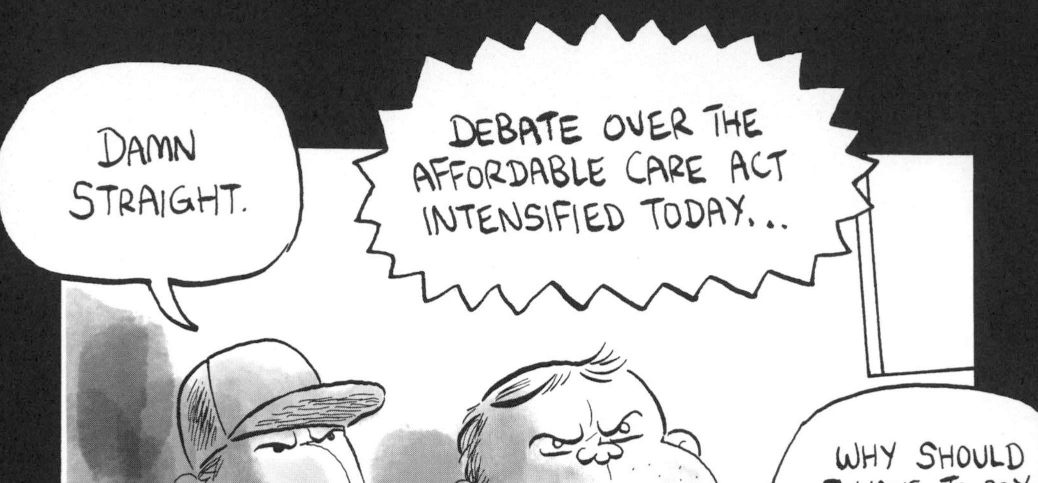
DEBATE OVER THE AFFORDABLE CARE ACT INTENSIFIED TODAY...
DAMN STRAIGHT.
WHY SHOULD **I** HAVE TO PAY FOR **THEIR** HEALTHCARE?

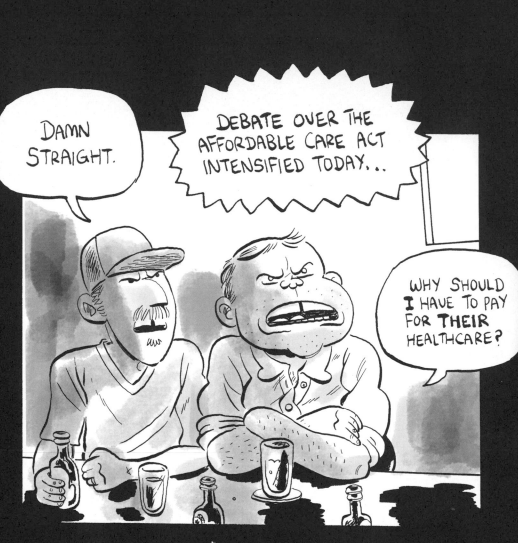

AMERICANS DON'T LOVE AN UNDERDOG.

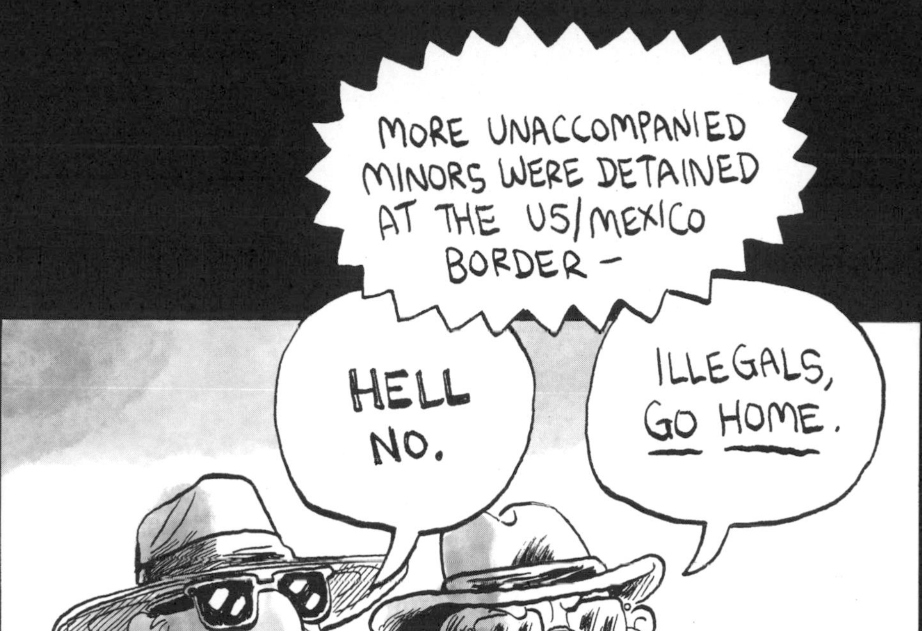
MORE UNACCOMPANIED MINORS WERE DETAINED AT THE US/MEXICO BORDER -
HELL NO.
ILLEGALS, GO HOME.
RETURN TO SENDER
USA
NO AMNEST

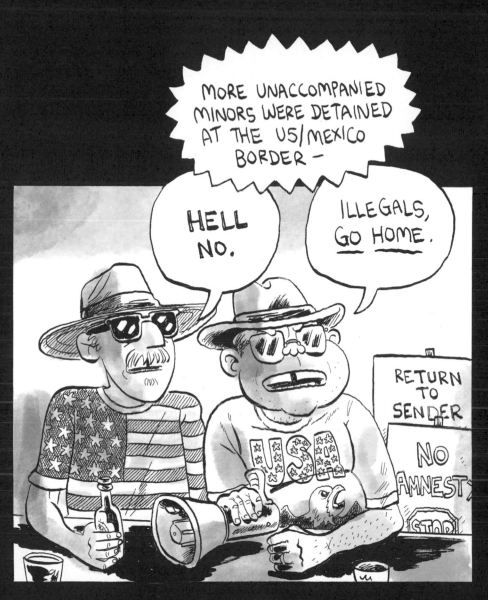

AMERICANS **DESPISE** AN UNDERDOG.

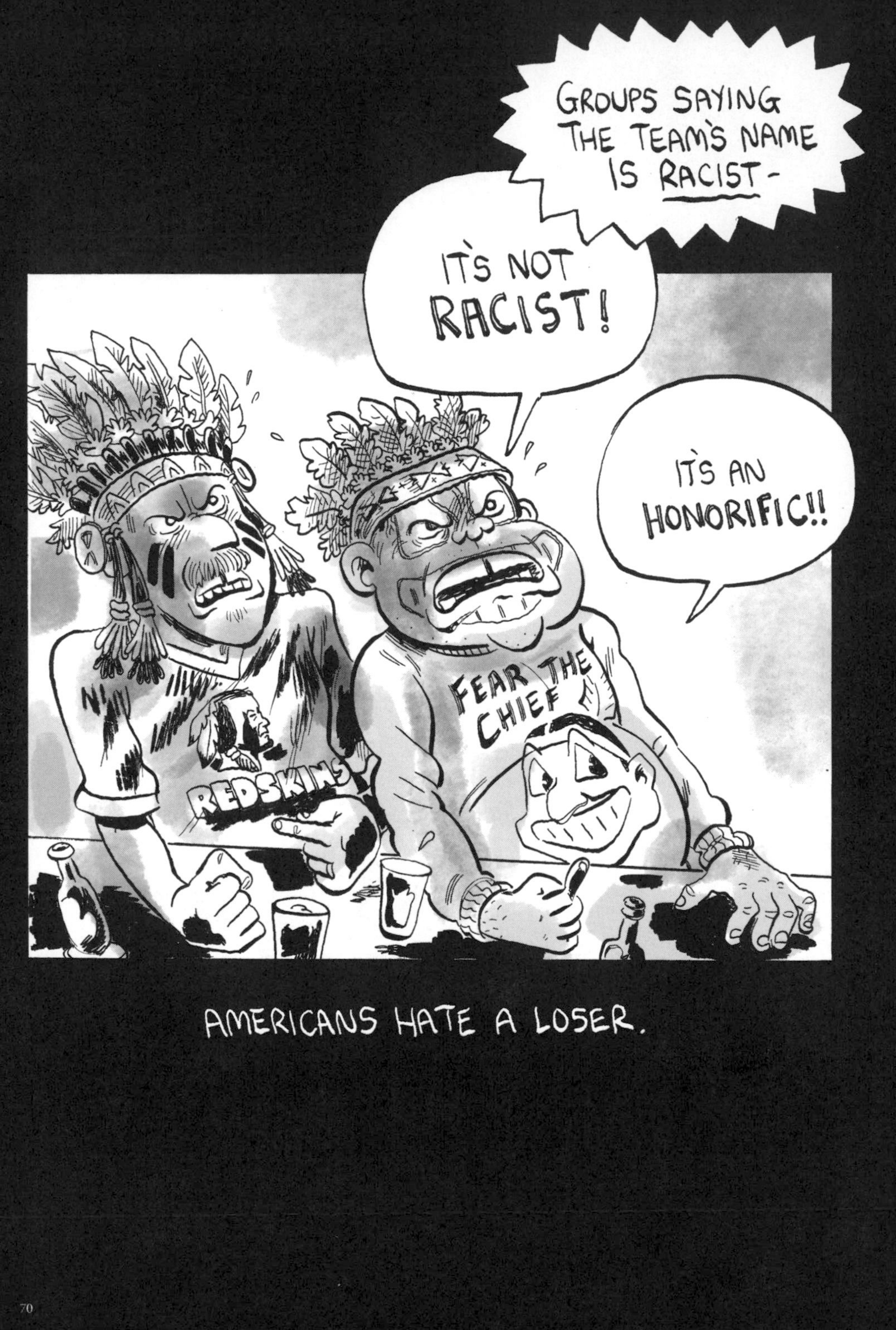
GROUPS SAYING THE TEAM'S NAME IS RACIST -
IT'S NOT RACIST!
IT'S AN HONORIFIC!!
REDSKINS
FEAR THE CHIEF

AMERICANS HATE A LOSER.

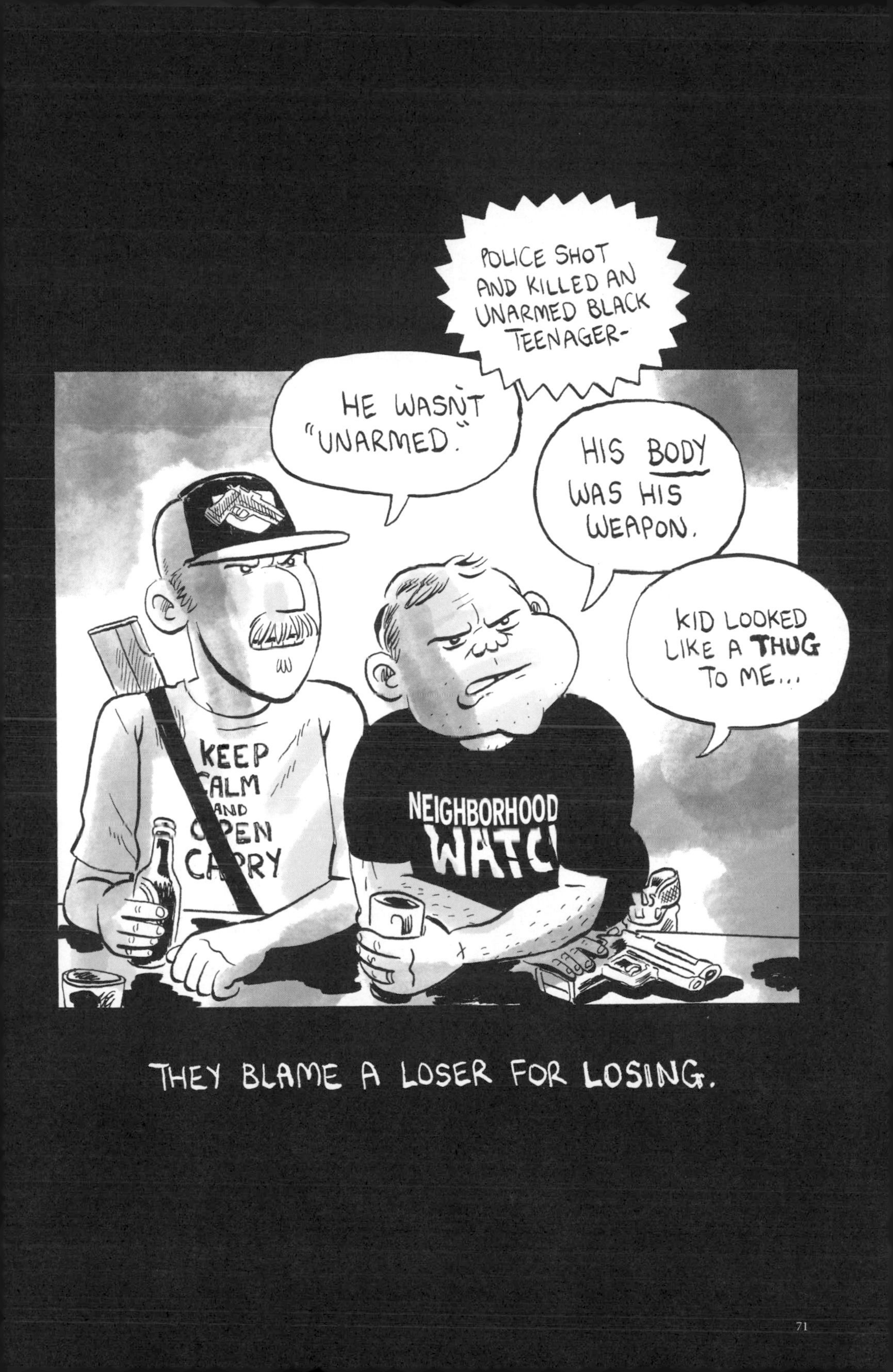
POLICE SHOT AND KILLED AN UNARMED BLACK TEENAGER-
HE WASN'T "UNARMED."
HIS BODY WAS HIS WEAPON.
KID LOOKED LIKE A THUG TO ME...
KEEP
NEIGHBORHOOD
WATC

THEY BLAME A LOSER FOR LOSING.

AMERICANS DON'T LOVE AN UNDERDOG –

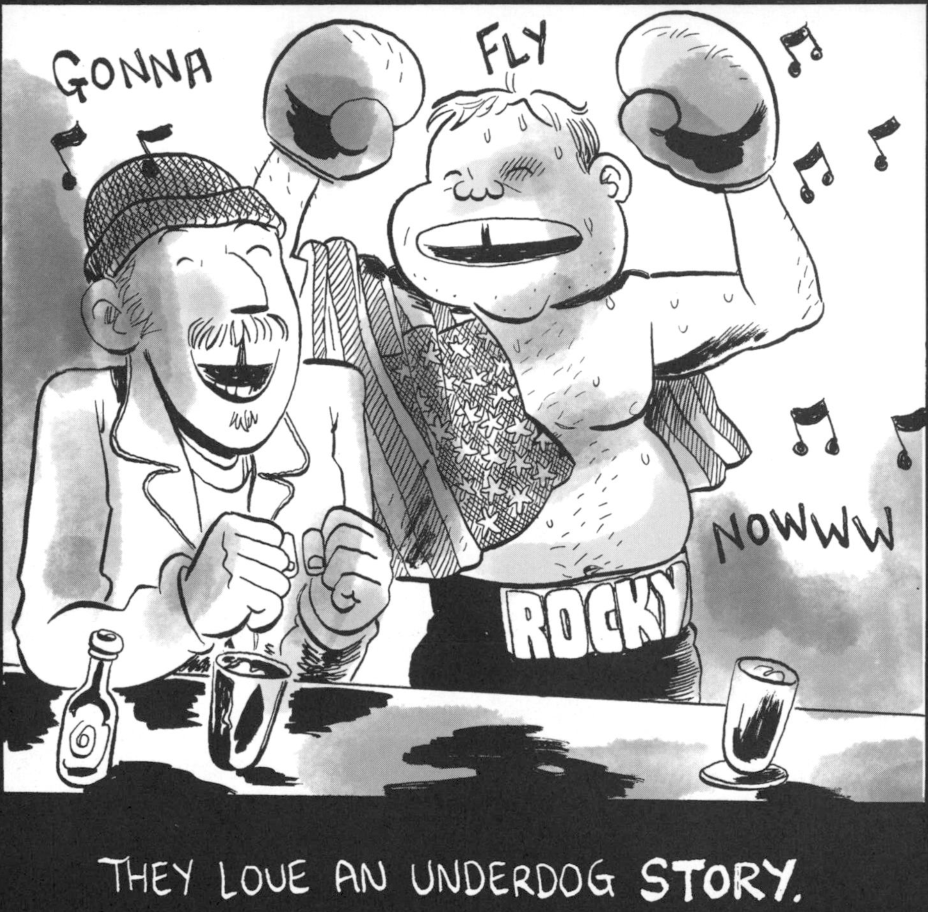
GONNA
FLY
NOWWW
ROCKY

THEY LOVE AN UNDERDOG **STORY.**

A STORY ABOUT THE LITTLE GUY,

OVERCOMING THE ODDS.

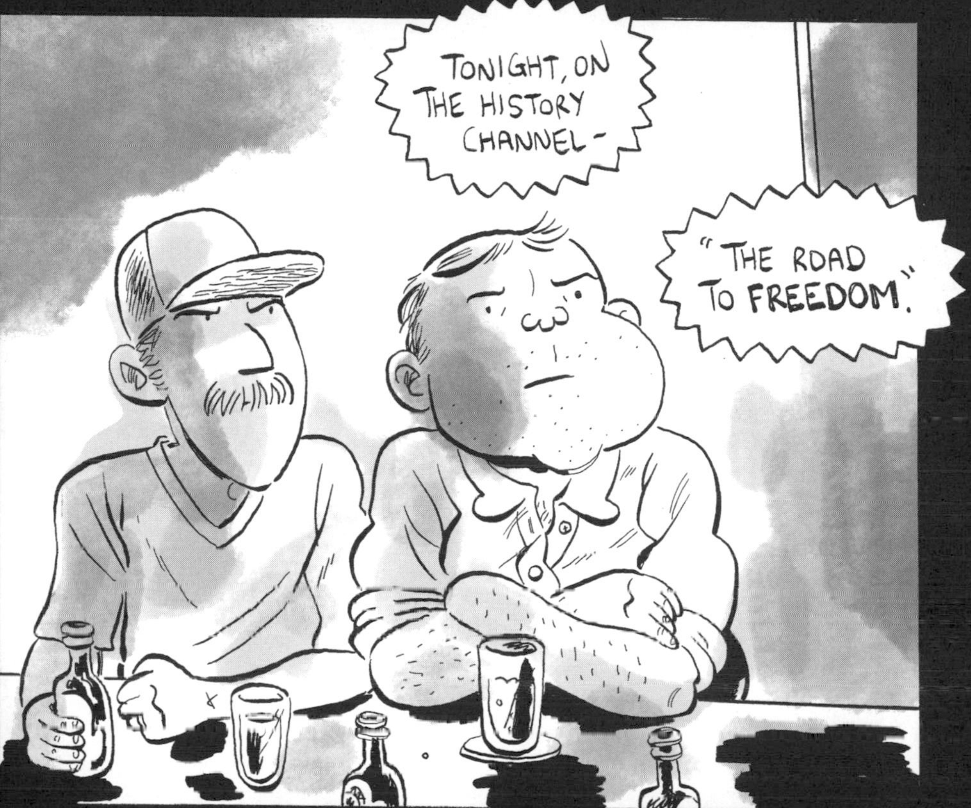
TONIGHT, ON THE HISTORY CHANNEL-
"THE ROAD TO **FREEDOM**".

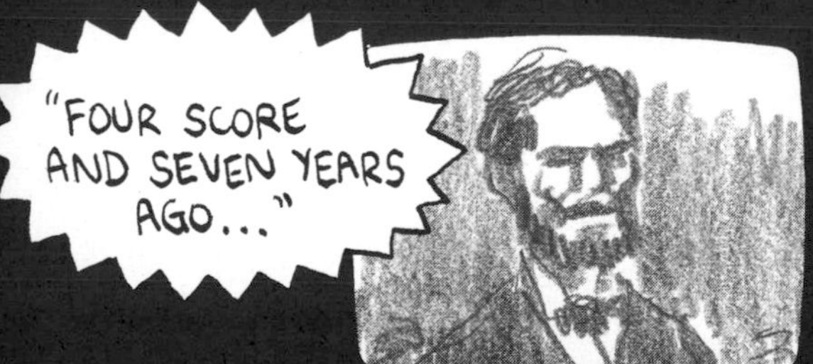
"FOUR SCORE AND SEVEN YEARS AGO..."

WHO, DESPITE EVERY IMPOSSIBLE **OBSTACLE** -

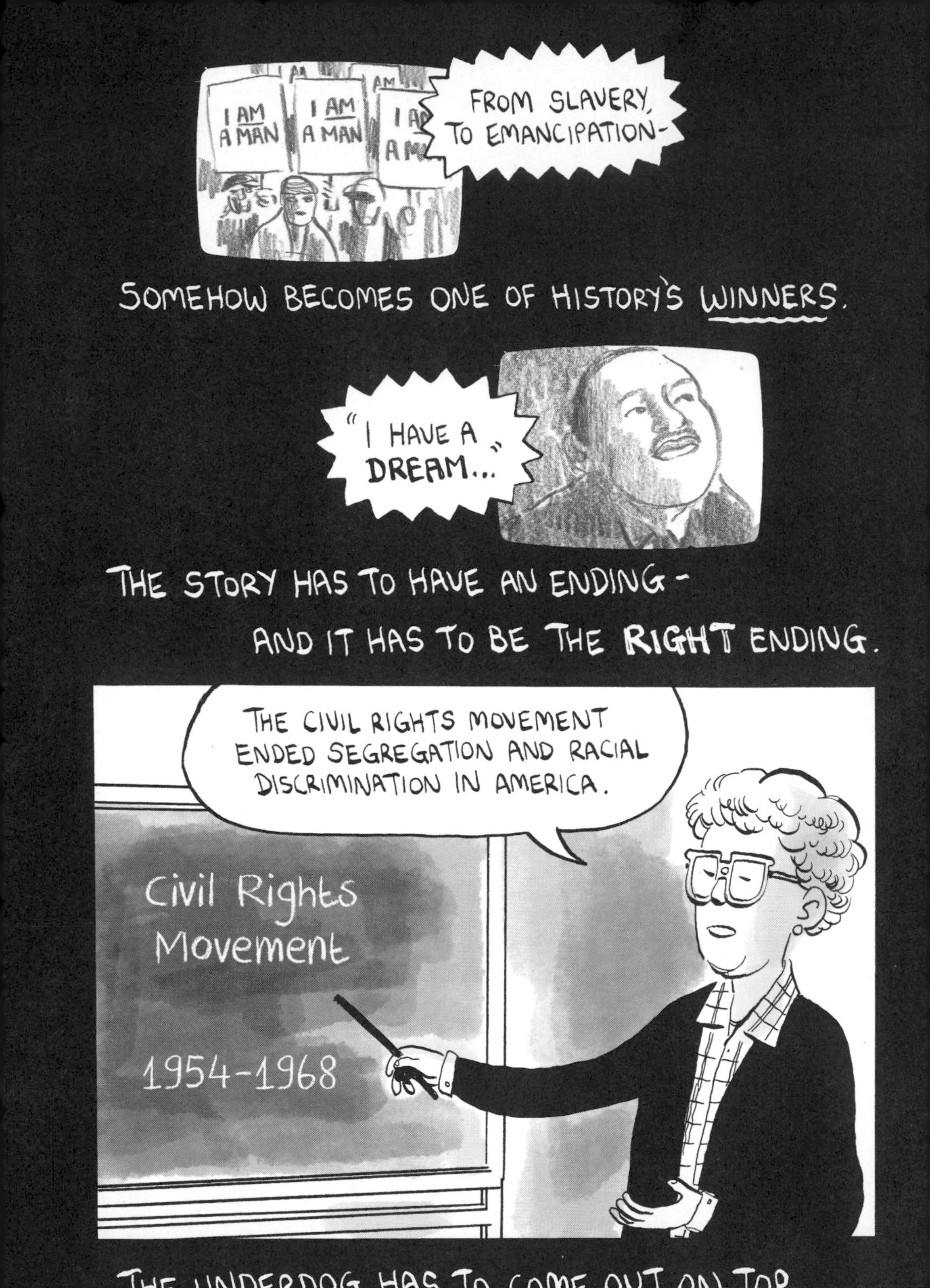
I AM A MAN
I AM A MAN
FROM SLAVERY, TO EMANCIPATION-
SOMEHOW BECOMES ONE OF HISTORY'S WINNERS.
"I HAVE A DREAM..."
THE STORY HAS TO HAVE AN ENDING -
AND IT HAS TO BE THE RIGHT ENDING.
THE CIVIL RIGHTS MOVEMENT ENDED SEGREGATION AND RACIAL DISCRIMINATION IN AMERICA.
Civil Rights Movement
1954-1968
THE UNDERDOG HAS TO COME OUT ON TOP.
EVERY OBSTACLE MUST BE OVERCOME.

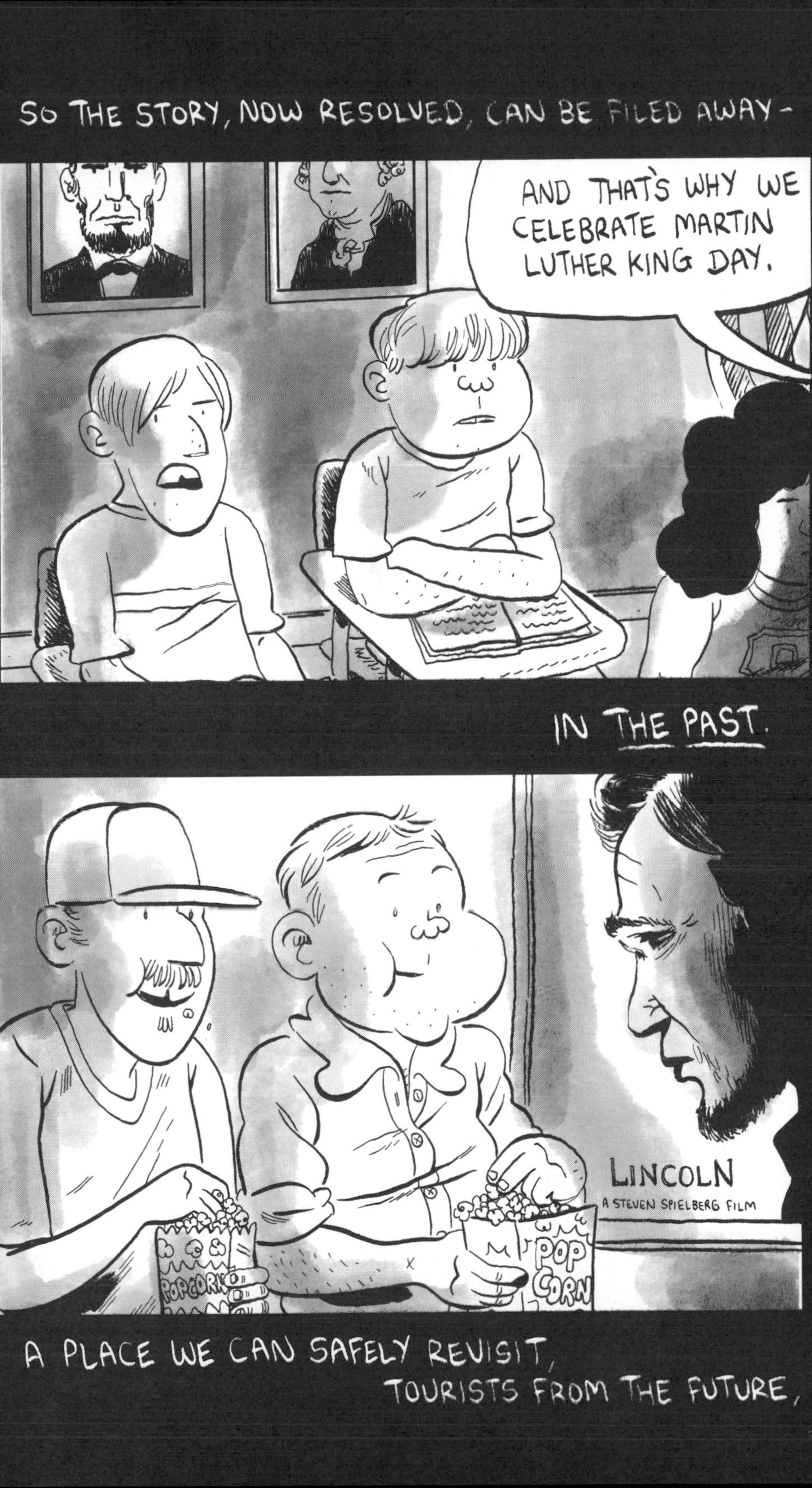
SO THE STORY, NOW RESOLVED, CAN BE FILED AWAY-
AND THAT'S WHY WE CELEBRATE MARTIN LUTHER KING DAY.
IN THE PAST.
LINCOLN
A STEVEN SPIELBERG FILM
POPCORN
POP CORN
A PLACE WE CAN SAFELY REVISIT,
TOURISTS FROM THE FUTURE,

FEELING GOOD ABOUT WISELY LIVING IN MORE ENLIGHTENED TIMES.

SUSPECTING, IN OUR GUTS,

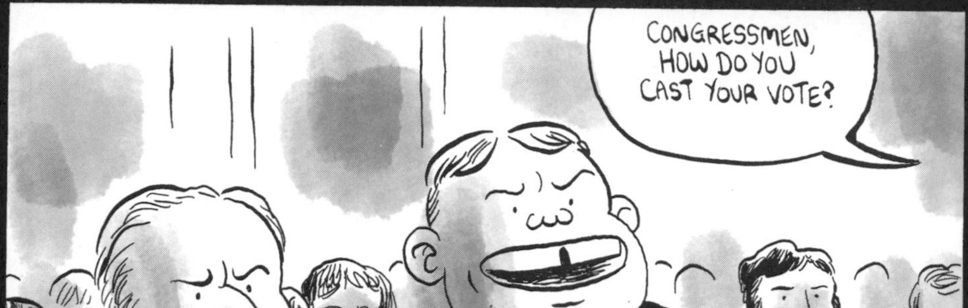
CONGRESSMEN, HOW DO YOU CAST YOUR VOTE?
WE VOTE YES!

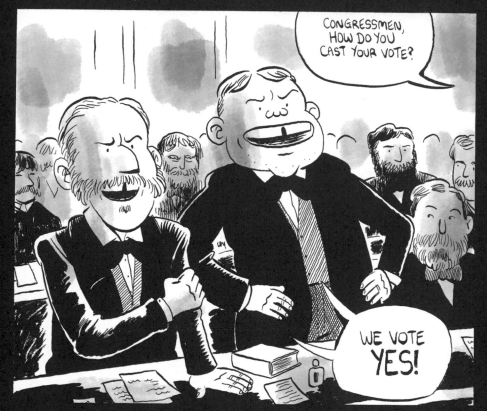

WE WOULD HAVE ALWAYS POSSESSED THE **MORAL FORESIGHT** TO SIDE WITH HISTORY'S UNDERDOGS.

AMERICANS LOVE AN UNDERDOG STORY.

BUT A GOOD STORY NEEDS OBSTACLES—

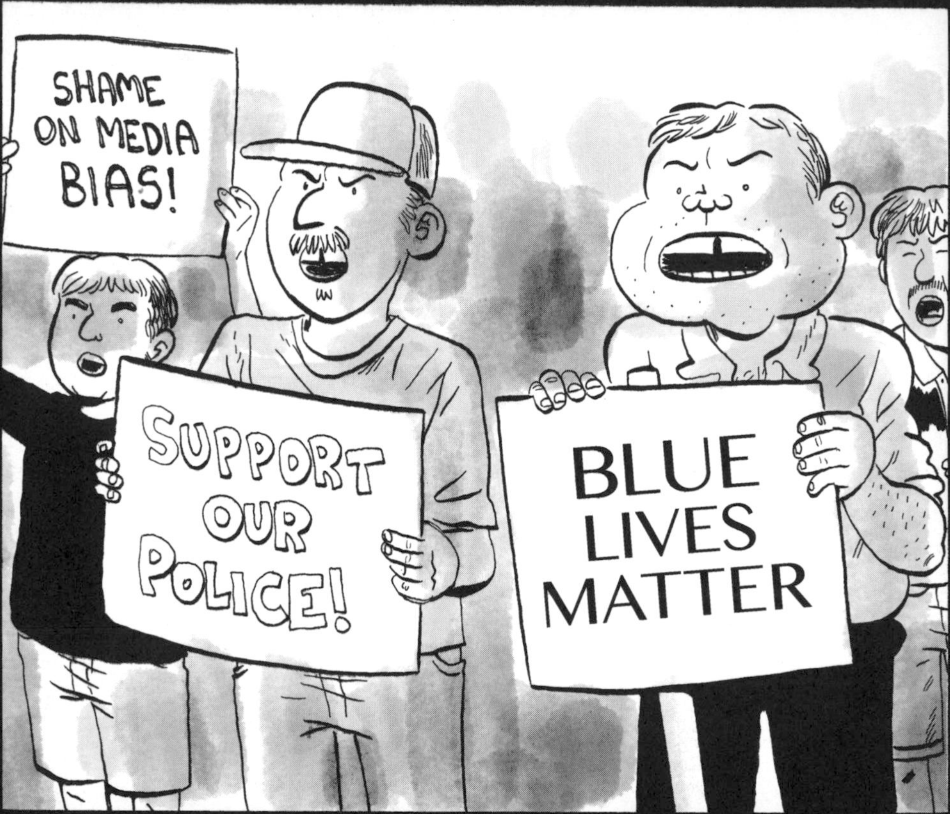
SHAME ON MEDIA BIAS!
SUPPORT OUR POLICE!
BLUE LIVES MATTER

AND AMERICANS ARE MORE THAN HAPPY TO PROVIDE THEM

WHEN I HEAR THE WORD **RIFLE** I THINK OF SOMETHING THAT LOOKS LIKE **THIS**:

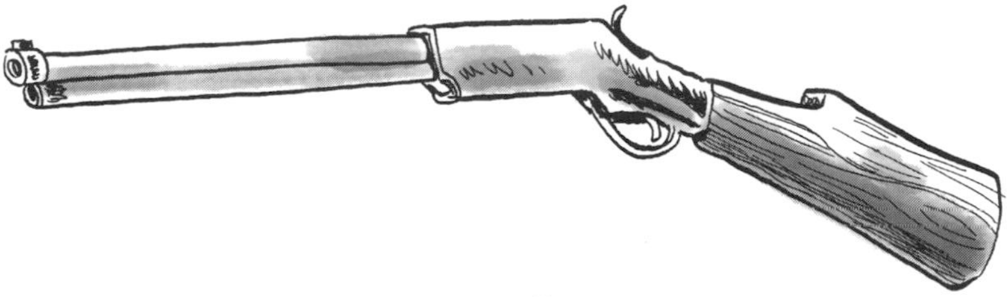

BUT, AS I UNDERSTAND IT, RIFLES MORE OFTEN LOOK A LOT LIKE **THIS**:

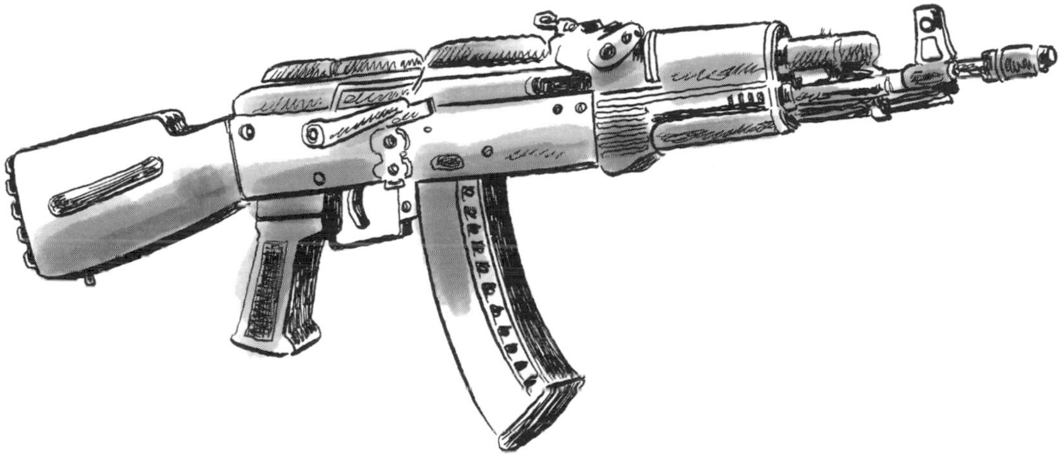

WHAT ON EARTH IS THIS THING?

WHAT KIND OF DISCONNECT DO YOU HAVE TO HAVE WITH REALITY TO THINK YOU NEED TO OWN ONE?

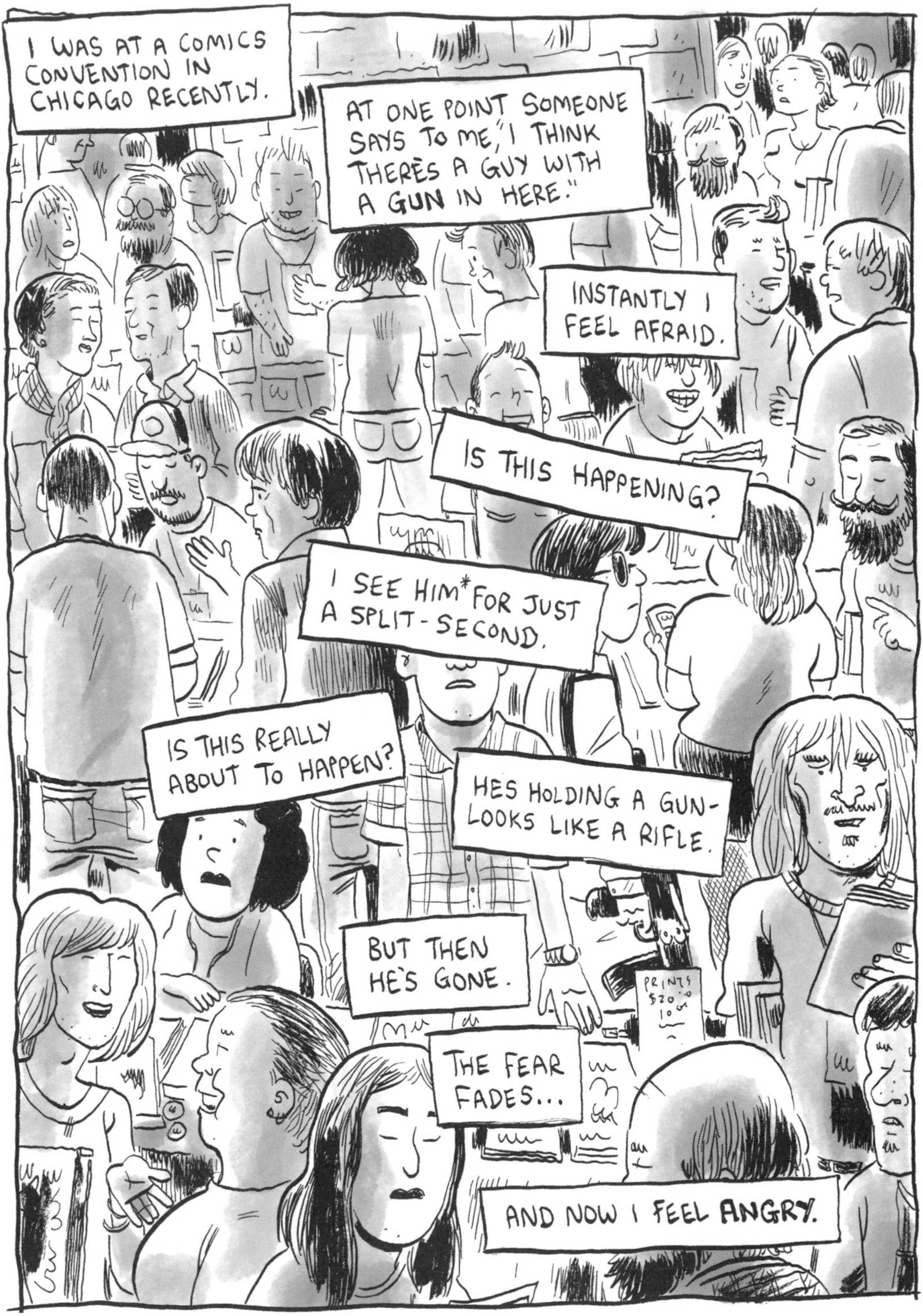
I WAS AT A COMICS CONVENTION IN CHICAGO RECENTLY.
AT ONE POINT SOMEONE SAYS TO ME, "I THINK THERE'S A GUY WITH A **GUN** IN HERE."
INSTANTLY I FEEL AFRAID.
IS THIS HAPPENING?
I SEE HIM* FOR JUST A SPLIT-SECOND.
IS THIS REALLY ABOUT TO HAPPEN?
HE'S HOLDING A GUN-LOOKS LIKE A RIFLE.
BUT THEN HE'S GONE.
PRINTS $20.00 10.00
THE FEAR FADES...
AND NOW I FEEL **ANGRY**.

* OF COURSE IT'S A HIM

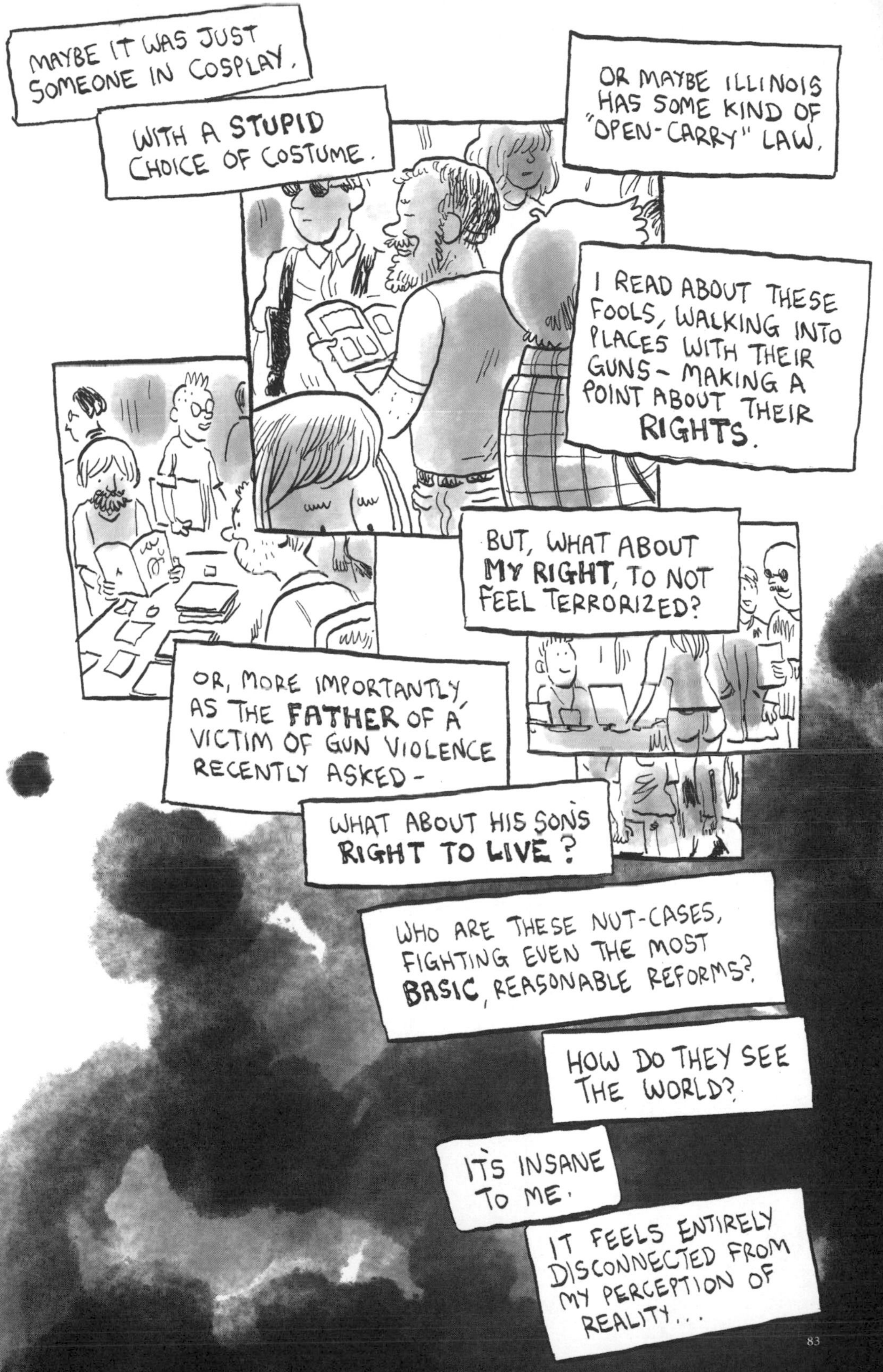
MAYBE IT WAS JUST SOMEONE IN COSPLAY,
WITH A **STUPID** CHOICE OF COSTUME.
OR MAYBE ILLINOIS HAS SOME KIND OF "OPEN-CARRY" LAW.
I READ ABOUT THESE FOOLS, WALKING INTO PLACES WITH THEIR GUNS - MAKING A POINT ABOUT THEIR **RIGHTS**.
BUT, WHAT ABOUT **MY RIGHT**, TO NOT FEEL TERRORIZED?
OR, MORE IMPORTANTLY, AS THE **FATHER** OF A VICTIM OF GUN VIOLENCE RECENTLY ASKED -
WHAT ABOUT HIS SON'S **RIGHT TO LIVE**?
WHO ARE THESE NUT-CASES, FIGHTING EVEN THE MOST **BASIC**, REASONABLE REFORMS?
HOW DO THEY SEE THE WORLD?
IT'S INSANE TO ME.
IT FEELS ENTIRELY DISCONNECTED FROM MY PERCEPTION OF REALITY...

BUT THEN I THINK
ABOUT THE **ISSUE** OF
MARRIAGE EQUALITY.

WHICH, AS A SUPPORTER,
FEELS LIKE A WAR
THAT IS BEING WON.

OPPONENTS ARE SEEING
NO EVIDENCE THAT
THEIR SIDE IS GOING
TO WIN OUT.

MORE STATES ADOPT
EQUALITY, OTHERS
OVERTURN EXISTING BANS.

PEOPLE OPPOSED TO GAY
MARRIAGE IN AMERICA...

WELL, IT FEELS LIKE THEY'RE
ON THE WRONG SIDE OF HISTORY.

NOTHING IS GOING THEIR
WAY... THEY'RE **LOSING.**

YET OPPONENTS OF
EQUALITY FIGHT ON.

WHAT DOES THAT SAY
ABOUT THOSE OF US
WHO'D LIKE TO SEE
GUN REGULATIONS CHANGE?

ARE WE TOO, ON THE WRONG
SIDE OF HISTORY?

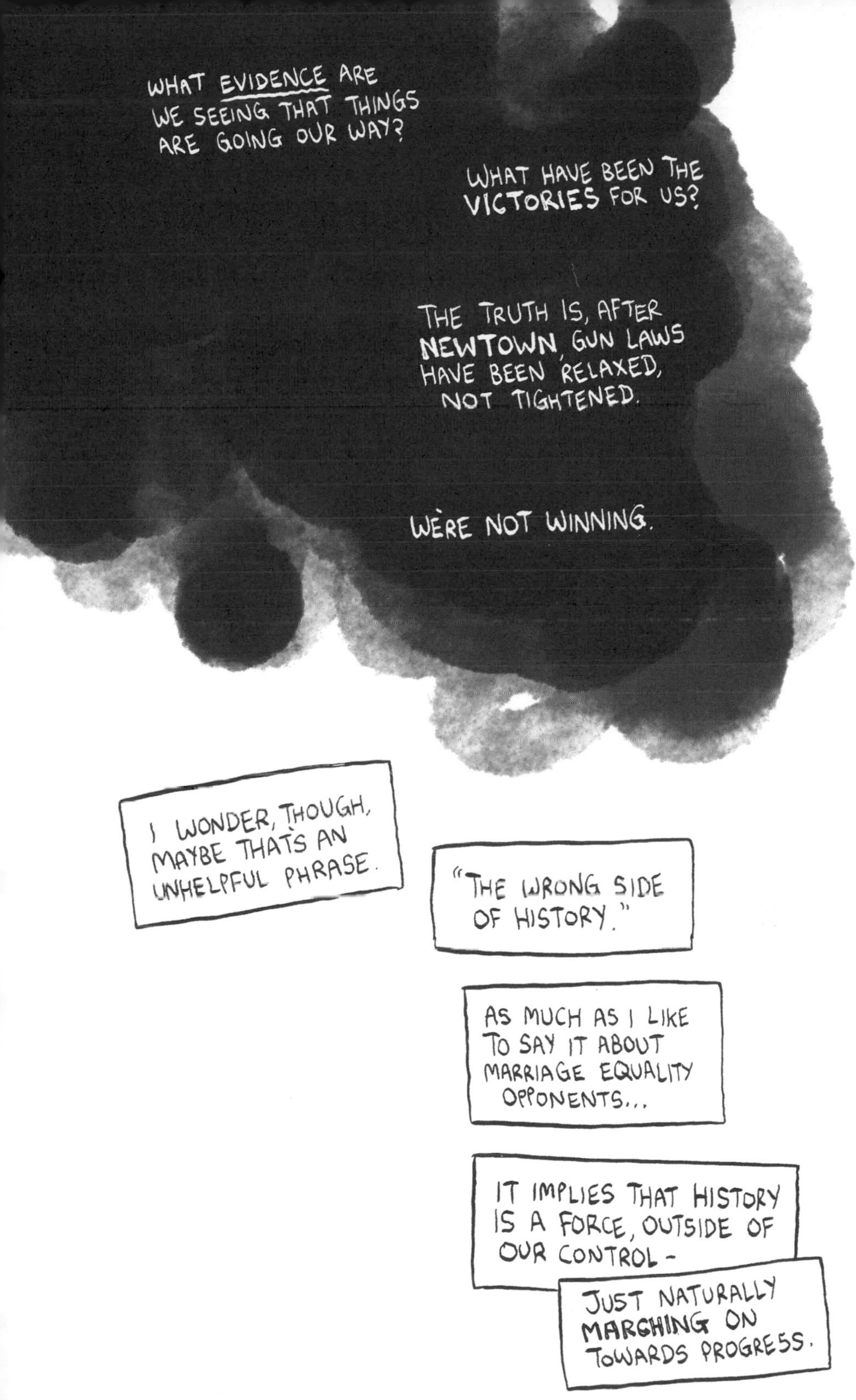
WHAT EVIDENCE ARE WE SEEING THAT THINGS ARE GOING OUR WAY?
WHAT HAVE BEEN THE VICTORIES FOR US?
THE TRUTH IS, AFTER NEWTOWN, GUN LAWS HAVE BEEN RELAXED, NOT TIGHTENED.
WE'RE NOT WINNING.
I WONDER, THOUGH, MAYBE THAT'S AN UNHELPFUL PHRASE.
"THE WRONG SIDE OF HISTORY."
AS MUCH AS I LIKE TO SAY IT ABOUT MARRIAGE EQUALITY OPPONENTS...
IT IMPLIES THAT HISTORY IS A FORCE, OUTSIDE OF OUR CONTROL -
JUST NATURALLY MARCHING ON TOWARDS PROGRESS.

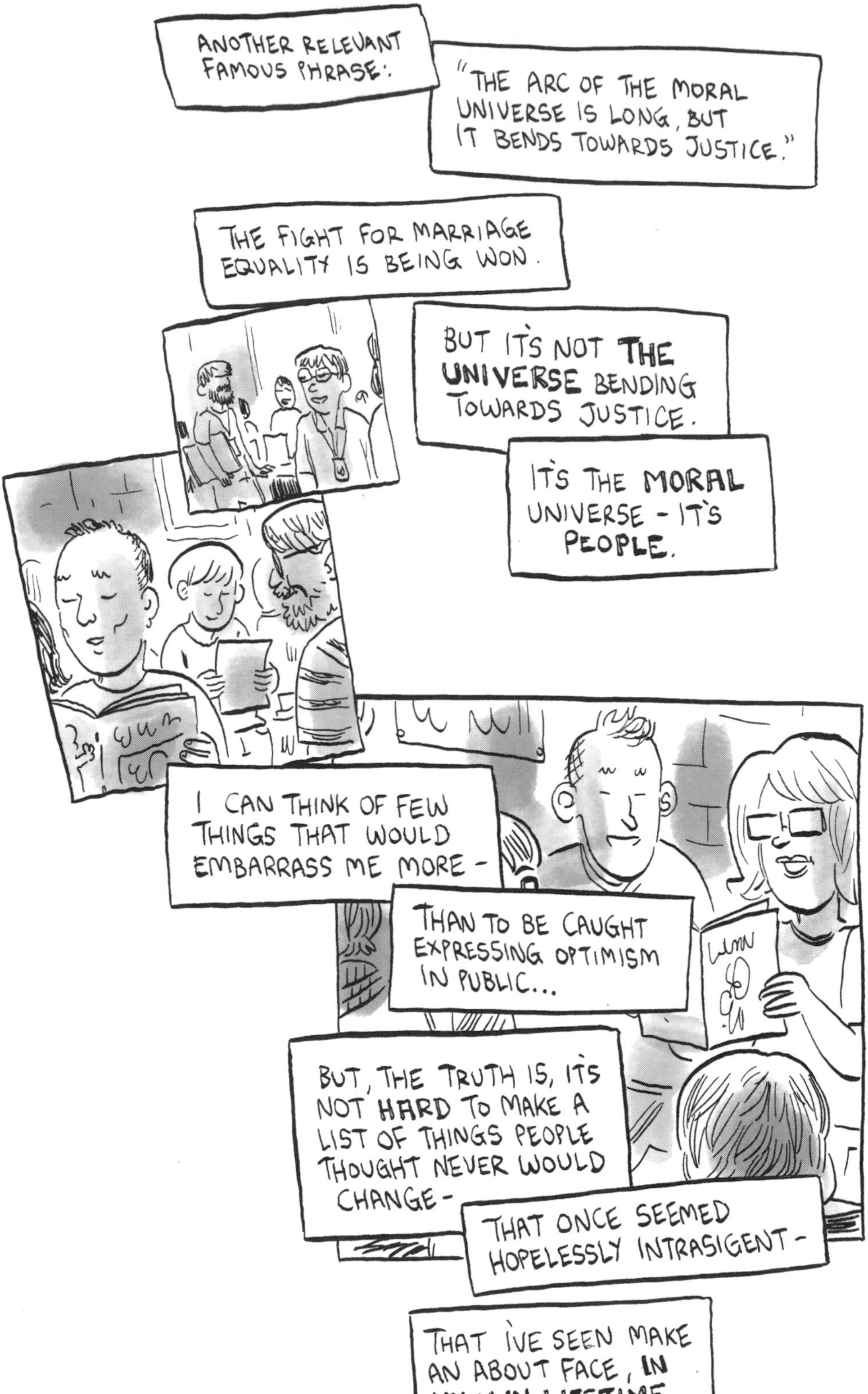
ANOTHER RELEVANT FAMOUS PHRASE:
"THE ARC OF THE MORAL UNIVERSE IS LONG, BUT IT BENDS TOWARDS JUSTICE."
THE FIGHT FOR MARRIAGE EQUALITY IS BEING WON.
BUT IT'S NOT **THE UNIVERSE** BENDING TOWARDS JUSTICE.
IT'S THE **MORAL** UNIVERSE - IT'S **PEOPLE**.
I CAN THINK OF FEW THINGS THAT WOULD EMBARRASS ME MORE -
THAN TO BE CAUGHT EXPRESSING OPTIMISM IN PUBLIC...
BUT, THE TRUTH IS, IT'S NOT **HARD** TO MAKE A LIST OF THINGS PEOPLE THOUGHT NEVER WOULD CHANGE -
THAT ONCE SEEMED HOPELESSLY INTRASIGENT -
THAT I'VE SEEN MAKE AN ABOUT FACE, **IN MY OWN LIFETIME**.

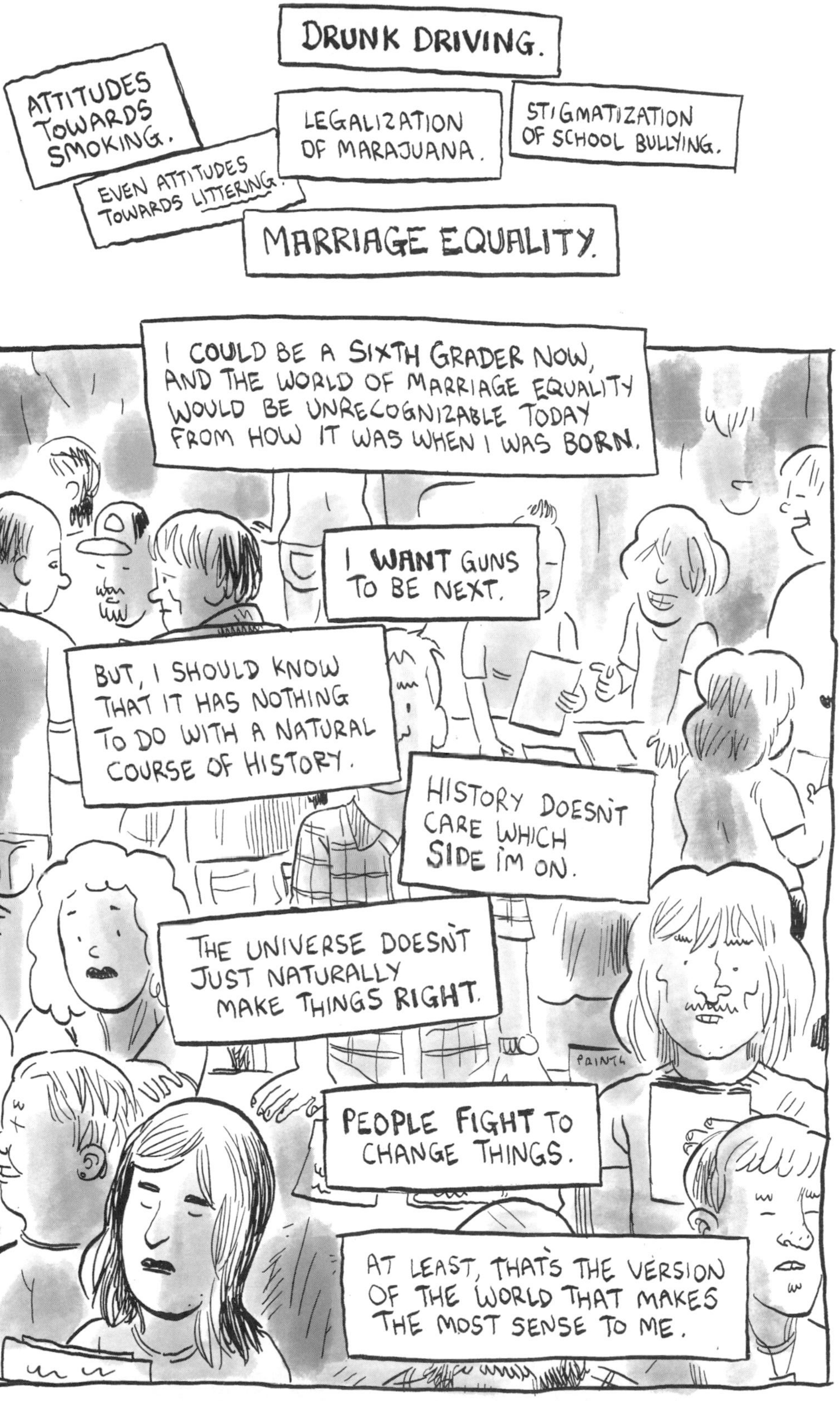
DRUNK DRIVING.
ATTITUDES TOWARDS SMOKING.
LEGALIZATION OF MARAJUANA.
STIGMATIZATION OF SCHOOL BULLYING.
EVEN ATTITUDES TOWARDS LITTERING.
MARRIAGE EQUALITY.
I COULD BE A SIXTH GRADER NOW, AND THE WORLD OF MARRIAGE EQUALITY WOULD BE UNRECOGNIZABLE TODAY FROM HOW IT WAS WHEN I WAS BORN.
I WANT GUNS TO BE NEXT.
BUT, I SHOULD KNOW THAT IT HAS NOTHING TO DO WITH A NATURAL COURSE OF HISTORY.
HISTORY DOESN'T CARE WHICH SIDE I'M ON.
THE UNIVERSE DOESN'T JUST NATURALLY MAKE THINGS RIGHT.
PEOPLE FIGHT TO CHANGE THINGS.
AT LEAST, THAT'S THE VERSION OF THE WORLD THAT MAKES THE MOST SENSE TO ME.

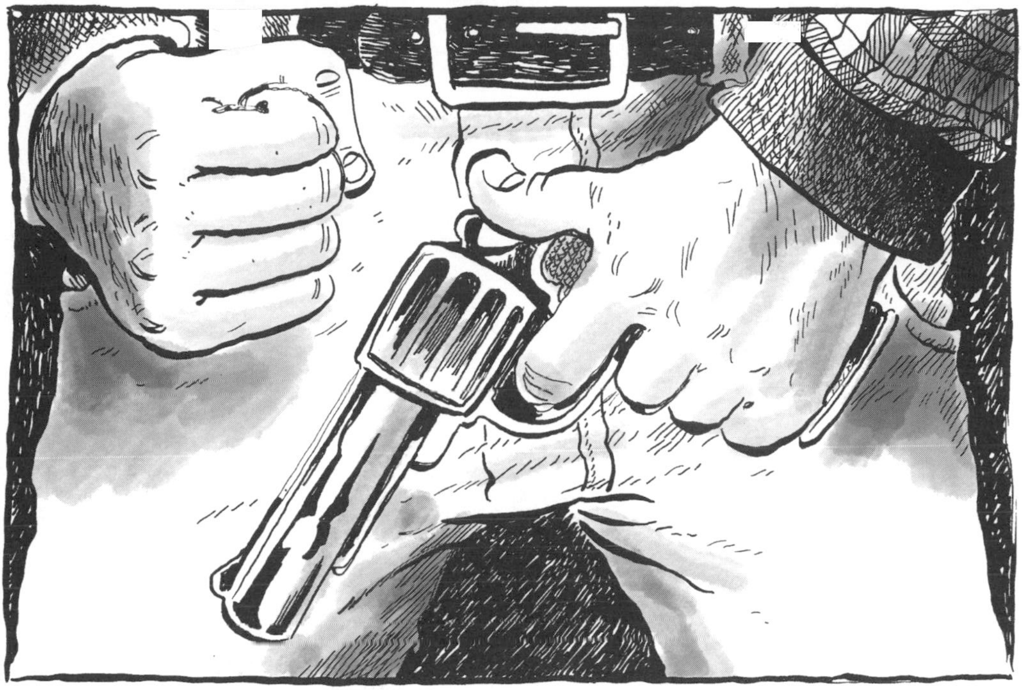

"overcompensating"

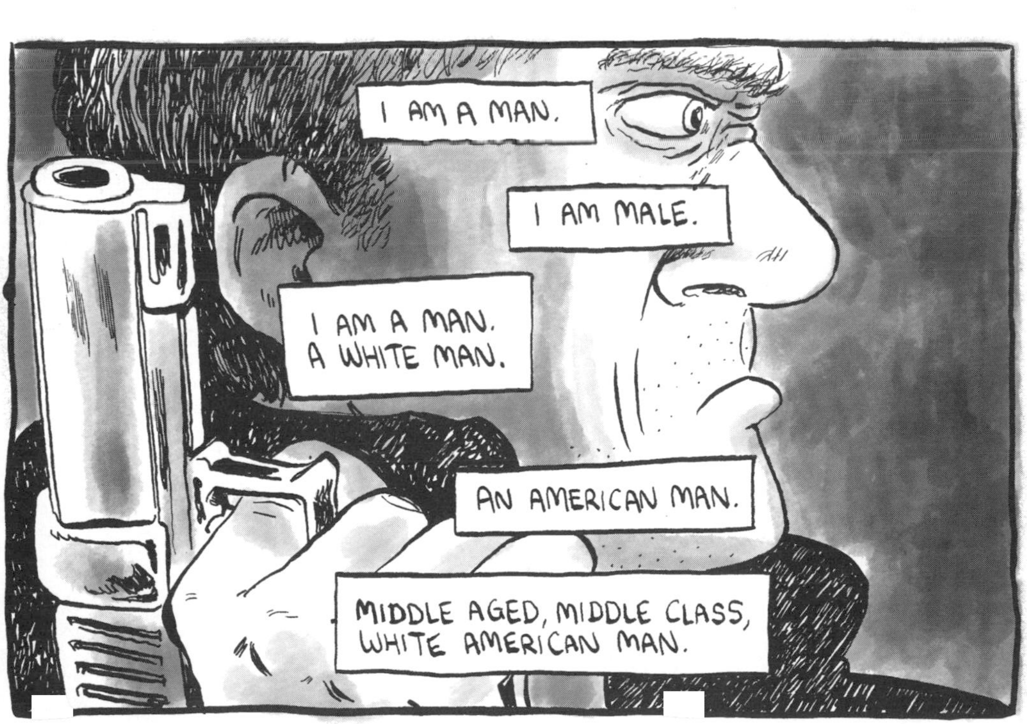
I AM A MAN.
I AM MALE.
I AM A MAN. A WHITE MAN.
AN AMERICAN MAN.
MIDDLE AGED, MIDDLE CLASS, WHITE AMERICAN MAN.

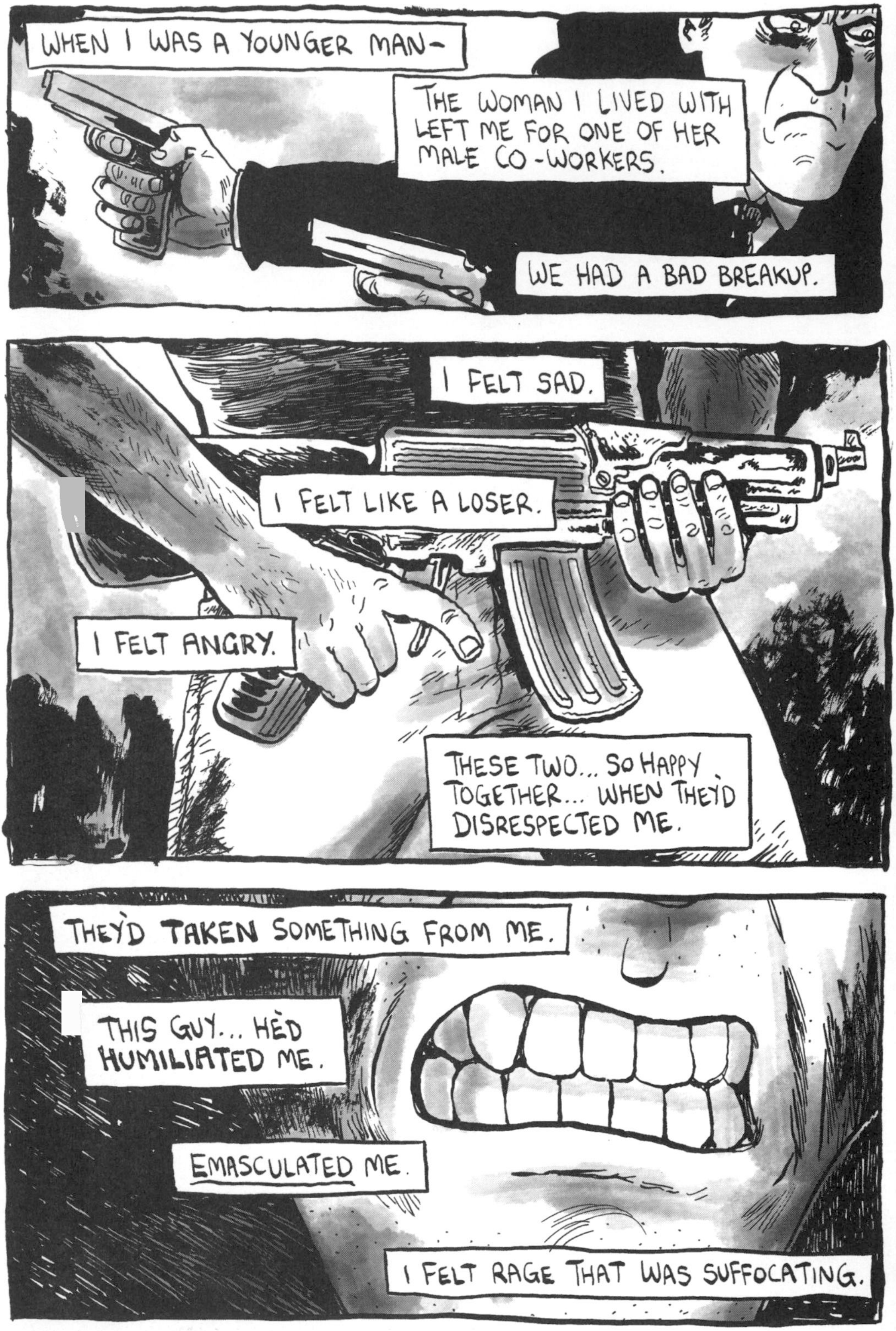
WHEN I WAS A YOUNGER MAN-
THE WOMAN I LIVED WITH LEFT ME FOR ONE OF HER MALE CO-WORKERS.
WE HAD A BAD BREAKUP.
I FELT SAD.
I FELT LIKE A LOSER.
I FELT ANGRY.
THESE TWO... SO HAPPY TOGETHER... WHEN THEY'D DISRESPECTED ME.
THEY'D TAKEN SOMETHING FROM ME.
THIS GUY... HE'D HUMILIATED ME.
EMASCULATED ME.
I FELT RAGE THAT WAS SUFFOCATING.

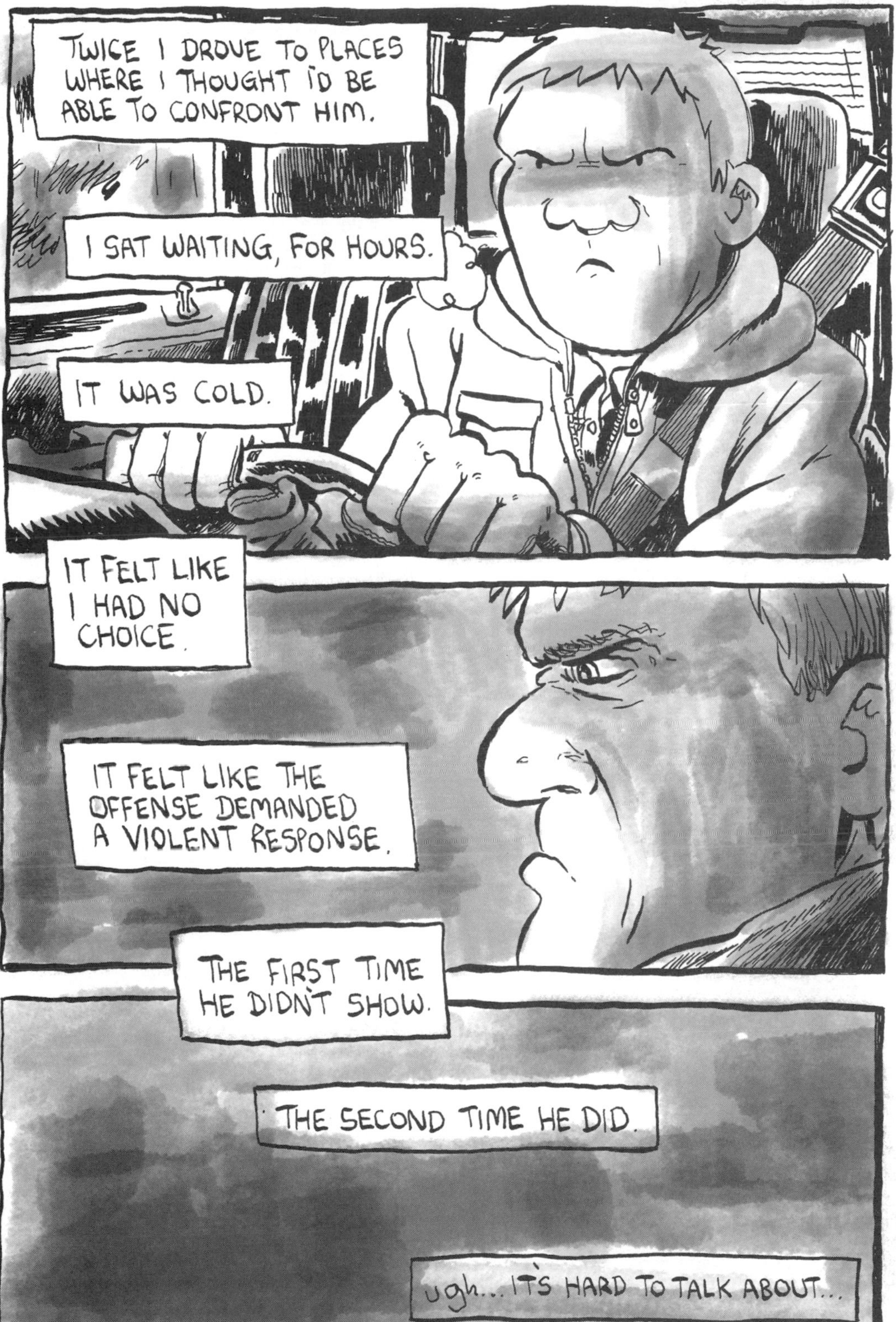
TWICE I DROVE TO PLACES WHERE I THOUGHT I'D BE ABLE TO CONFRONT HIM.
I SAT WAITING, FOR HOURS.
IT WAS COLD.
IT FELT LIKE I HAD NO CHOICE.
IT FELT LIKE THE OFFENSE DEMANDED A VIOLENT RESPONSE.
THE FIRST TIME HE DIDN'T SHOW.
THE SECOND TIME HE DID.
ugh... IT'S HARD TO TALK ABOUT...

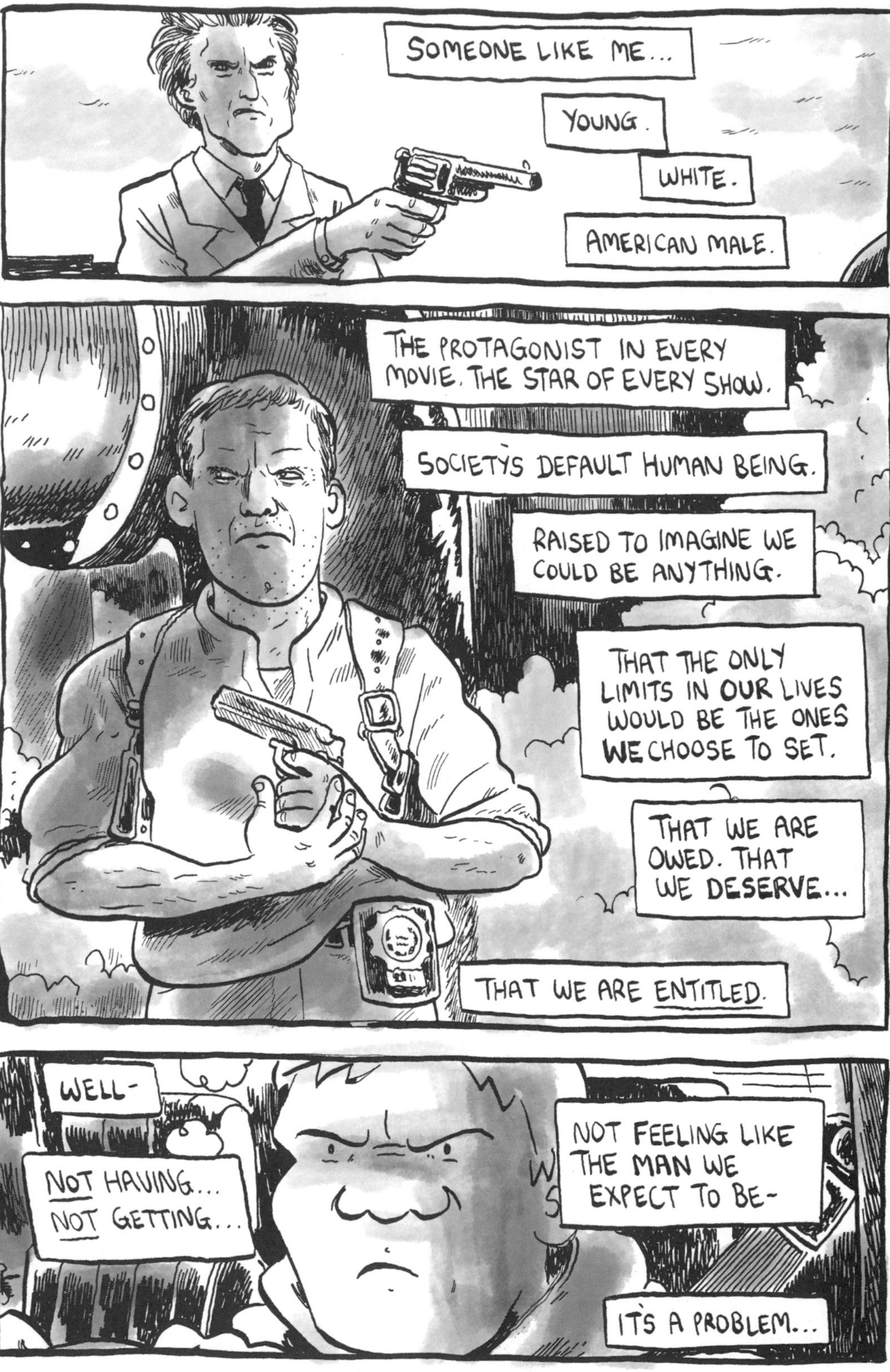
SOMEONE LIKE ME...
YOUNG.
WHITE.
AMERICAN MALE.
THE PROTAGONIST IN EVERY MOVIE. THE STAR OF EVERY SHOW.
SOCIETY'S DEFAULT HUMAN BEING.
RAISED TO IMAGINE WE COULD BE ANYTHING.
THAT THE ONLY LIMITS IN OUR LIVES WOULD BE THE ONES WE CHOOSE TO SET.
THAT WE ARE OWED. THAT WE DESERVE...
THAT WE ARE ENTITLED.
WELL-
NOT HAVING... NOT GETTING...
NOT FEELING LIKE THE MAN WE EXPECT TO BE-
IT'S A PROBLEM...

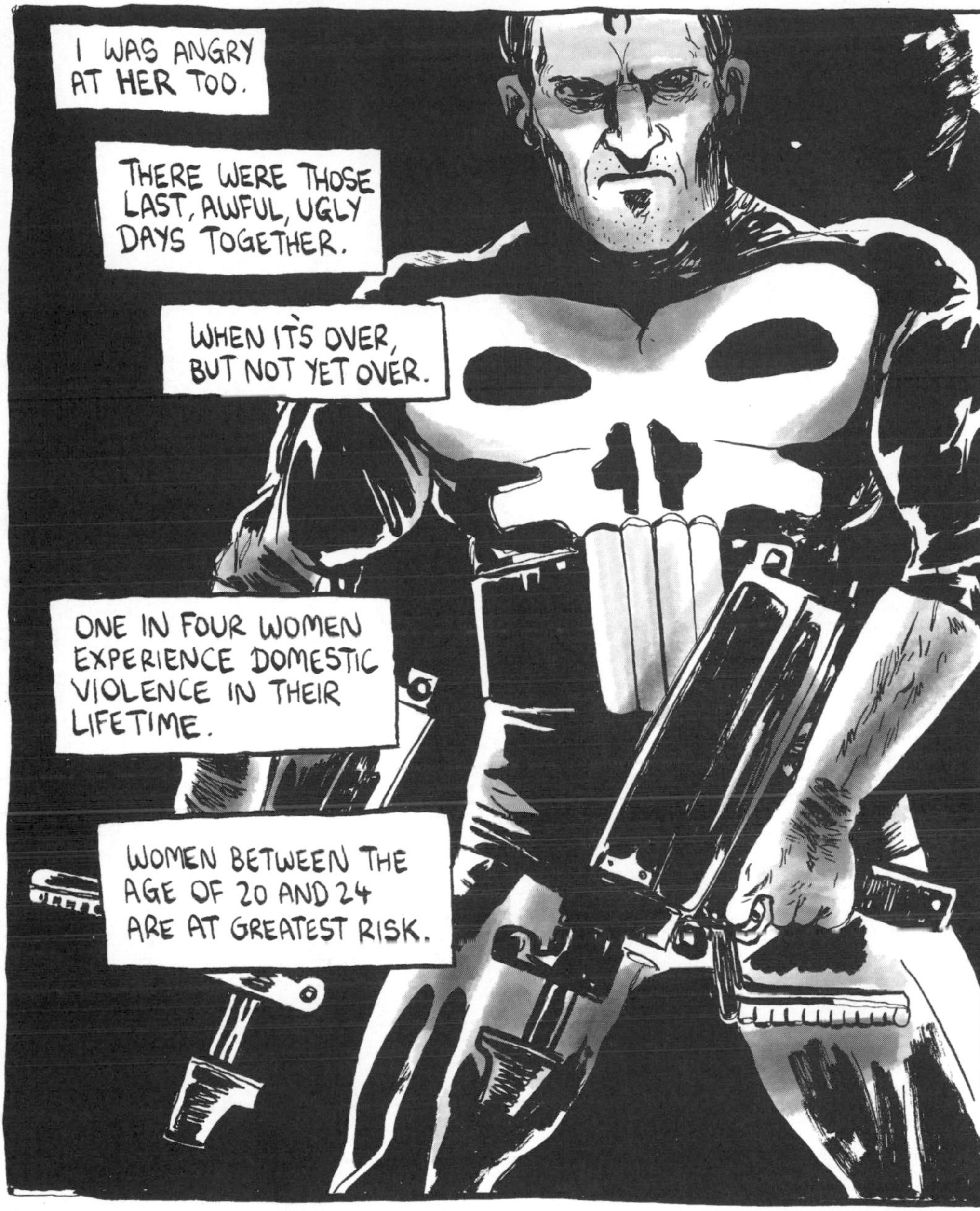
I WAS ANGRY AT HER TOO.
THERE WERE THOSE LAST, AWFUL, UGLY DAYS TOGETHER.
WHEN IT'S OVER, BUT NOT YET OVER.
ONE IN FOUR WOMEN EXPERIENCE DOMESTIC VIOLENCE IN THEIR LIFETIME.
WOMEN BETWEEN THE AGE OF 20 AND 24 ARE AT GREATEST RISK.

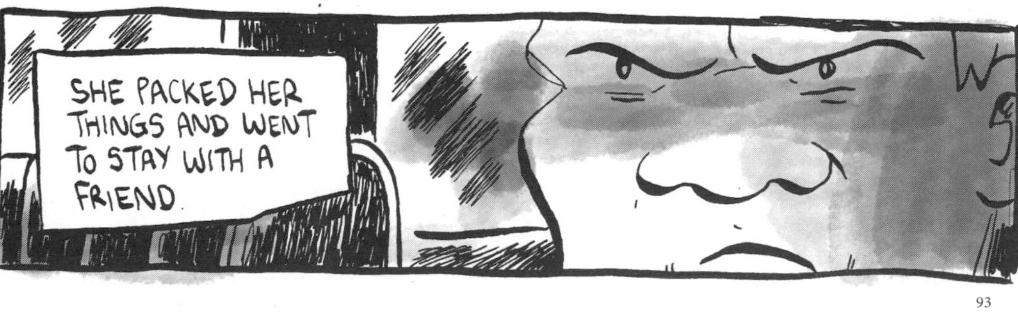
SHE PACKED HER THINGS AND WENT TO STAY WITH A FRIEND.

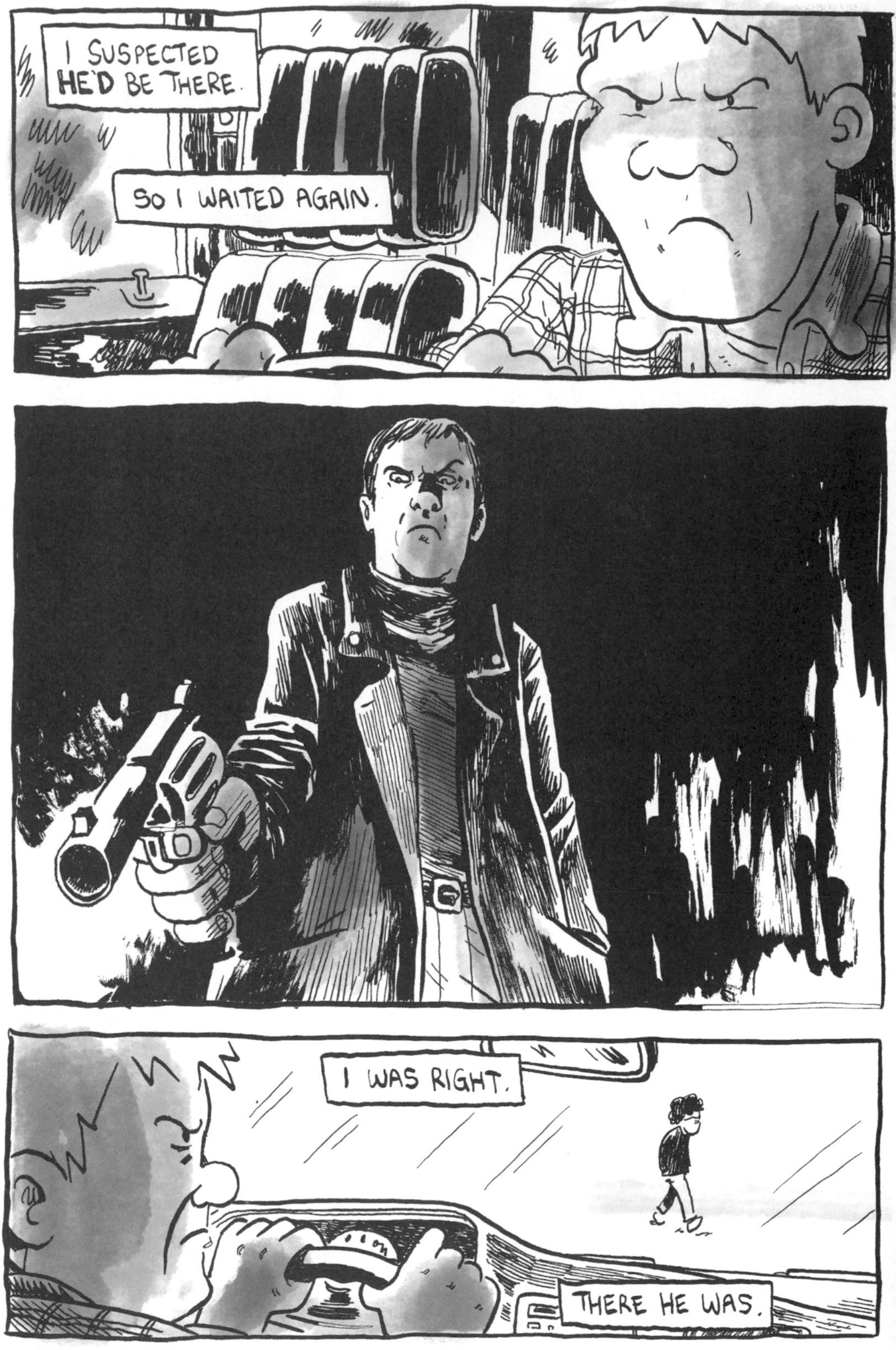
I SUSPECTED HE'D BE THERE.
SO I WAITED AGAIN.
I WAS RIGHT.
THERE HE WAS.

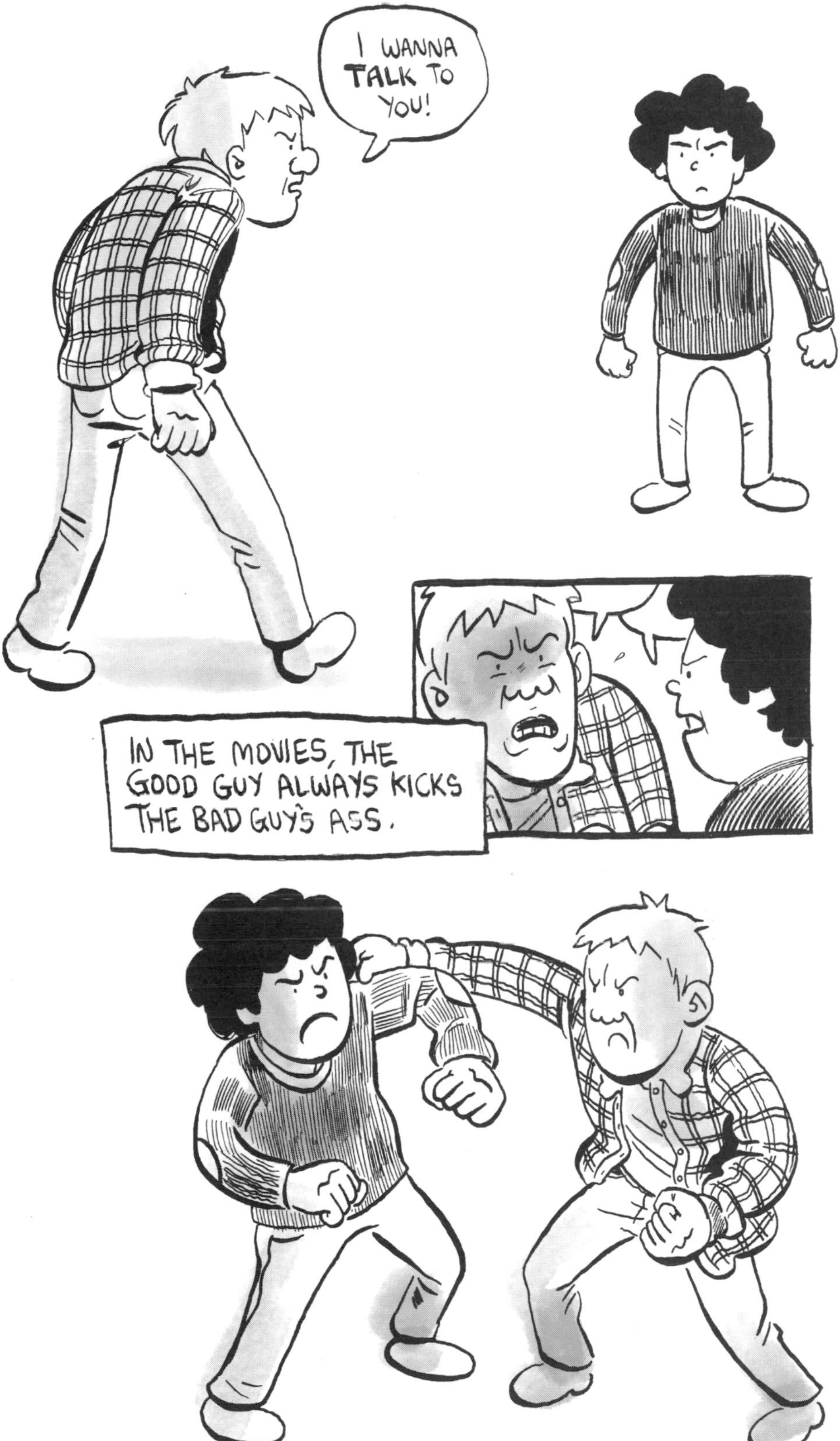
I WANNA TALK TO YOU!
IN THE MOVIES, THE GOOD GUY ALWAYS KICKS THE BAD GUY'S ASS.

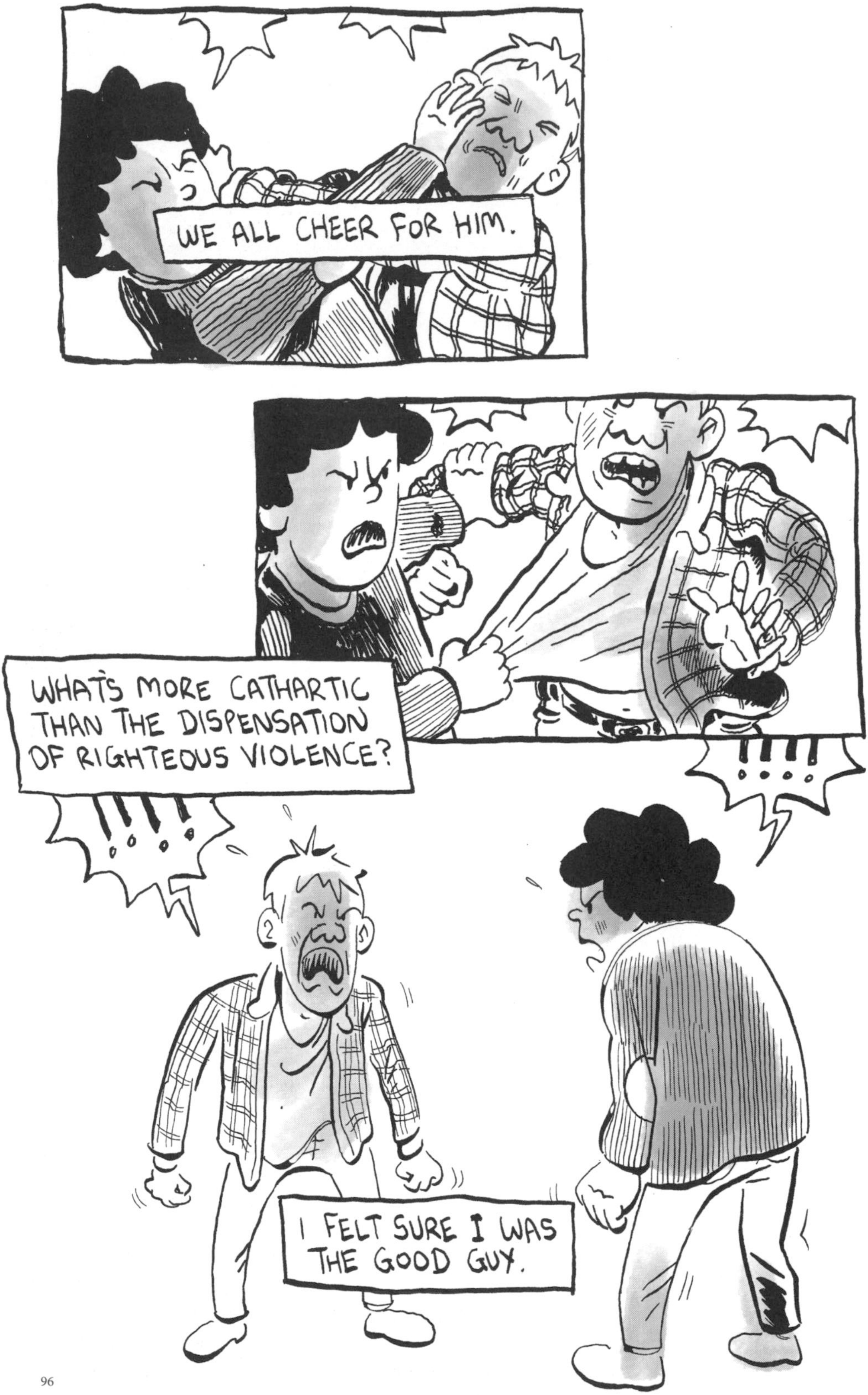

WE ALL CHEER FOR HIM.
WHAT'S MORE CATHARTIC THAN THE DISPENSATION OF RIGHTEOUS VIOLENCE?
!!!!
!!!!
I FELT SURE I WAS THE GOOD GUY.

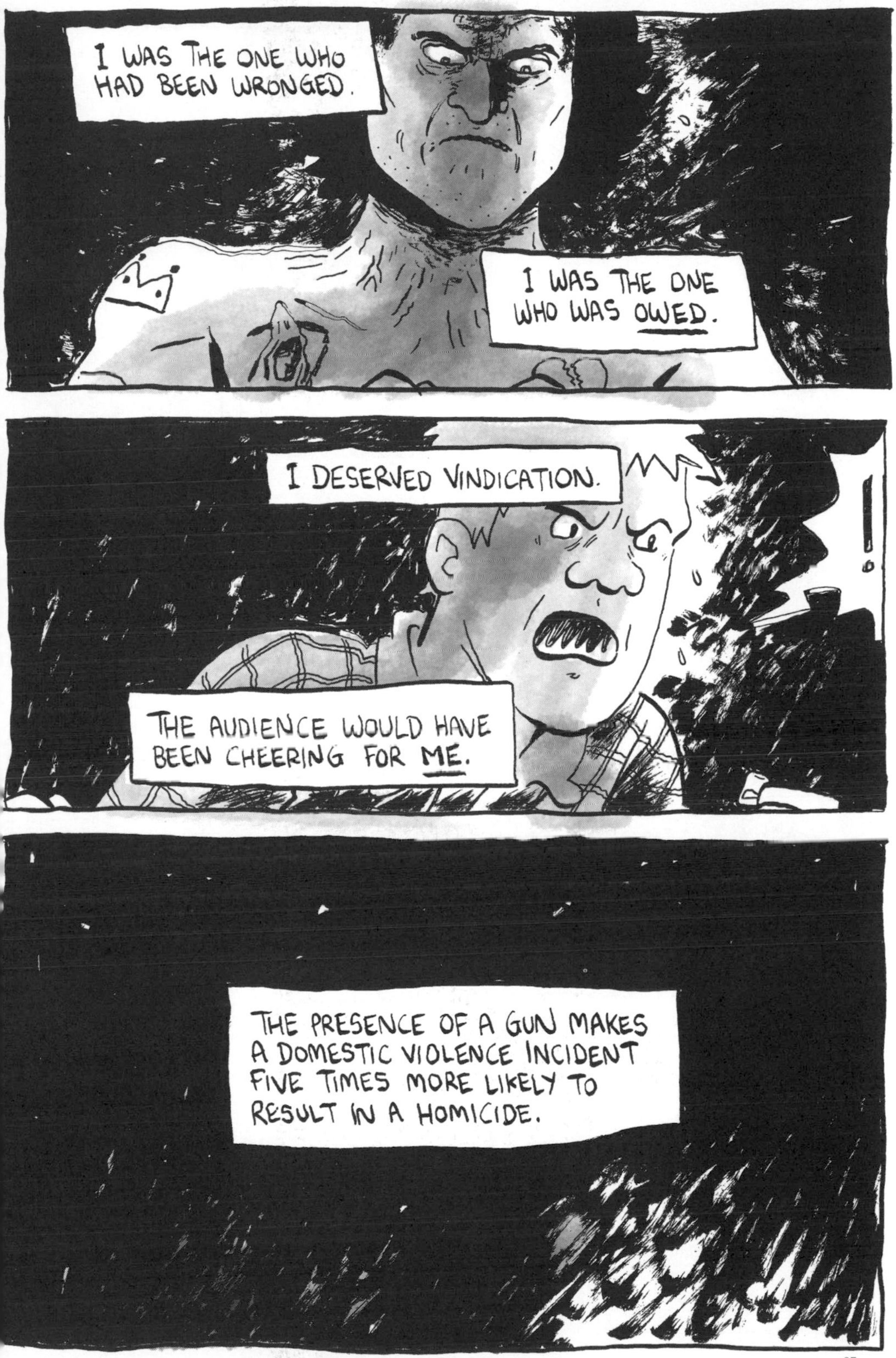
I WAS THE ONE WHO HAD BEEN WRONGED.
I WAS THE ONE WHO WAS OWED.
I DESERVED VINDICATION.
THE AUDIENCE WOULD HAVE BEEN CHEERING FOR ME.
THE PRESENCE OF A GUN MAKES A DOMESTIC VIOLENCE INCIDENT FIVE TIMES MORE LIKELY TO RESULT IN A HOMICIDE.

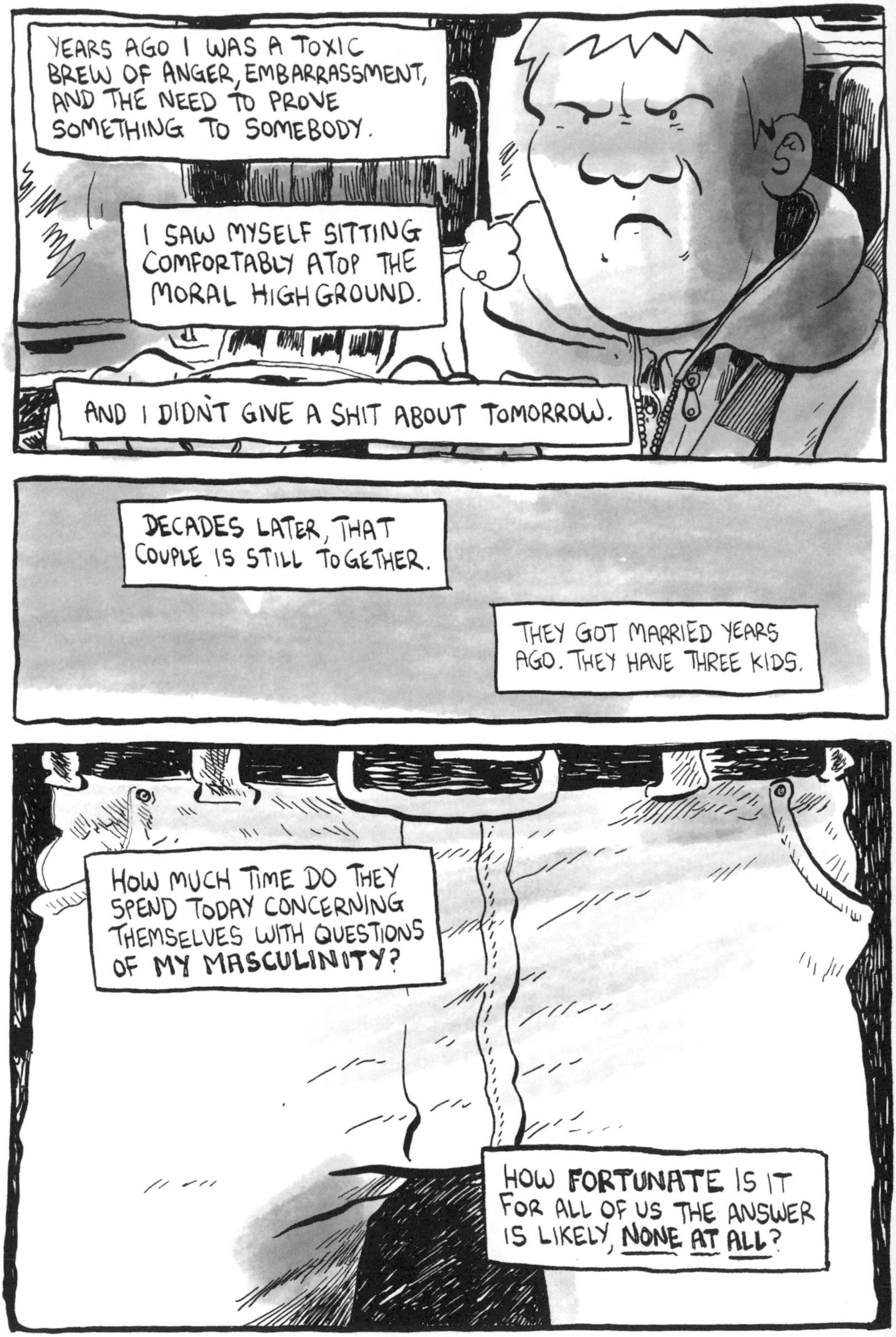
YEARS AGO I WAS A TOXIC BREW OF ANGER, EMBARRASSMENT, AND THE NEED TO PROVE SOMETHING TO SOMEBODY.
I SAW MYSELF SITTING COMFORTABLY ATOP THE MORAL HIGHGROUND.
AND I DIDN'T GIVE A SHIT ABOUT TOMORROW.
DECADES LATER, THAT COUPLE IS STILL TOGETHER.
THEY GOT MARRIED YEARS AGO. THEY HAVE THREE KIDS.
HOW MUCH TIME DO THEY SPEND TODAY CONCERNING THEMSELVES WITH QUESTIONS OF MY MASCULINITY?
HOW FORTUNATE IS IT FOR ALL OF US THE ANSWER IS LIKELY, NONE AT ALL?

JUNE 22ND, 2014

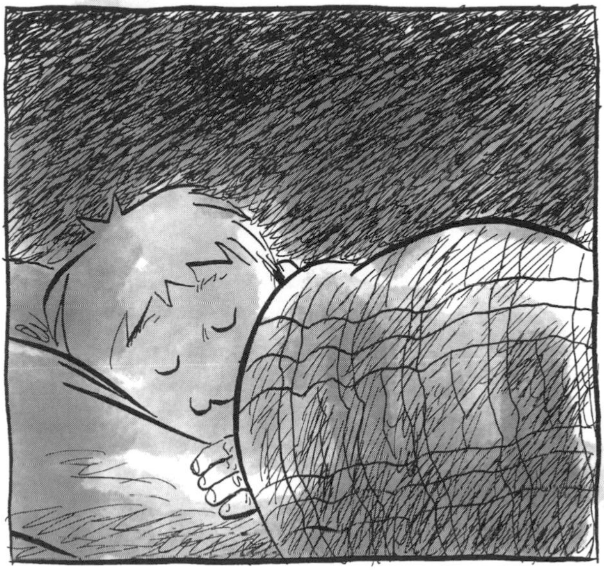

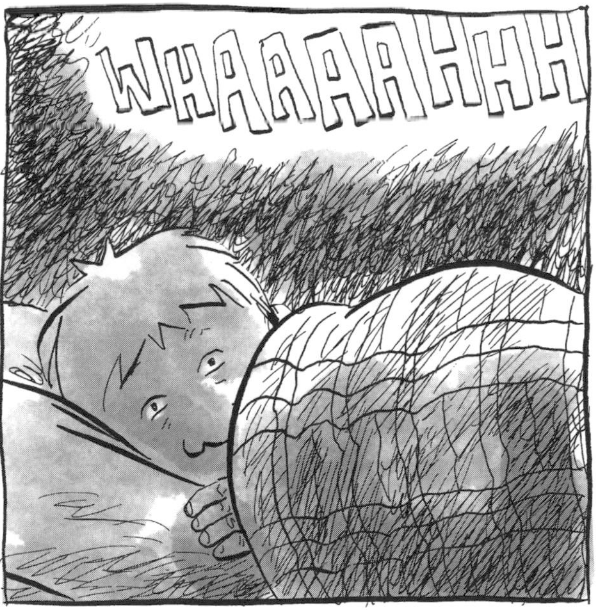
WHAAAAAHHH

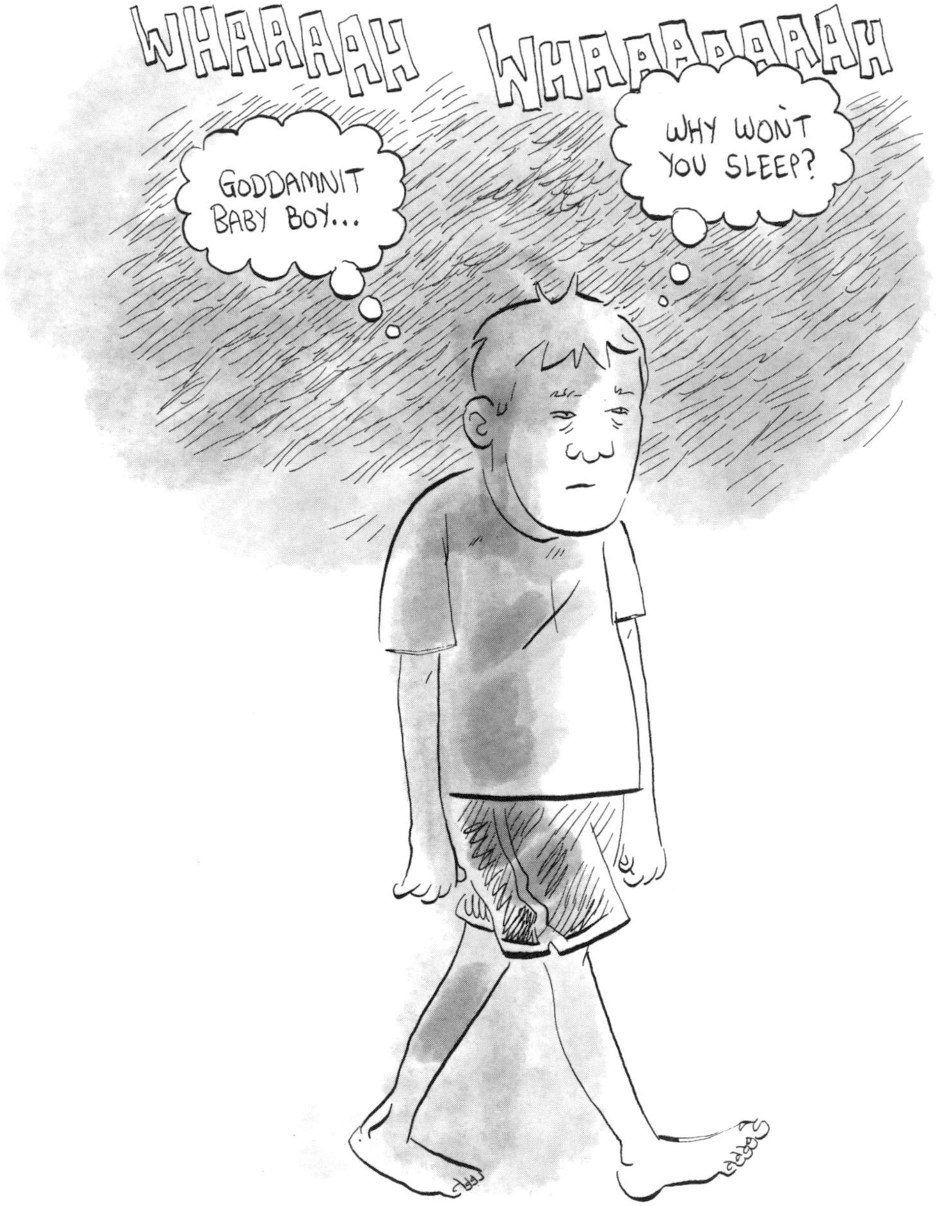
WHAAAAAH
GODDAMNIT BABY BOY...
WHAAAAAAAAH
WHY WON'T YOU SLEEP?

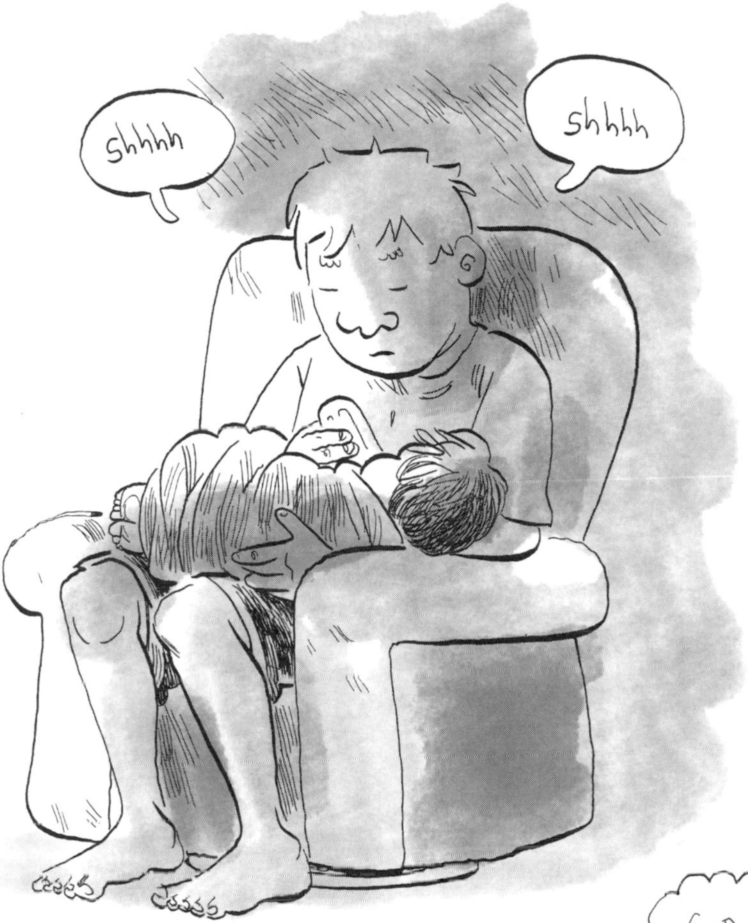
Shhhh
Shhhh

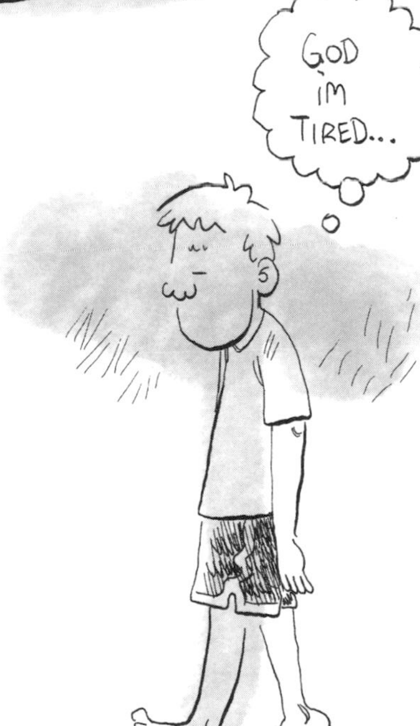
GOD IM TIRED...

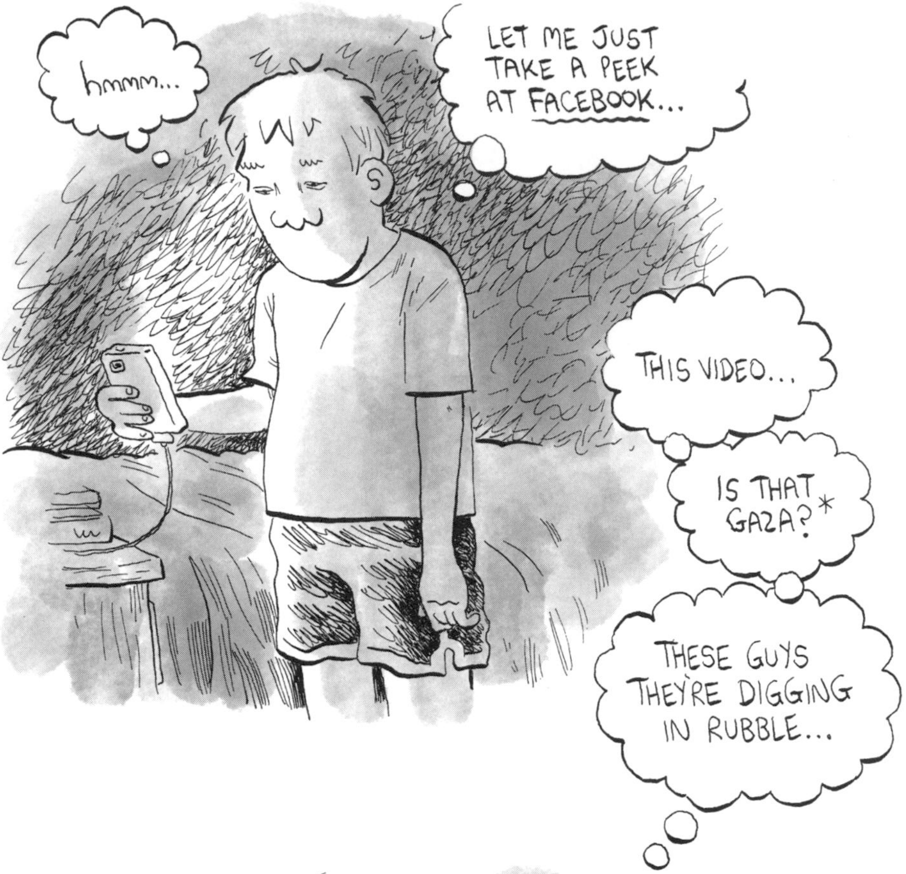
hmmm...
LET ME JUST TAKE A PEEK AT FACEBOOK...
THIS VIDEO...
IS THAT GAZA?*
THESE GUYS THEY'RE DIGGING IN RUBBLE...

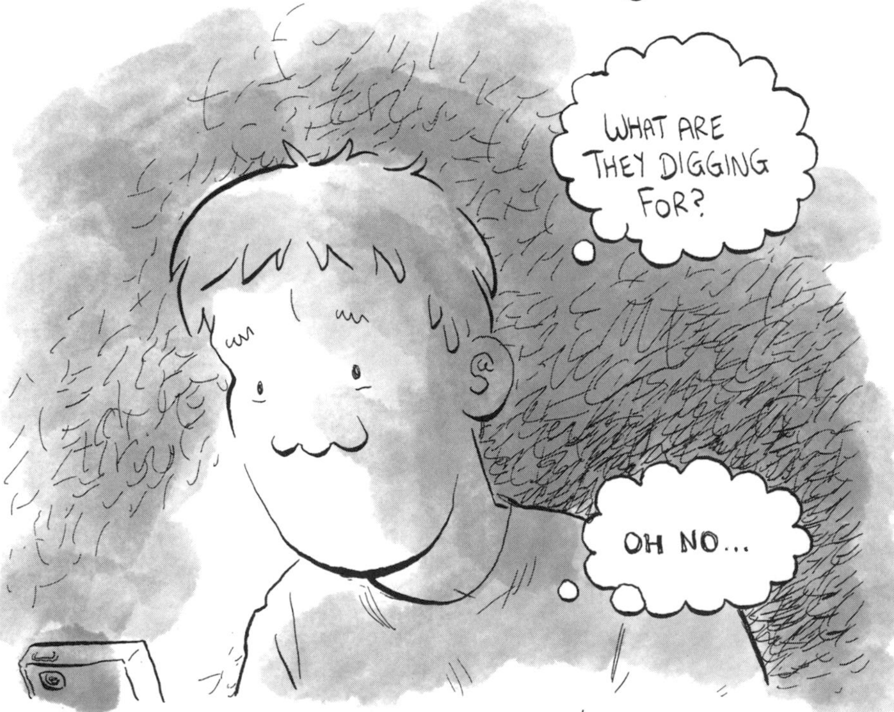
WHAT ARE THEY DIGGING FOR?
OH NO...

*IT WAS SYRIA

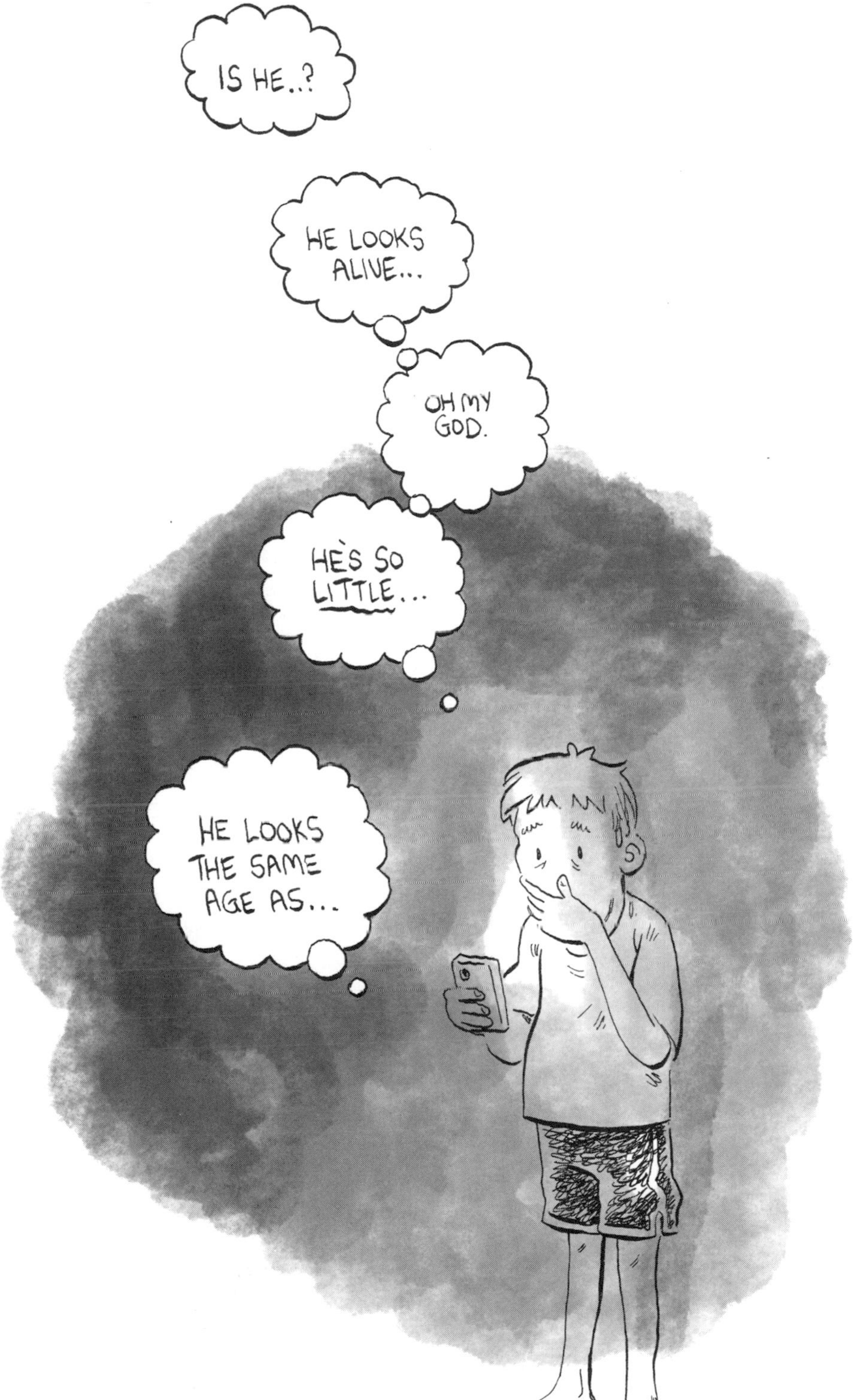
IS HE..?
HE LOOKS ALIVE...
OH MY GOD.
HE'S SO LITTLE...
HE LOOKS THE SAME AGE AS...

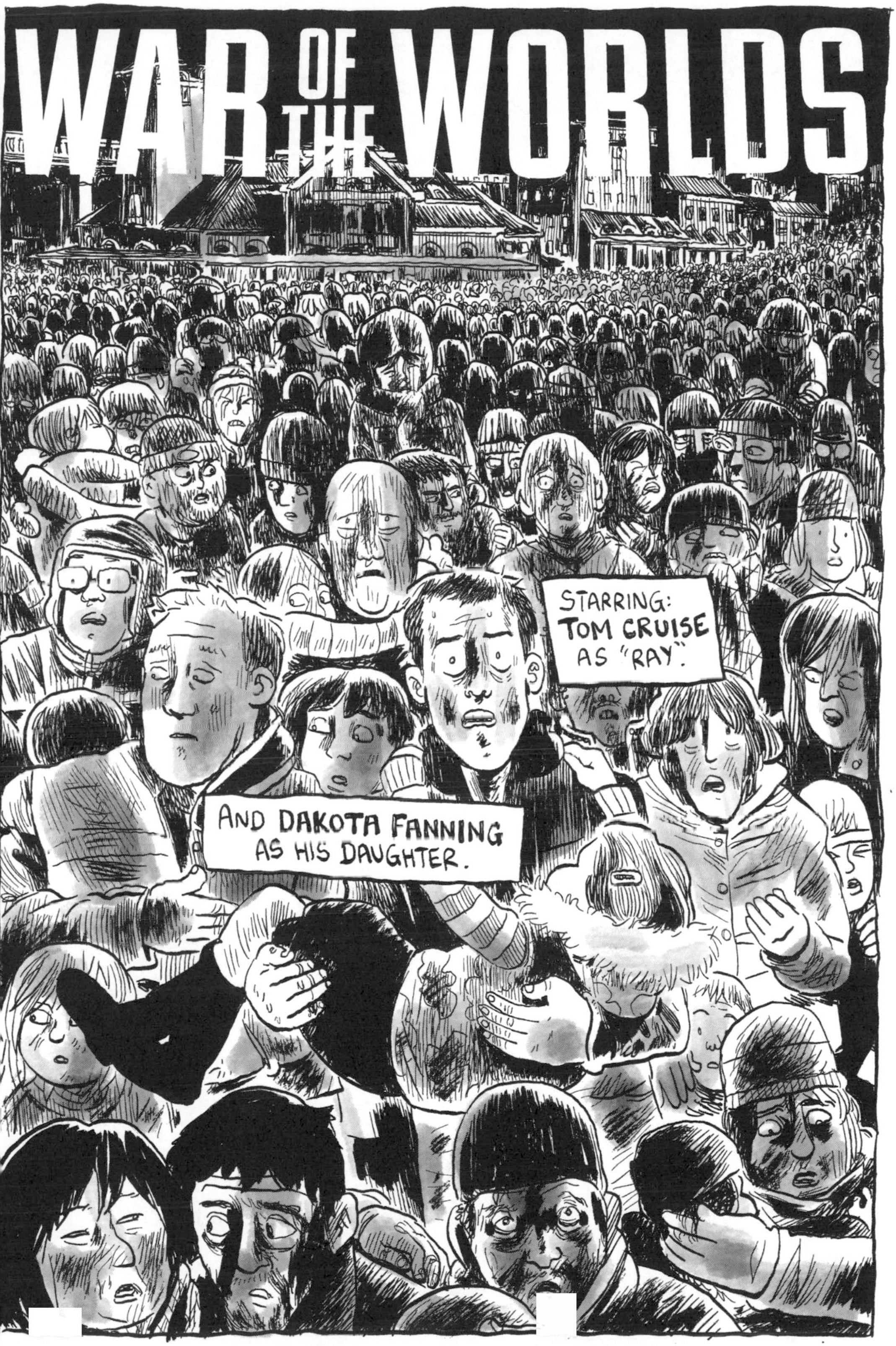
WAR OF THE WORLDS
STARRING: TOM CRUISE AS "RAY".
AND DAKOTA FANNING AS HIS DAUGHTER.

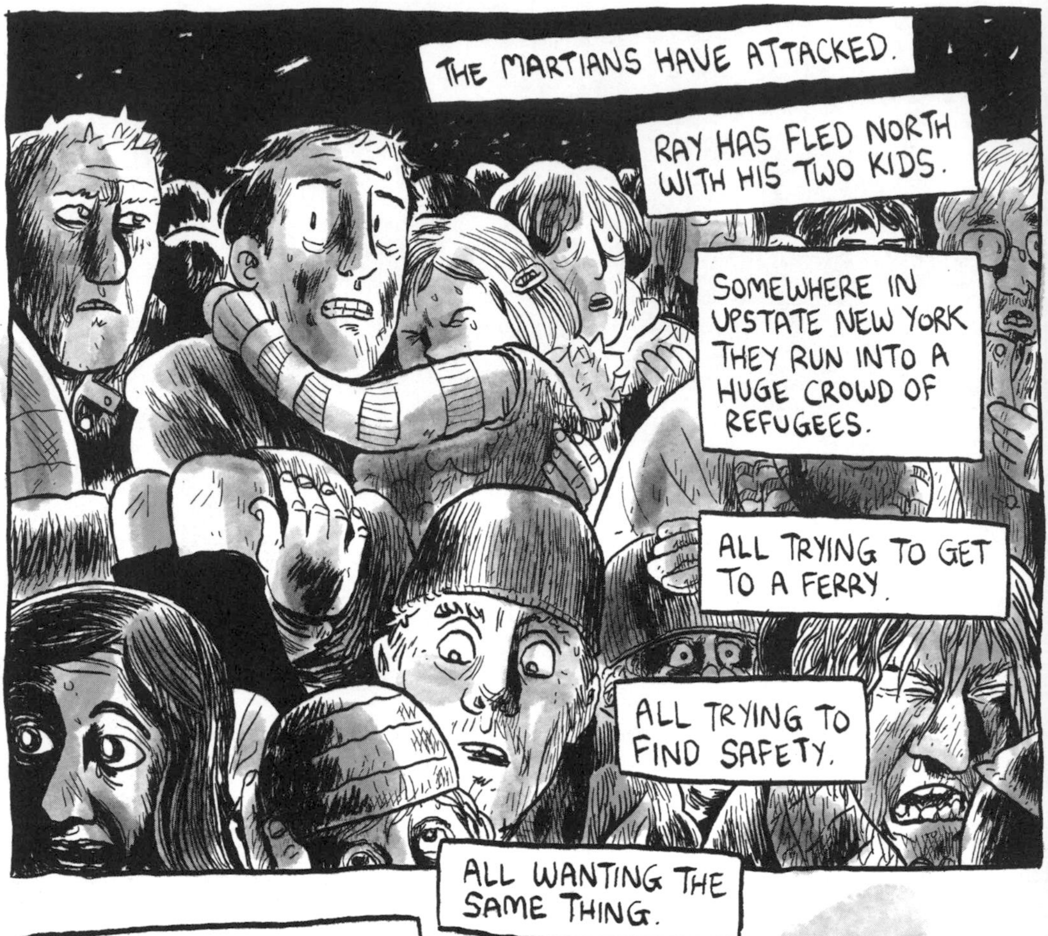
THE MARTIANS HAVE ATTACKED.
RAY HAS FLED NORTH WITH HIS TWO KIDS.
SOMEWHERE IN UPSTATE NEW YORK THEY RUN INTO A HUGE CROWD OF REFUGEES.
ALL TRYING TO GET TO A FERRY.
ALL TRYING TO FIND SAFETY.
ALL WANTING THE SAME THING.

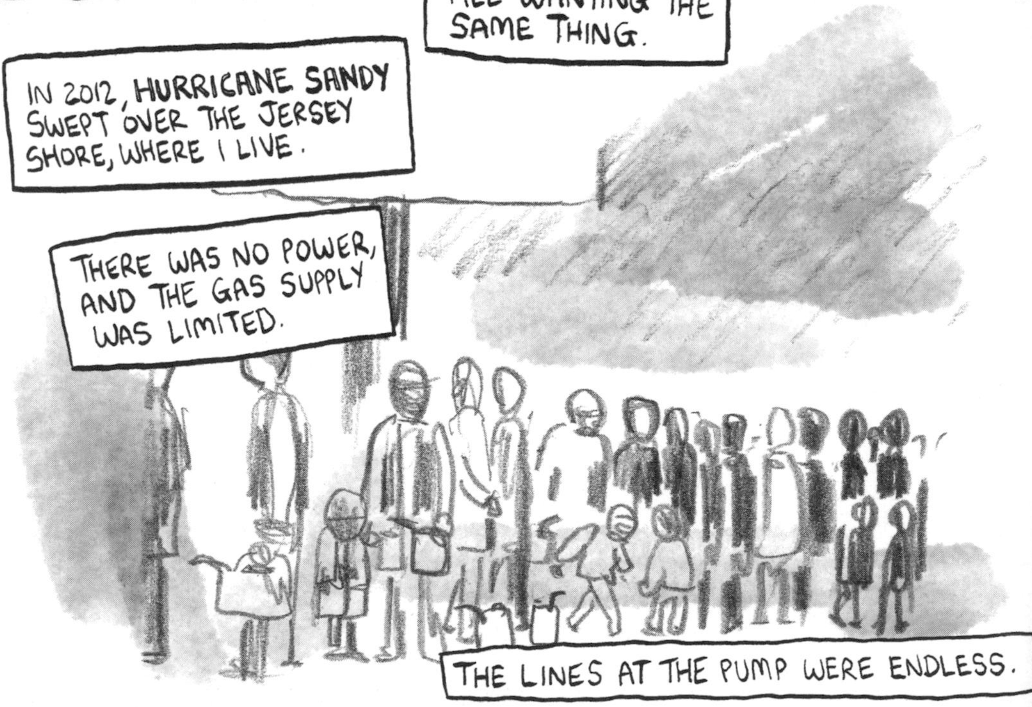
IN 2012, HURRICANE SANDY SWEPT OVER THE JERSEY SHORE, WHERE I LIVE.
THERE WAS NO POWER, AND THE GAS SUPPLY WAS LIMITED.
THE LINES AT THE PUMP WERE ENDLESS.

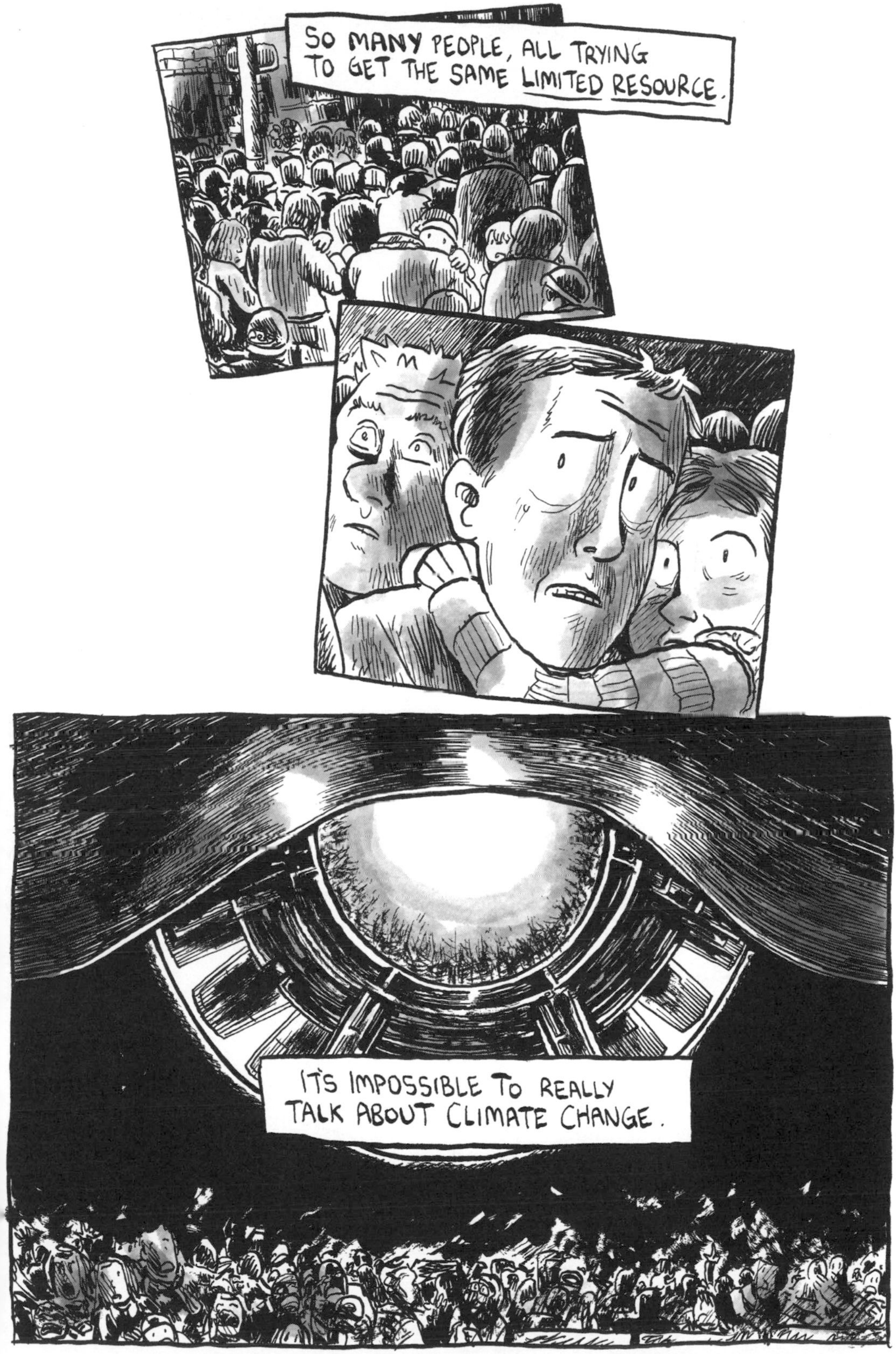
SO MANY PEOPLE, ALL TRYING TO GET THE SAME LIMITED RESOURCE.
IT'S IMPOSSIBLE TO REALLY TALK ABOUT CLIMATE CHANGE.

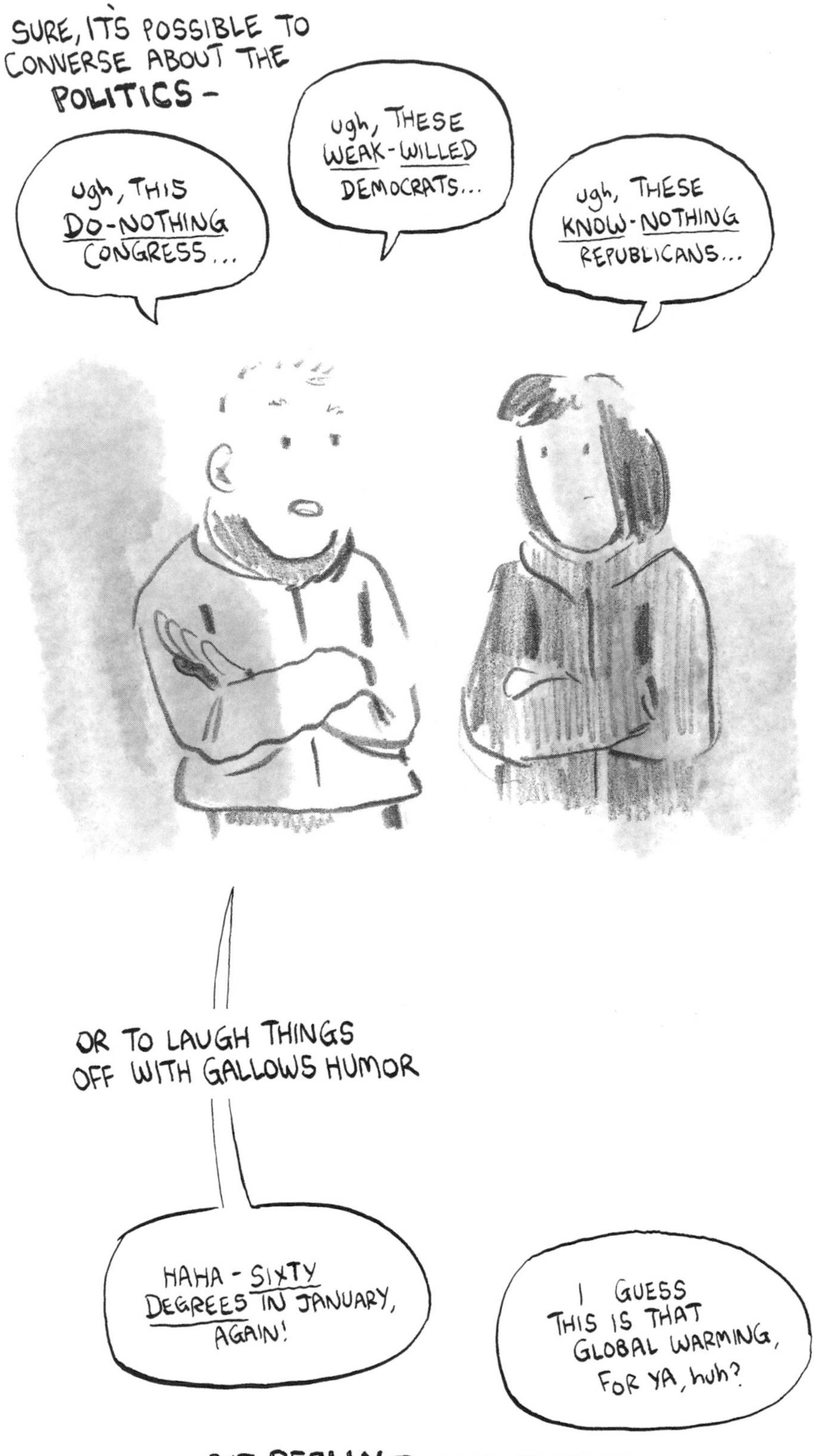
SURE, IT'S POSSIBLE TO CONVERSE ABOUT THE POLITICS -
ugh, THIS DO-NOTHING CONGRESS...
ugh, THESE WEAK-WILLED DEMOCRATS...
ugh, THESE KNOW-NOTHING REPUBLICANS...
OR TO LAUGH THINGS OFF WITH GALLOWS HUMOR
HAHA - SIXTY DEGREES IN JANUARY, AGAIN!
I GUESS THIS IS THAT GLOBAL WARMING, FOR YA, huh?
BUT REALLY TALKING ABOUT IT...

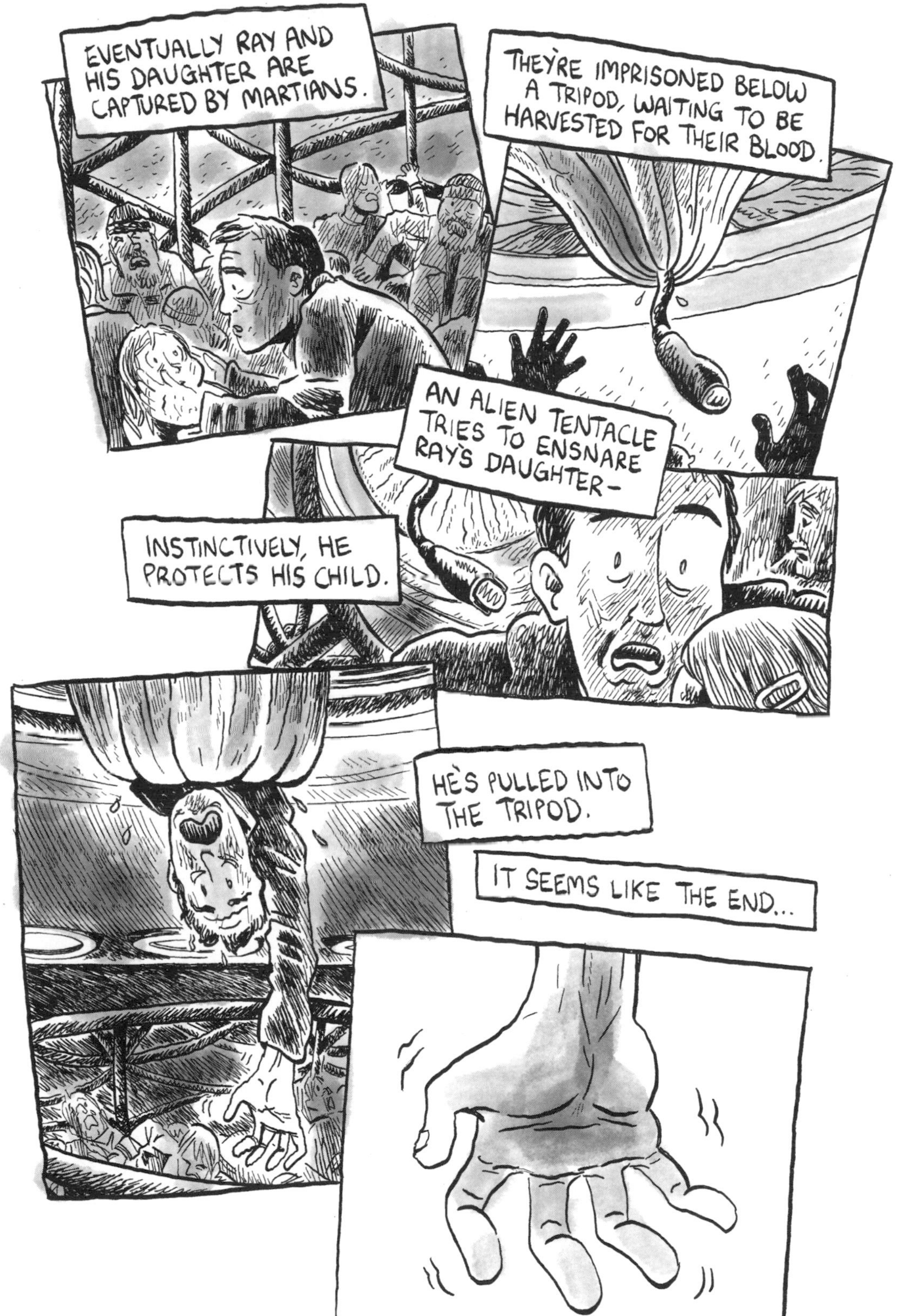
EVENTUALLY RAY AND HIS DAUGHTER ARE CAPTURED BY MARTIANS.
THEY'RE IMPRISONED BELOW A TRIPOD, WAITING TO BE HARVESTED FOR THEIR BLOOD.
AN ALIEN TENTACLE TRIES TO ENSNARE RAY'S DAUGHTER-
INSTINCTIVELY, HE PROTECTS HIS CHILD.
HE'S PULLED INTO THE TRIPOD.
IT SEEMS LIKE THE END...

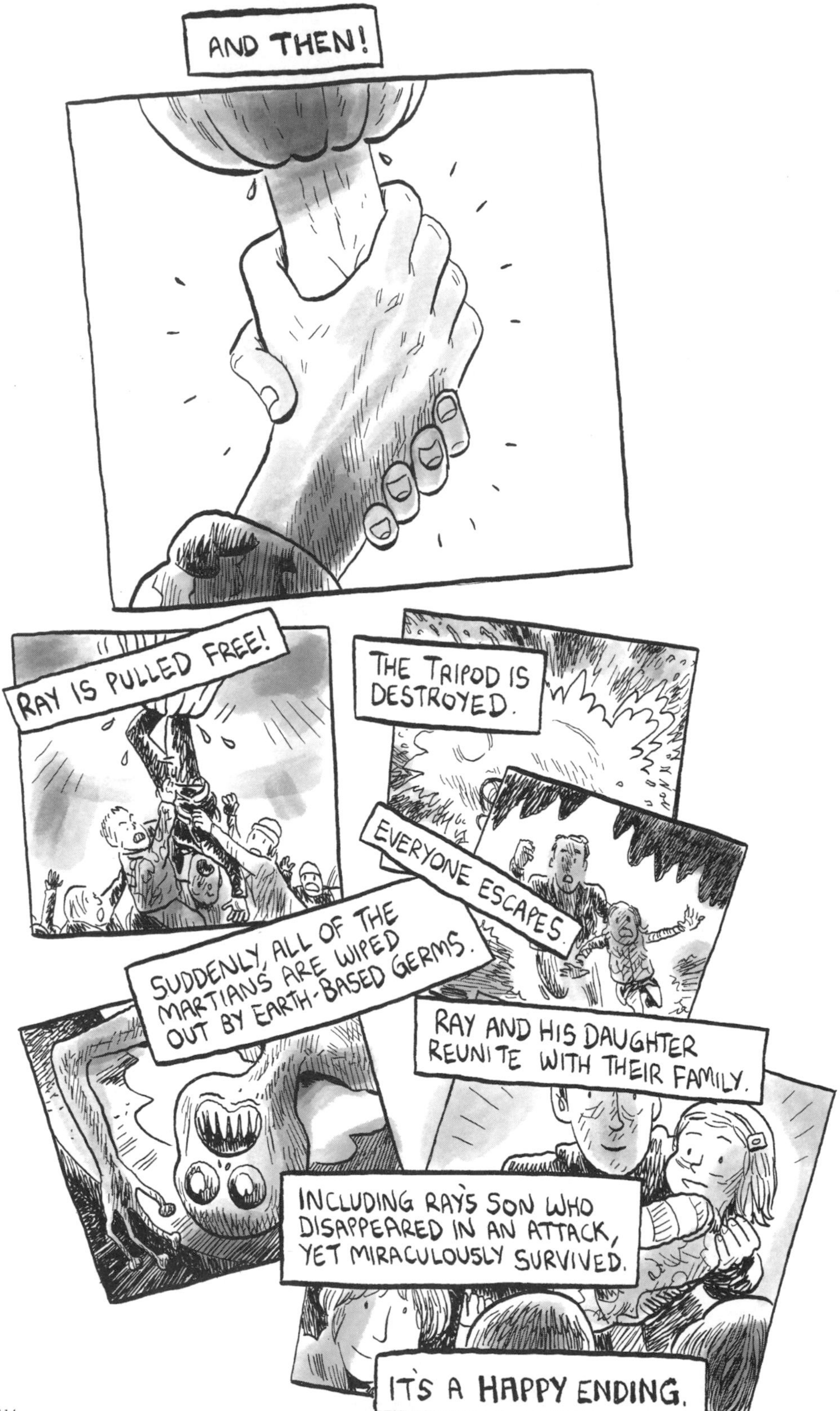
AND THEN!
RAY IS PULLED FREE!
THE TRIPOD IS DESTROYED.
EVERYONE ESCAPES.
SUDDENLY, ALL OF THE MARTIANS ARE WIPED OUT BY EARTH-BASED GERMS.
RAY AND HIS DAUGHTER REUNITE WITH THEIR FAMILY.
INCLUDING RAY'S SON WHO DISAPPEARED IN AN ATTACK, YET MIRACULOUSLY SURVIVED.
IT'S A HAPPY ENDING.

IT'S TOO HAPPY.

IT'S WISH FULFILLMENT.

IT'S THE FANTASY THAT PLAYS THROUGH THE FATHER'S MIND AS HE DIES—

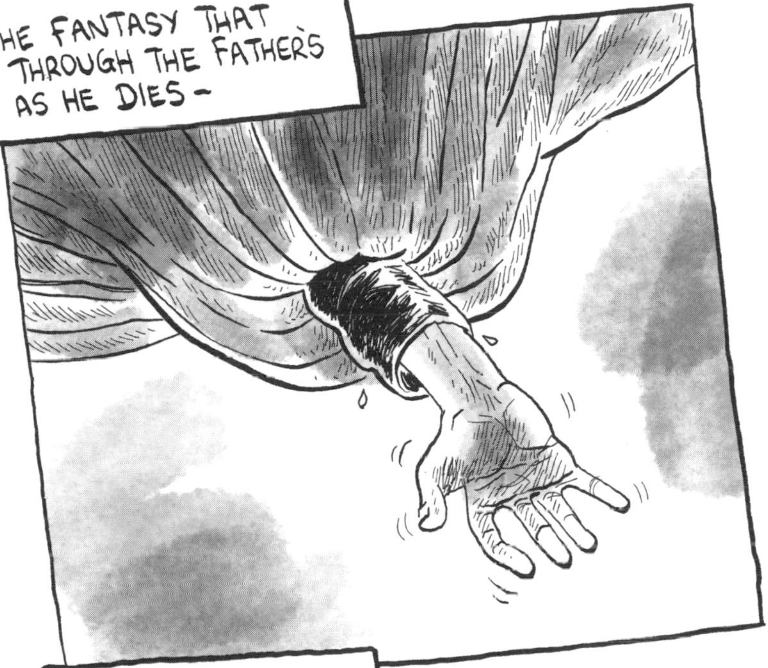

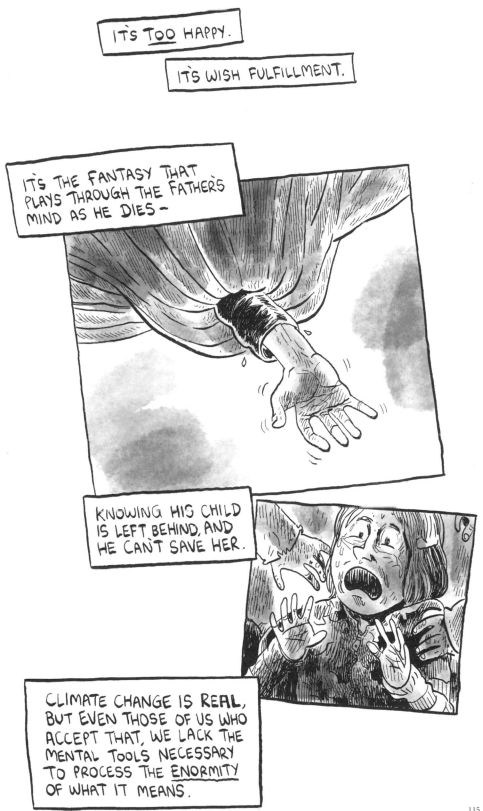

KNOWING HIS CHILD IS LEFT BEHIND, AND HE CAN'T SAVE HER.

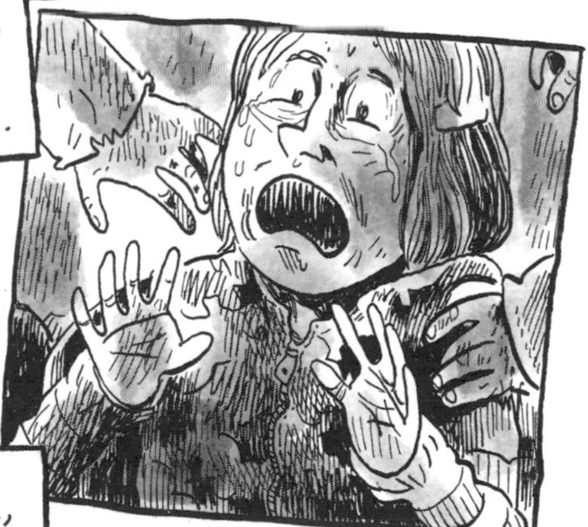

CLIMATE CHANGE IS **REAL**, BUT EVEN THOSE OF US WHO ACCEPT THAT, WE LACK THE MENTAL TOOLS NECESSARY TO PROCESS THE ENORMITY OF WHAT IT MEANS.

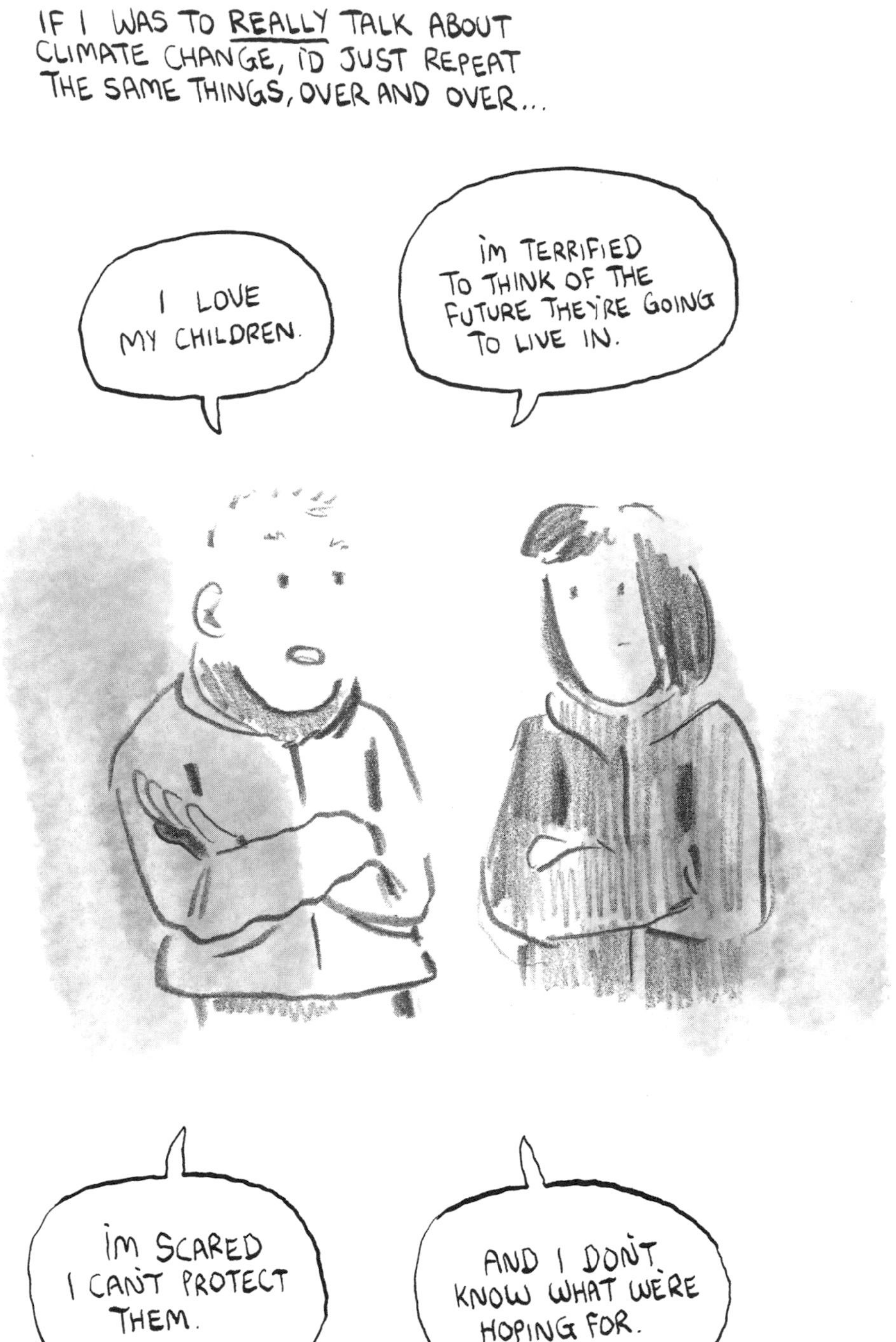
IF I WAS TO REALLY TALK ABOUT CLIMATE CHANGE, I'D JUST REPEAT THE SAME THINGS, OVER AND OVER...
I LOVE MY CHILDREN.
I'M TERRIFIED TO THINK OF THE FUTURE THEY'RE GOING TO LIVE IN.
I'M SCARED I CAN'T PROTECT THEM.
AND I DON'T KNOW WHAT WE'RE HOPING FOR.

"I can only accept it for about one second a day."

DR TIMOTHY MORTON, DISCUSSING THE SIXTH MASS EXTINCTION EVENT –

WHICH WE ARE CURRENTLY IN.

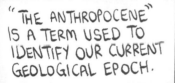

"THE ANTHROPOCENE" IS A TERM USED TO IDENTIFY OUR CURRENT GEOLOGICAL EPOCH.

THOUGH THERE'S SOME DEBATE –

MANY SCIENTISTS DATE THE START OF THE ANTHROPOCENE TO THE 1790'S –

WHEN HUMAN BEINGS FIRST BEGAN BURNING FOSSIL FUELS AND PUMPING CARBON INTO THE ATMOSPHERE.

The Age of Man

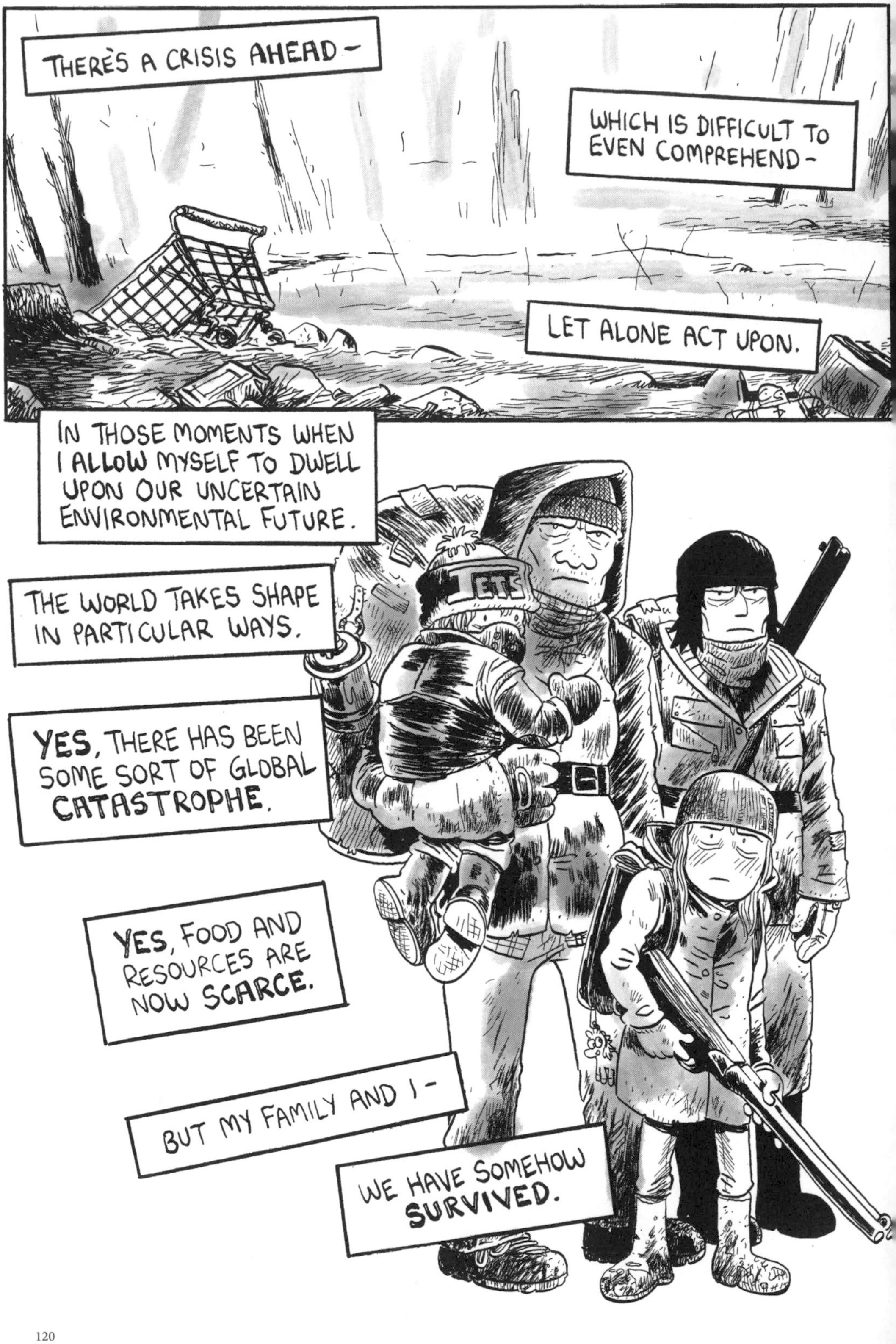
THERE'S A CRISIS AHEAD -
WHICH IS DIFFICULT TO EVEN COMPREHEND -
LET ALONE ACT UPON.
IN THOSE MOMENTS WHEN I ALLOW MYSELF TO DWELL UPON OUR UNCERTAIN ENVIRONMENTAL FUTURE.
JETS
THE WORLD TAKES SHAPE IN PARTICULAR WAYS.
YES, THERE HAS BEEN SOME SORT OF GLOBAL CATASTROPHE.
YES, FOOD AND RESOURCES ARE NOW SCARCE.
BUT MY FAMILY AND I -
WE HAVE SOMEHOW SURVIVED.

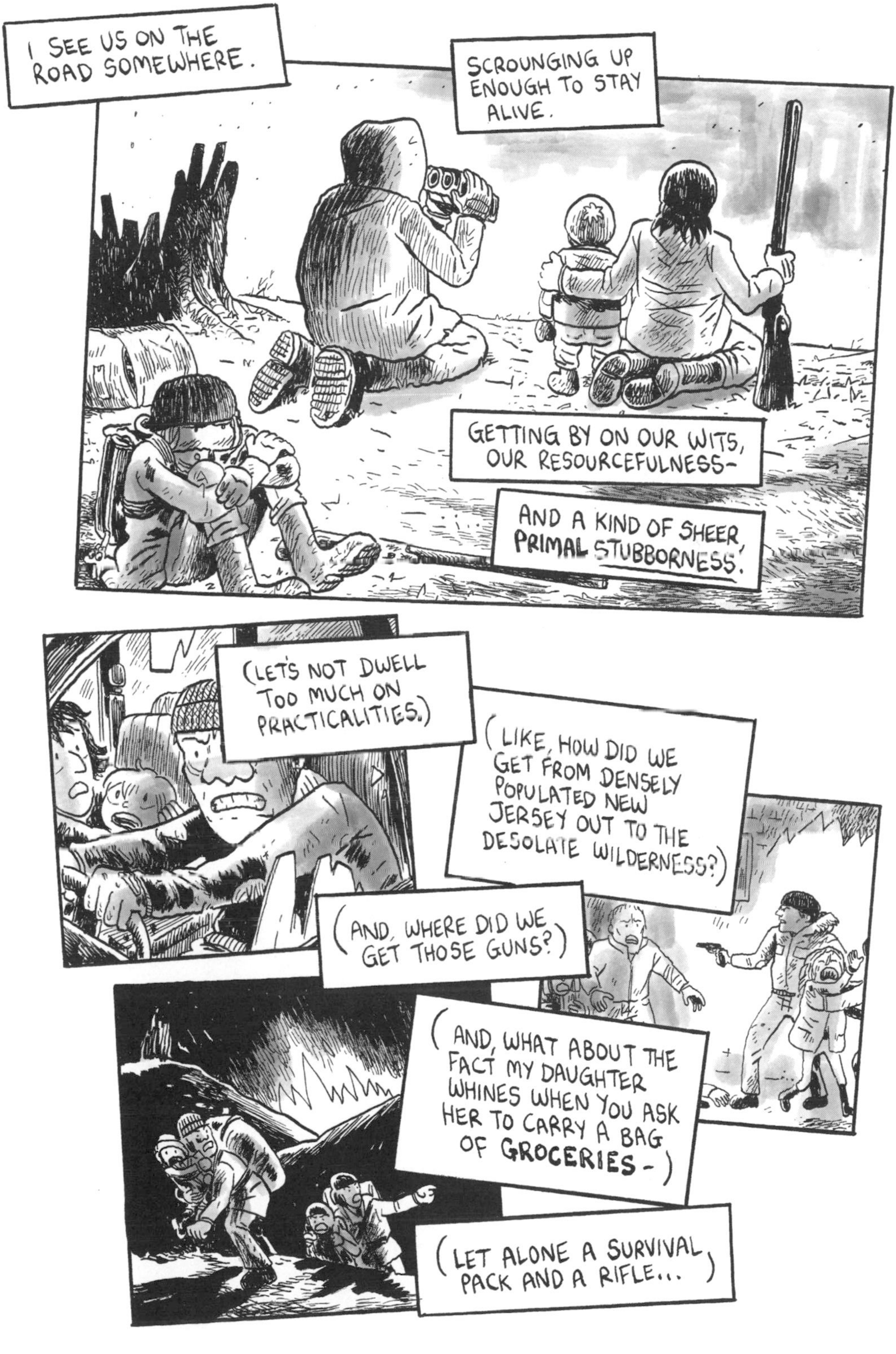
I SEE US ON THE ROAD SOMEWHERE.
SCROUNGING UP ENOUGH TO STAY ALIVE.
GETTING BY ON OUR WITS, OUR RESOURCEFULNESS-
AND A KIND OF SHEER PRIMAL STUBBORNESS.
(LET'S NOT DWELL TOO MUCH ON PRACTICALITIES.)
(LIKE, HOW DID WE GET FROM DENSELY POPULATED NEW JERSEY OUT TO THE DESOLATE WILDERNESS?)
(AND, WHERE DID WE GET THOSE GUNS?)
(AND, WHAT ABOUT THE FACT MY DAUGHTER WHINES WHEN YOU ASK HER TO CARRY A BAG OF GROCERIES -)
(LET ALONE A SURVIVAL PACK AND A RIFLE...)

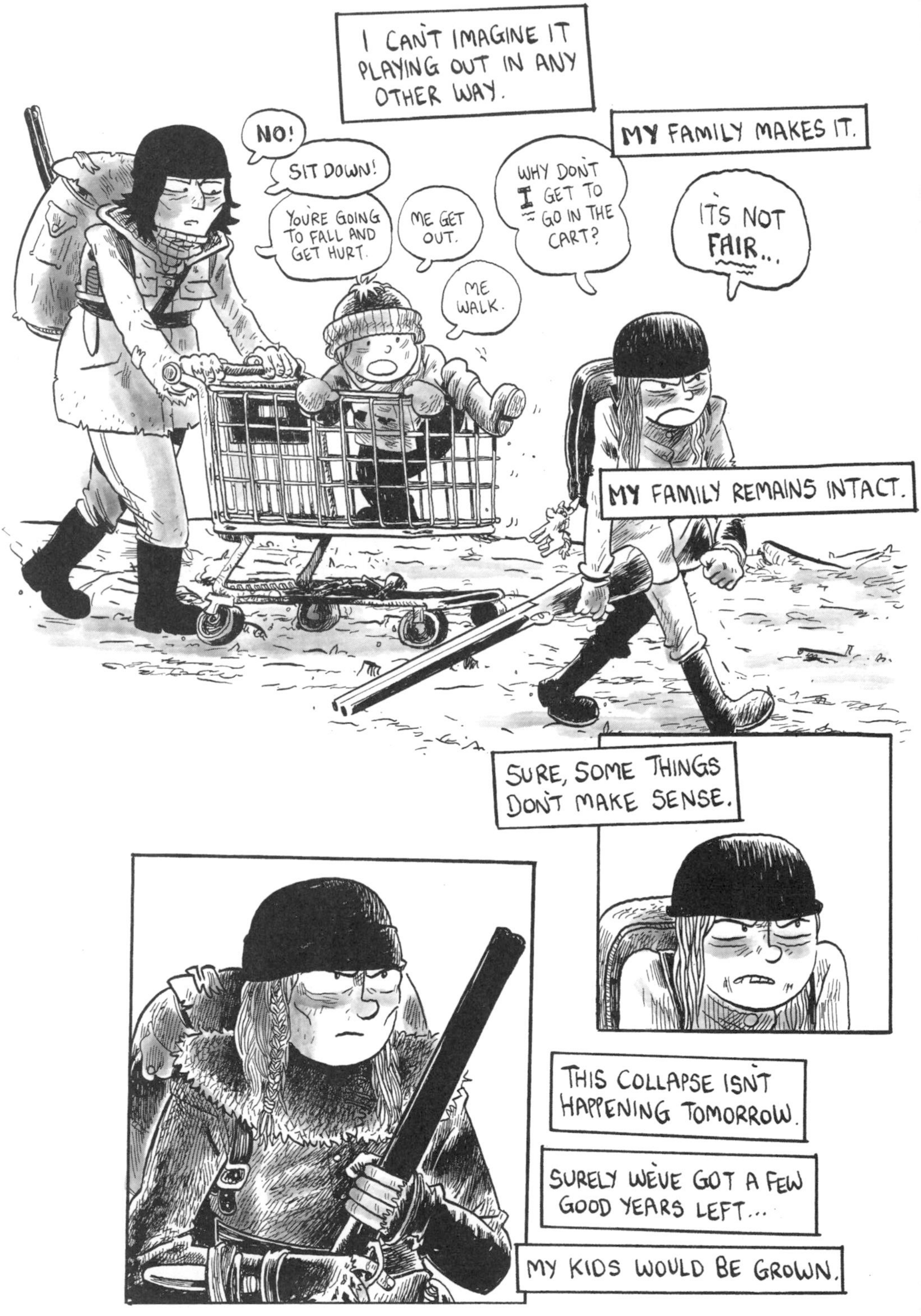
I CAN'T IMAGINE IT PLAYING OUT IN ANY OTHER WAY.
MY FAMILY MAKES IT.
NO!
SIT DOWN!
YOU'RE GOING TO FALL AND GET HURT.
ME GET OUT.
ME WALK.
WHY DON'T I GET TO GO IN THE CART?
IT'S NOT FAIR...
MY FAMILY REMAINS INTACT.
SURE, SOME THINGS DON'T MAKE SENSE.
THIS COLLAPSE ISN'T HAPPENING TOMORROW.
SURELY WE'VE GOT A FEW GOOD YEARS LEFT...
MY KIDS WOULD BE GROWN.

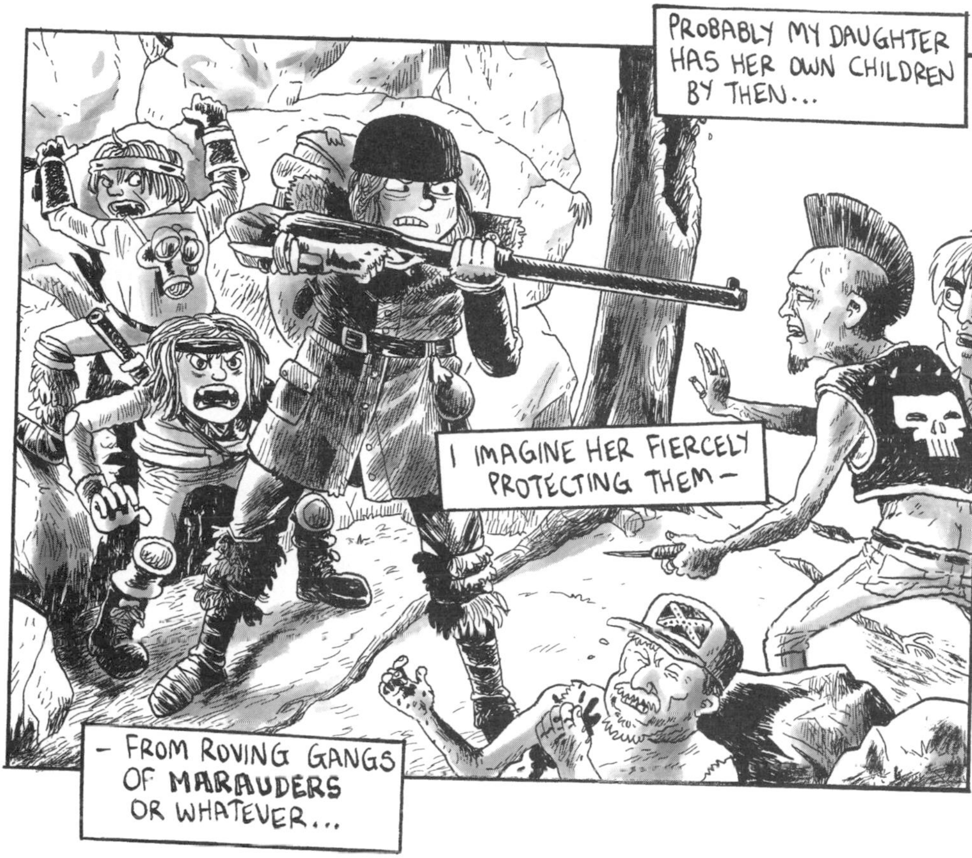
PROBABLY MY DAUGHTER HAS HER OWN CHILDREN BY THEN...
I IMAGINE HER FIERCELY PROTECTING THEM—
— FROM ROVING GANGS OF MARAUDERS OR WHATEVER...

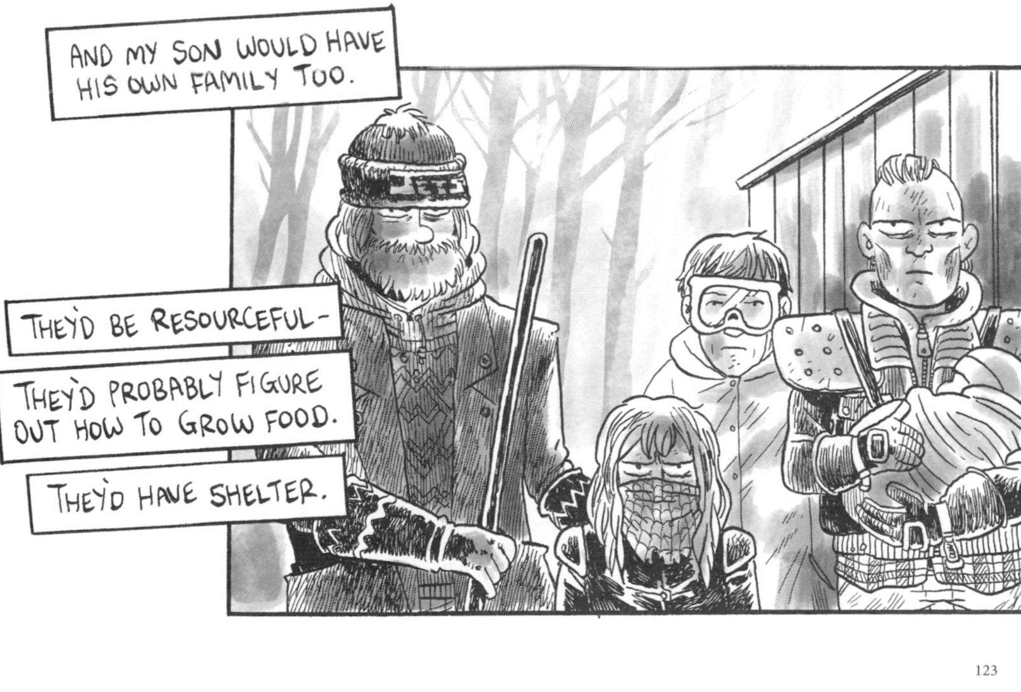
AND MY SON WOULD HAVE HIS OWN FAMILY TOO.
THEY'D BE RESOURCEFUL—
THEY'D PROBABLY FIGURE OUT HOW TO GROW FOOD.
THEY'D HAVE SHELTER.

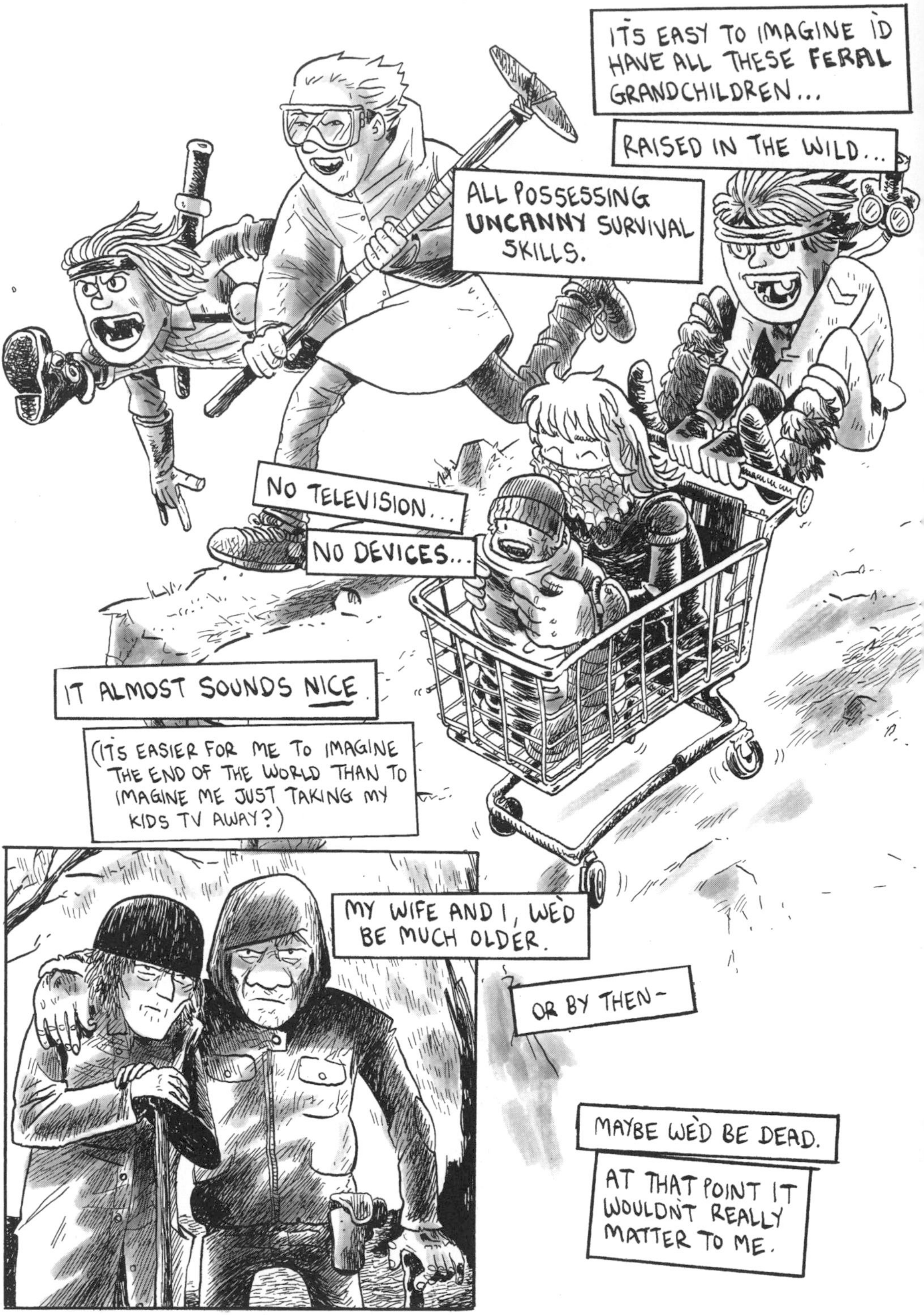
IT'S EASY TO IMAGINE I'D HAVE ALL THESE **FERAL** GRANDCHILDREN...
RAISED IN THE WILD...
ALL POSSESSING **UNCANNY** SURVIVAL SKILLS.
NO TELEVISION...
NO DEVICES...
IT ALMOST SOUNDS NICE.
(IT'S EASIER FOR ME TO IMAGINE THE END OF THE WORLD THAN TO IMAGINE ME JUST TAKING MY KIDS TV AWAY?)
MY WIFE AND I, WE'D BE MUCH OLDER.
OR BY THEN-
MAYBE WE'D BE DEAD.
AT THAT POINT IT WOULDN'T REALLY MATTER TO ME.

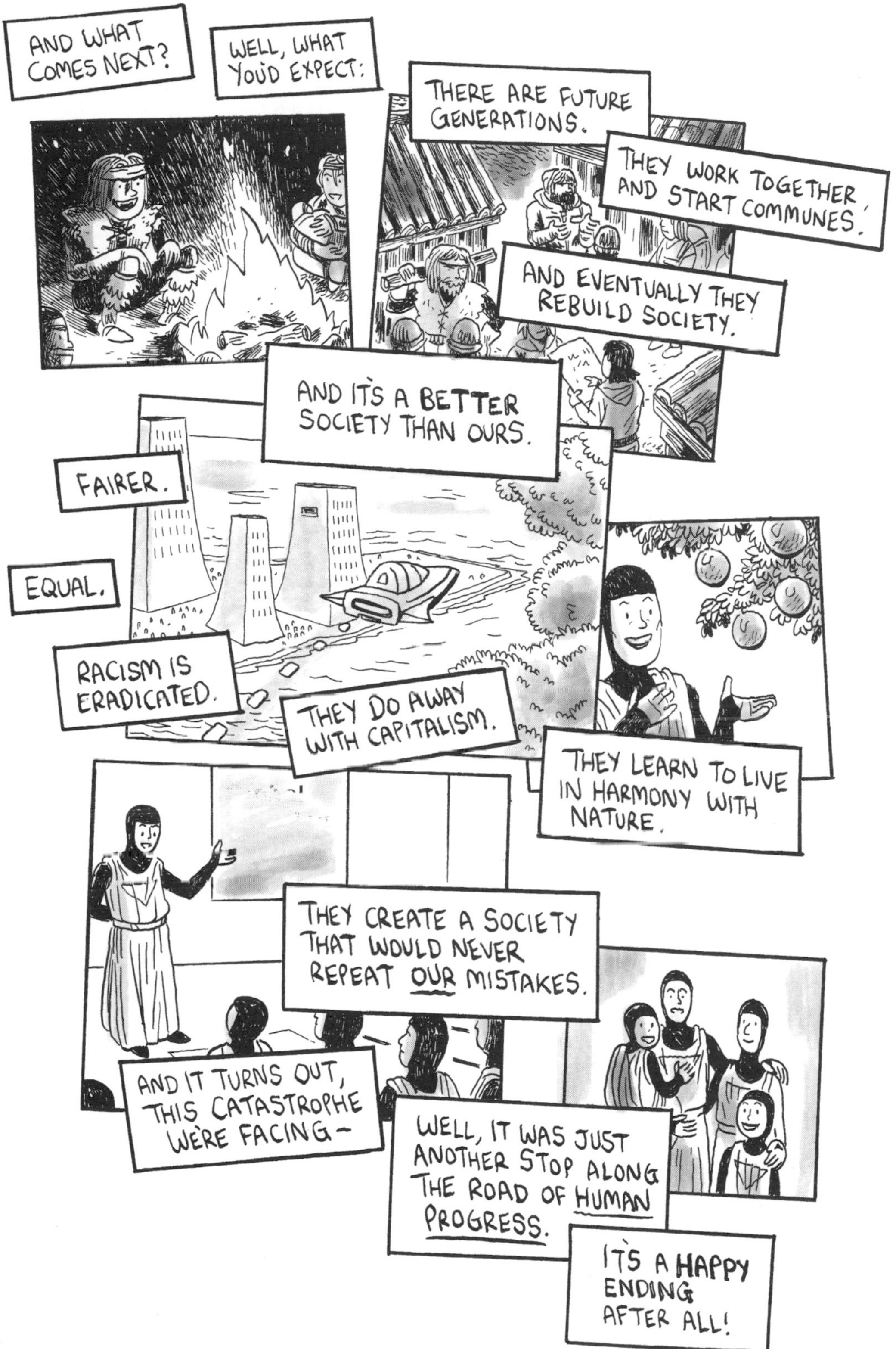
AND WHAT COMES NEXT?
WELL, WHAT YOU'D EXPECT:
THERE ARE FUTURE GENERATIONS.
THEY WORK TOGETHER, AND START COMMUNES.
AND EVENTUALLY THEY REBUILD SOCIETY.
AND IT'S A BETTER SOCIETY THAN OURS.
FAIRER.
EQUAL.
RACISM IS ERADICATED.
THEY DO AWAY WITH CAPITALISM.
THEY LEARN TO LIVE IN HARMONY WITH NATURE.
THEY CREATE A SOCIETY THAT WOULD NEVER REPEAT OUR MISTAKES.
AND IT TURNS OUT, THIS CATASTROPHE WE'RE FACING—
WELL, IT WAS JUST ANOTHER STOP ALONG THE ROAD OF HUMAN PROGRESS.
IT'S A HAPPY ENDING AFTER ALL!

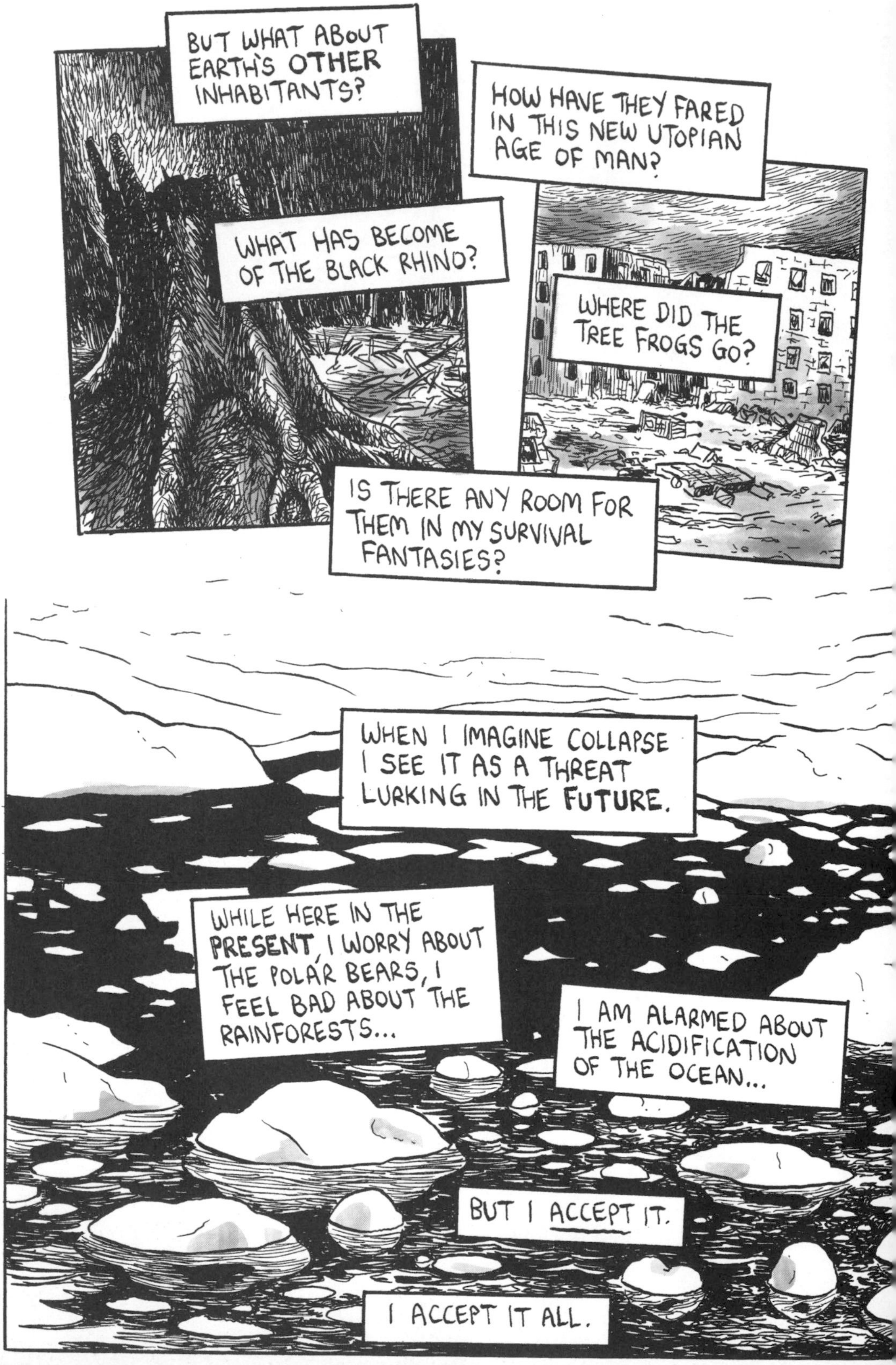
BUT WHAT ABOUT EARTH'S **OTHER** INHABITANTS?
HOW HAVE THEY FARED IN THIS NEW UTOPIAN AGE OF MAN?
WHAT HAS BECOME OF THE BLACK RHINO?
WHERE DID THE TREE FROGS GO?
IS THERE ANY ROOM FOR THEM IN MY SURVIVAL FANTASIES?
WHEN I IMAGINE COLLAPSE I SEE IT AS A THREAT LURKING IN THE **FUTURE**.
WHILE HERE IN THE **PRESENT**, I WORRY ABOUT THE POLAR BEARS, I FEEL BAD ABOUT THE RAINFORESTS...
I AM ALARMED ABOUT THE ACIDIFICATION OF THE OCEAN...
BUT I ACCEPT IT.
I ACCEPT IT ALL.

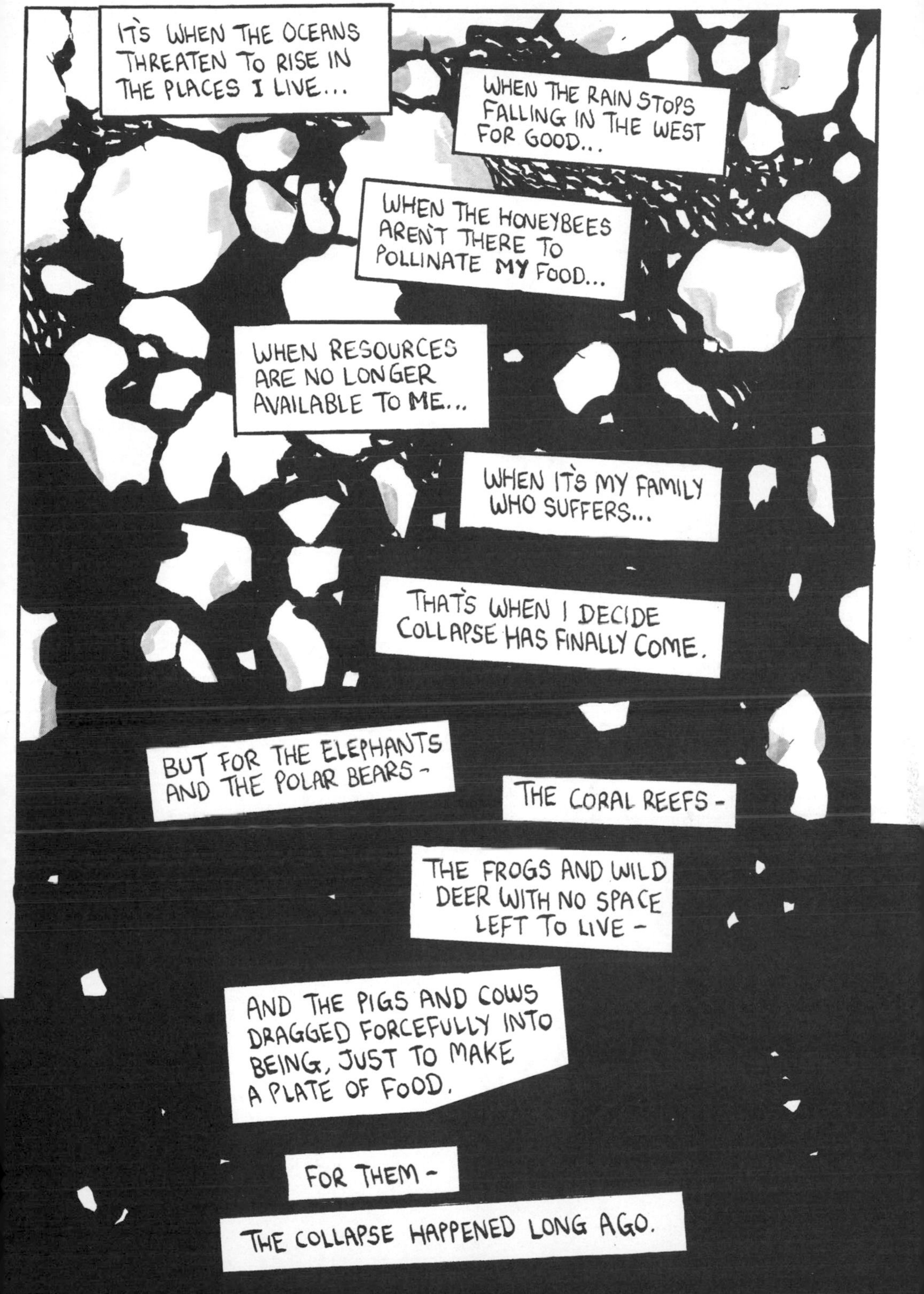
IT'S WHEN THE OCEANS THREATEN TO RISE IN THE PLACES I LIVE...
WHEN THE RAIN STOPS FALLING IN THE WEST FOR GOOD...
WHEN THE HONEYBEES AREN'T THERE TO POLLINATE MY FOOD...
WHEN RESOURCES ARE NO LONGER AVAILABLE TO ME...
WHEN IT'S MY FAMILY WHO SUFFERS...
THAT'S WHEN I DECIDE COLLAPSE HAS FINALLY COME.
BUT FOR THE ELEPHANTS AND THE POLAR BEARS -
THE CORAL REEFS -
THE FROGS AND WILD DEER WITH NO SPACE LEFT TO LIVE -
AND THE PIGS AND COWS DRAGGED FORCEFULLY INTO BEING, JUST TO MAKE A PLATE OF FOOD.
FOR THEM -
THE COLLAPSE HAPPENED LONG AGO.

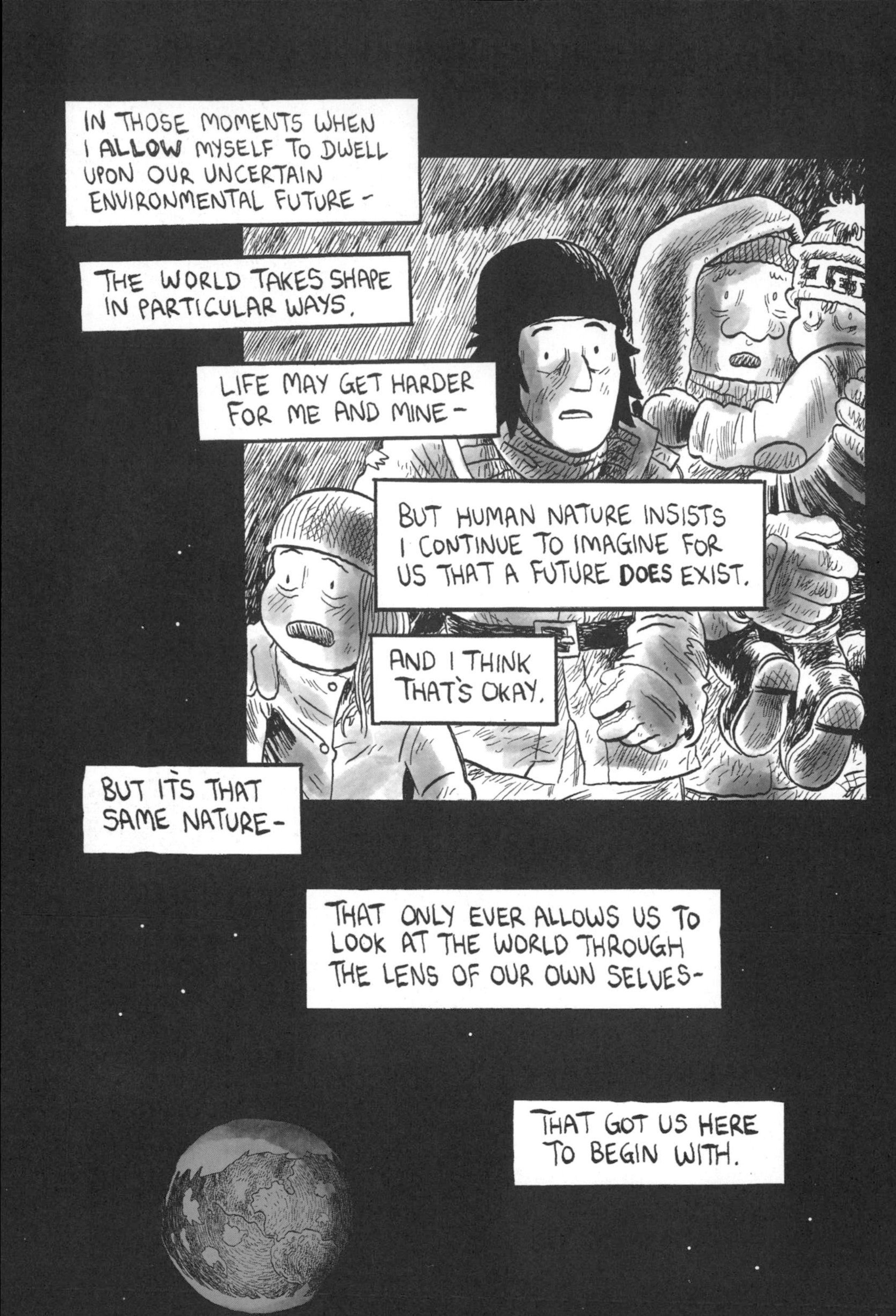
IN THOSE MOMENTS WHEN I **ALLOW** MYSELF TO DWELL UPON OUR UNCERTAIN ENVIRONMENTAL FUTURE -
THE WORLD TAKES SHAPE IN PARTICULAR WAYS.
LIFE MAY GET HARDER FOR ME AND MINE -
BUT HUMAN NATURE INSISTS I CONTINUE TO IMAGINE FOR US THAT A FUTURE **DOES** EXIST.
AND I THINK THAT'S OKAY.
BUT IT'S THAT SAME NATURE -
THAT ONLY EVER ALLOWS US TO LOOK AT THE WORLD THROUGH THE LENS OF OUR OWN SELVES -
THAT GOT US HERE TO BEGIN WITH.

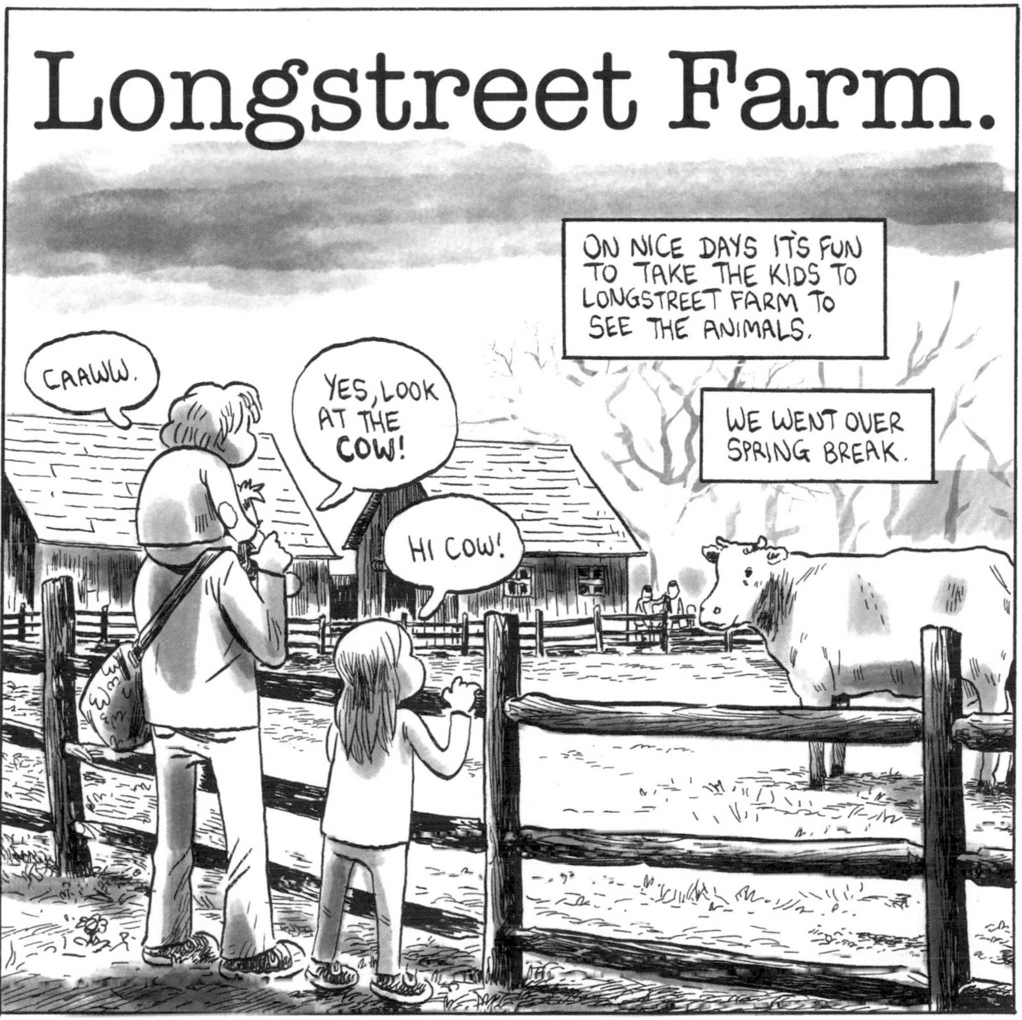
Longstreet Farm.
ON NICE DAYS IT'S FUN TO TAKE THE KIDS TO LONGSTREET FARM TO SEE THE ANIMALS.
CAAWW.
YES, LOOK AT THE COW!
HI COW!
WE WENT OVER SPRING BREAK.

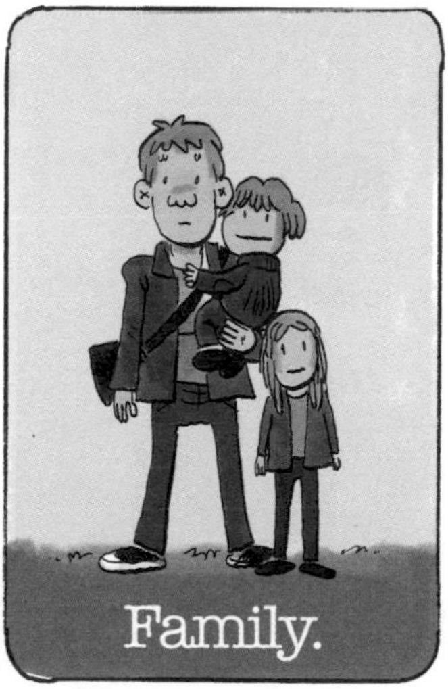
Family.

LONGSTREET IS A WORKING FACSIMILE OF AN ANIMAL FARM FROM THE 1890'S.

THE PEOPLE WHO WORK THERE USE TRADITIONAL FARMING METHODS AND WEAR PERIOD DRESS.

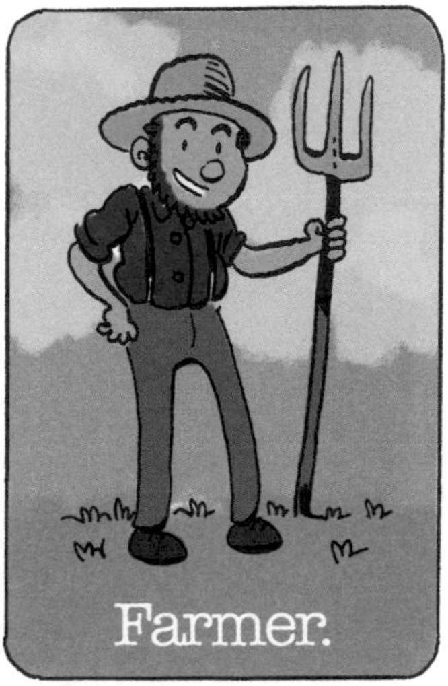
Farmer.

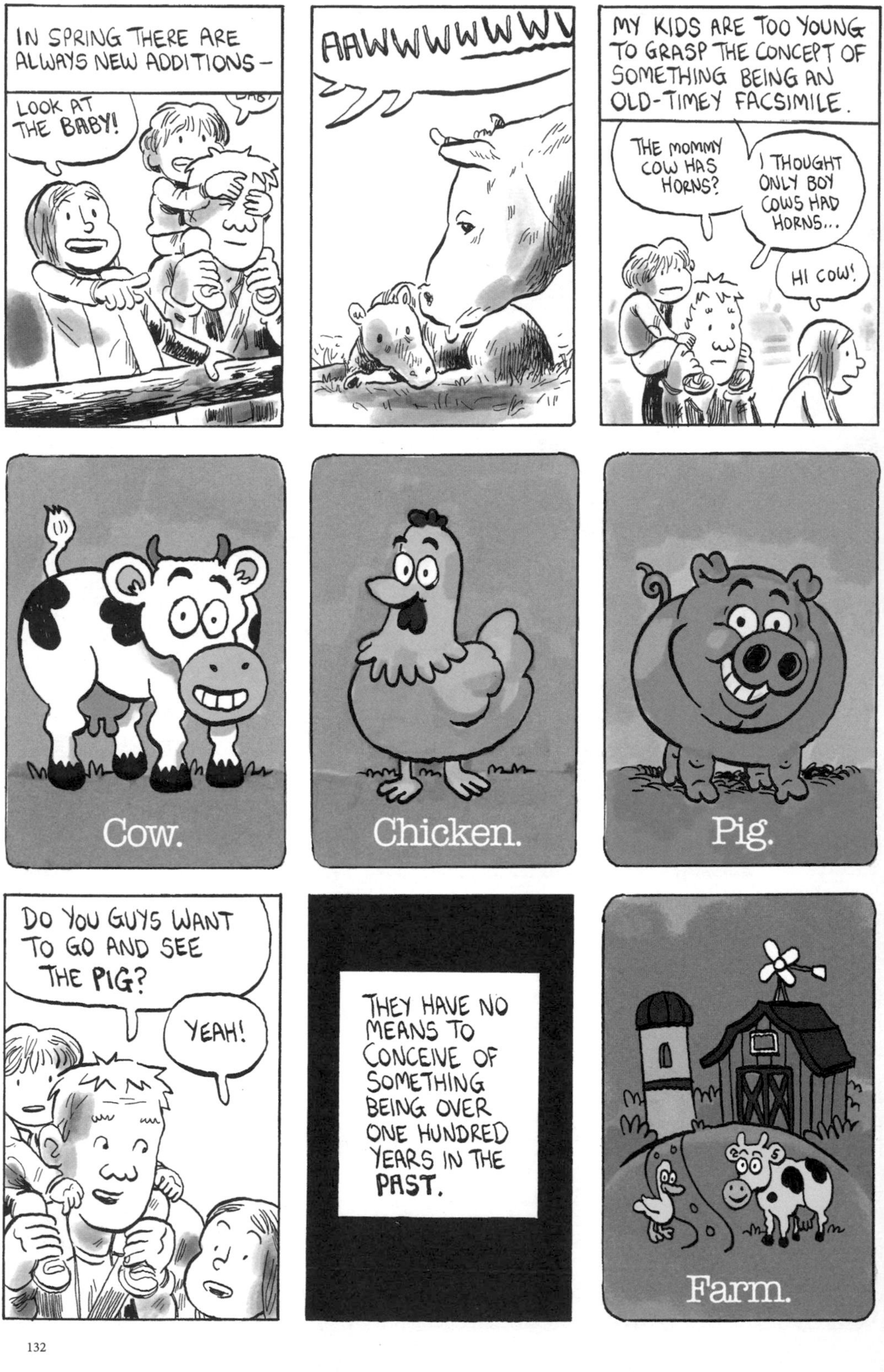

IN SPRING THERE ARE ALWAYS NEW ADDITIONS–
LOOK AT THE BABY!
AAWWWWWWW
MY KIDS ARE TOO YOUNG TO GRASP THE CONCEPT OF SOMETHING BEING AN OLD-TIMEY FACSIMILE.
THE MOMMY COW HAS HORNS?
I THOUGHT ONLY BOY COWS HAD HORNS...
HI COW!
Cow.
Chicken.
Pig.
DO YOU GUYS WANT TO GO AND SEE THE PIG?
YEAH!
THEY HAVE NO MEANS TO CONCEIVE OF SOMETHING BEING OVER ONE HUNDRED YEARS IN THE PAST.
Farm.

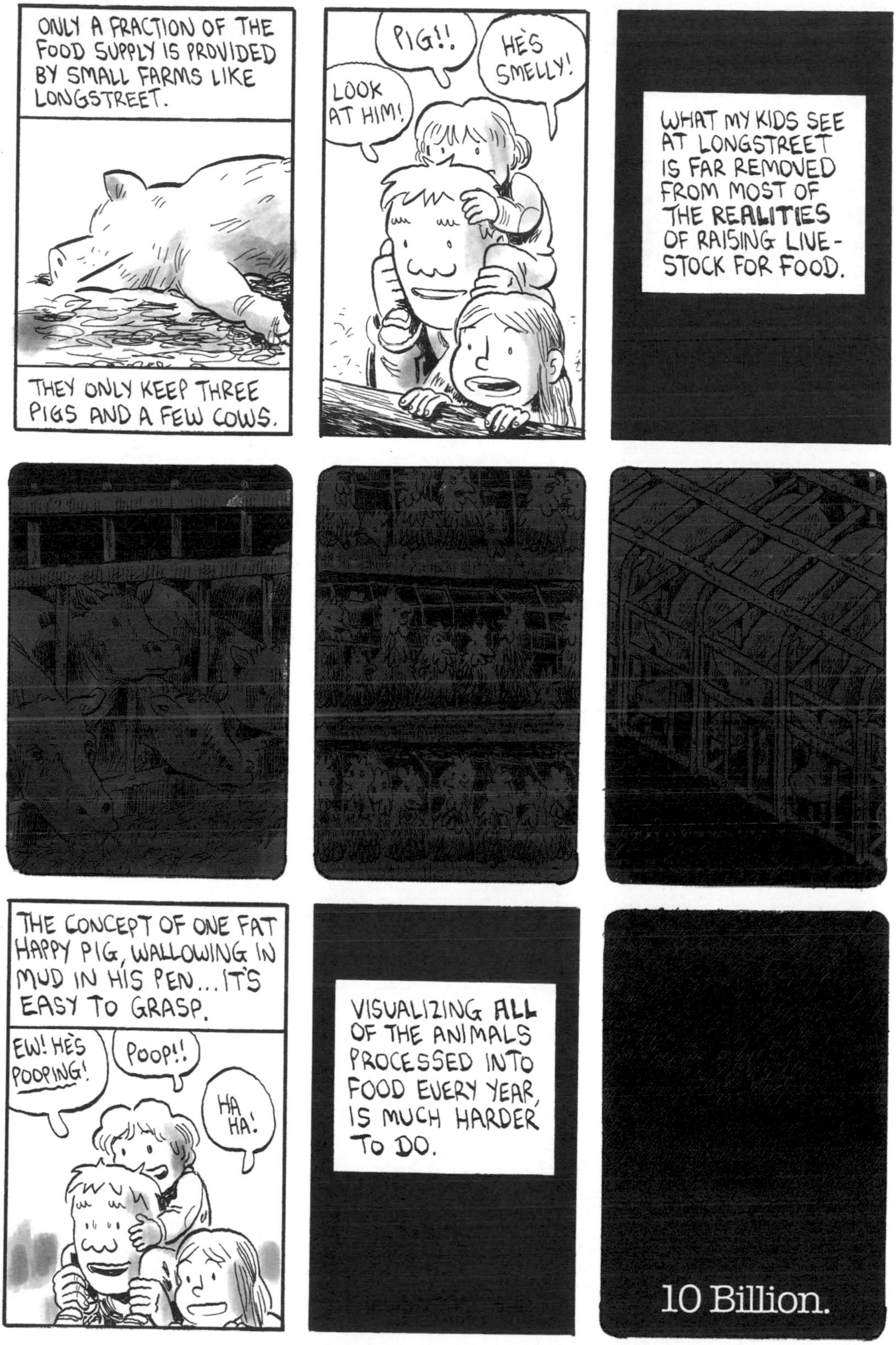
ONLY A FRACTION OF THE FOOD SUPPLY IS PROVIDED BY SMALL FARMS LIKE LONGSTREET.
THEY ONLY KEEP THREE PIGS AND A FEW COWS.
LOOK AT HIM!
PIG!!
HE'S SMELLY!
WHAT MY KIDS SEE AT LONGSTREET IS FAR REMOVED FROM MOST OF THE **REALITIES** OF RAISING LIVE-STOCK FOR FOOD.
THE CONCEPT OF ONE FAT HAPPY PIG, WALLOWING IN MUD IN HIS PEN... IT'S EASY TO GRASP.
EW! HE'S POOPING!
POOP!!
HA HA!
VISUALIZING **ALL** OF THE ANIMALS PROCESSED INTO FOOD EVERY YEAR, IS MUCH HARDER TO DO.
10 Billion.

BILLIONS OF SHORT AND BRUTAL LIVES.

PIGS THAT BECOME FOOD RARELY LIVE LONGER THAN THREE TO SIX MONTHS.

THEY SPEND THE ENTIRETY OF THEIR BRIEF LIVES CONFINED IN SMALL CAGES.

THEIR ONLY EXPERIENCE IS SUFFERING.

WHAT IS IT WE HAVE THAT MAKES **OUR** LIVES PRECIOUS?

WHAT MAKES **OUR** SUFFERING LEGITIMATE AND THEIRS NOT?

An Immortal Soul.

WE ARE SET **APART** FROM THE ANIMALS.

People.

THEY AREN'T LIVING **REAL** LIVES AS WE DO.

Animals.

God said, "Let us r
r THEY WERE PUT age,
a HERE FOR US. ess.
And let them have
dominion over the
of the sea and over
birds of the heaven
over the livestock
and over all the ea
and over every cre
thing that creeps o
the earth.

FOR OUR USE.

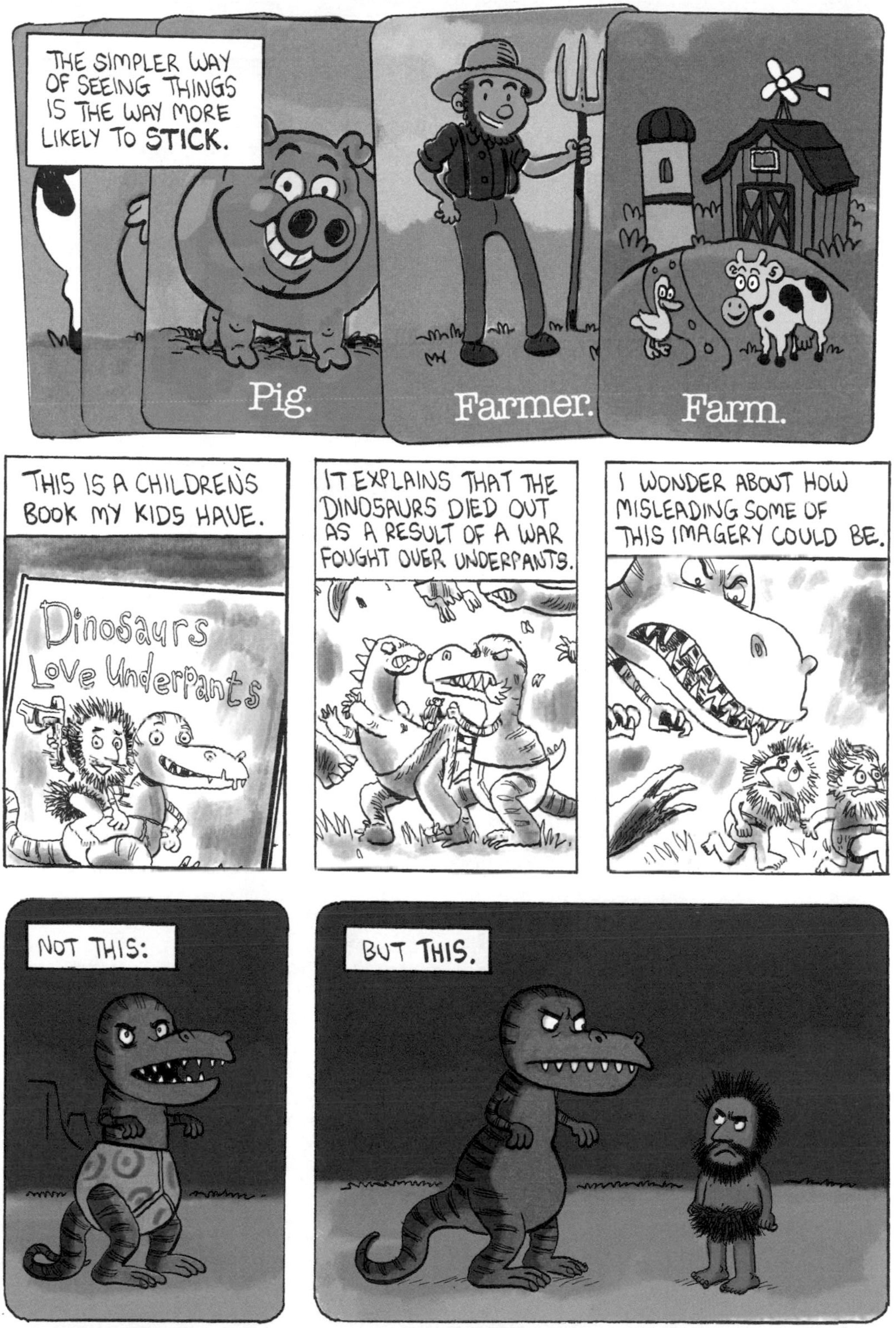
THE SIMPLER WAY OF SEEING THINGS IS THE WAY MORE LIKELY TO STICK.
Pig.
Farmer.
Farm.
THIS IS A CHILDREN'S BOOK MY KIDS HAVE.
Dinosaurs Love Underpants
IT EXPLAINS THAT THE DINOSAURS DIED OUT AS A RESULT OF A WAR FOUGHT OVER UNDERPANTS.
I WONDER ABOUT HOW MISLEADING SOME OF THIS IMAGERY COULD BE.
NOT THIS:
BUT THIS.

DINOSAURS AND HUMAN BEINGS DID NOT CO-EXIST.

AND WHILE I KNOW THIS—

AND CAN MENTALLY DISCONNECT THE TWO—

Dinosaur.

Human.

LIKE EVERYBODY—

Egypti...

Gree...

Roman...

Jesus

Middle Ages.

MY ABILITY TO CONSTRUCT A COMPLEX MENTAL BRIDGE OF HISTORY—

IMPROVES THE CLOSER THE PIECES ARE TO PRESENT DAY.

Revolutio...

Ci...

Worl...

Now.

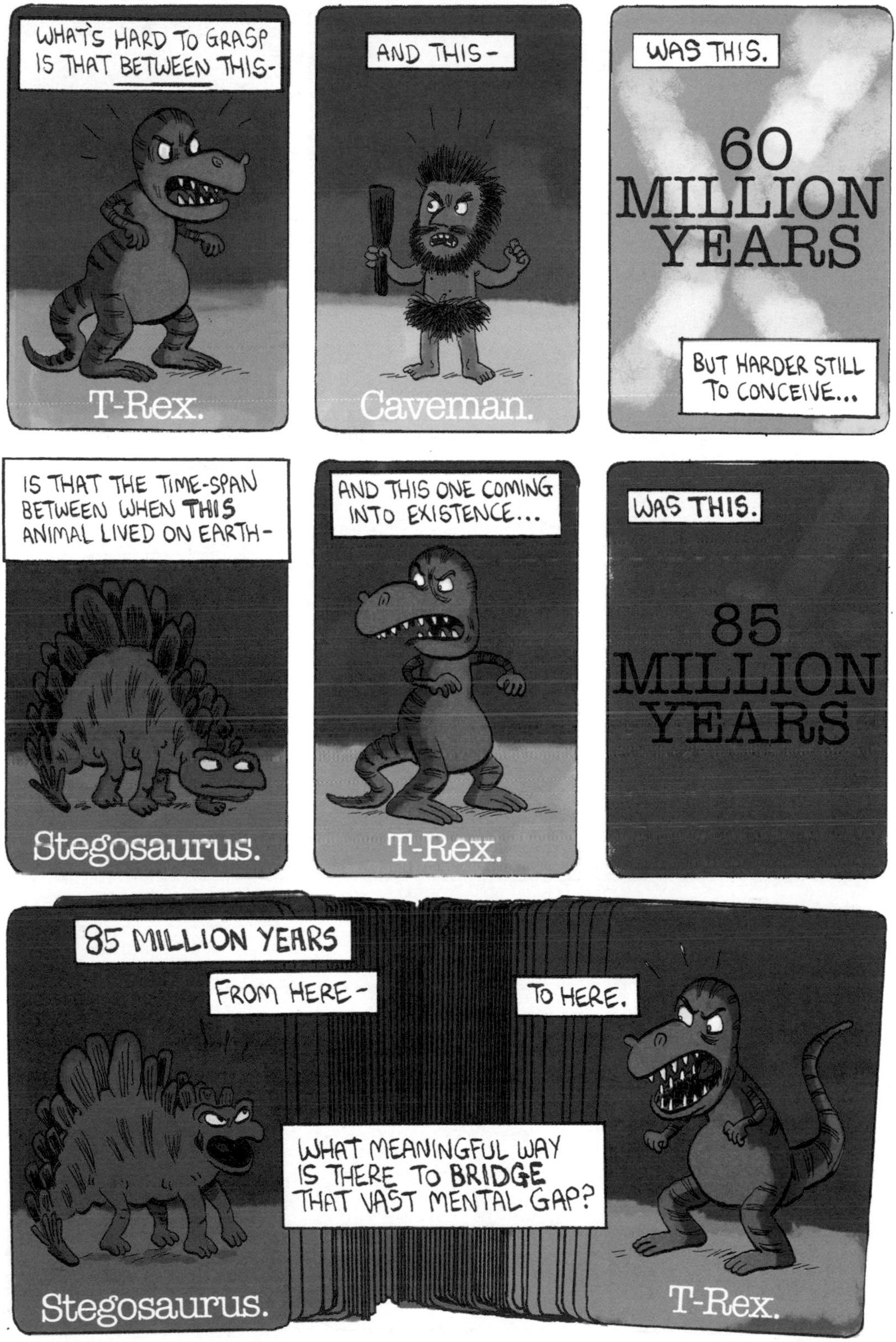
WHAT'S HARD TO GRASP IS THAT BETWEEN THIS-
T-Rex.
AND THIS-
Caveman.
WAS THIS.
60 MILLION YEARS
BUT HARDER STILL TO CONCEIVE...
IS THAT THE TIME-SPAN BETWEEN WHEN THIS ANIMAL LIVED ON EARTH-
Stegosaurus.
AND THIS ONE COMING INTO EXISTENCE...
T-Rex.
WAS THIS.
85 MILLION YEARS
85 MILLION YEARS
FROM HERE-
TO HERE.
Stegosaurus.
WHAT MEANINGFUL WAY IS THERE TO BRIDGE THAT VAST MENTAL GAP?
T-Rex.

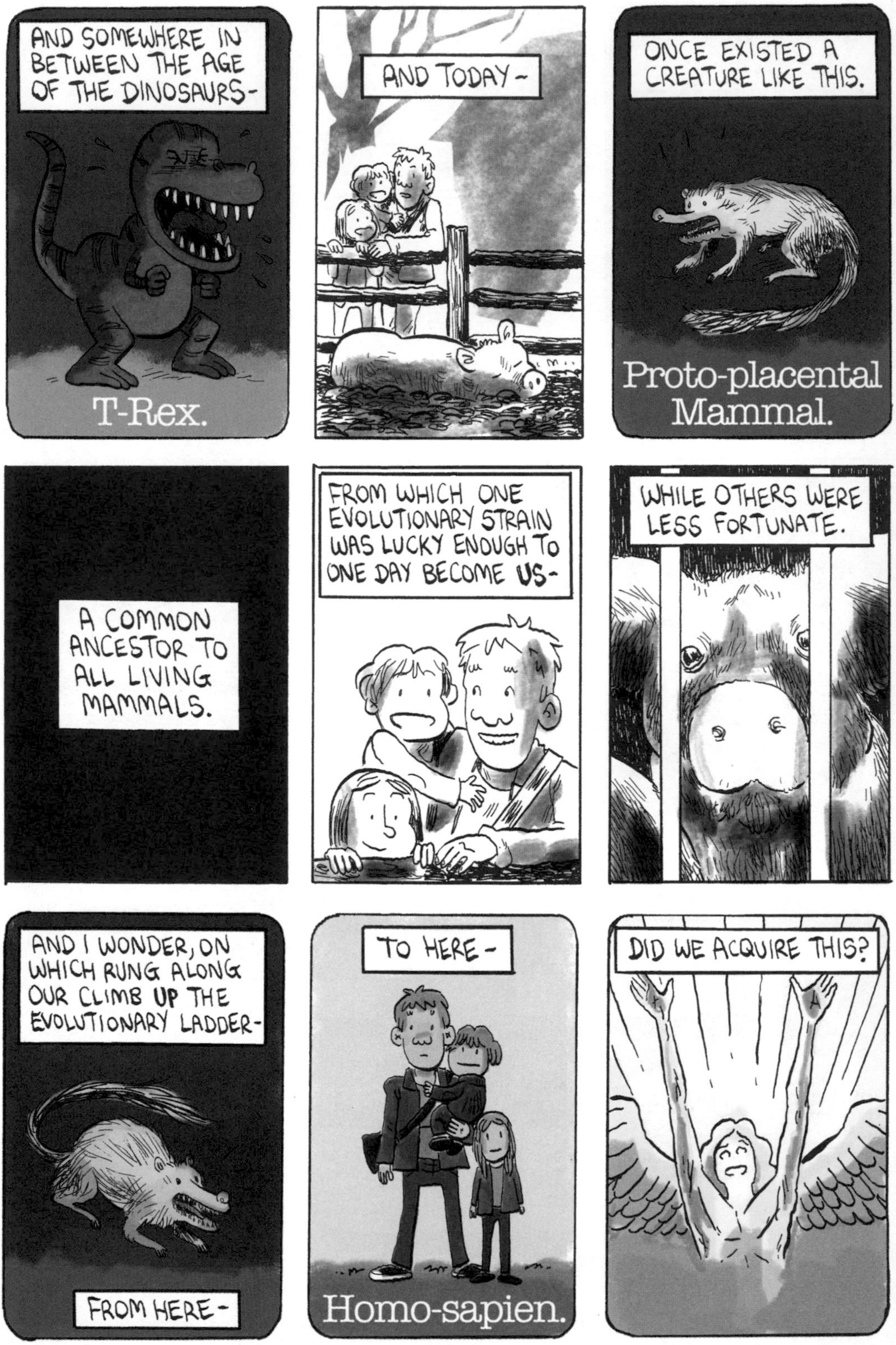
AND SOMEWHERE IN BETWEEN THE AGE OF THE DINOSAURS-
T-Rex.
AND TODAY-
ONCE EXISTED A CREATURE LIKE THIS.
Proto-placental Mammal.
A COMMON ANCESTOR TO ALL LIVING MAMMALS.
FROM WHICH ONE EVOLUTIONARY STRAIN WAS LUCKY ENOUGH TO ONE DAY BECOME US-
WHILE OTHERS WERE LESS FORTUNATE.
AND I WONDER, ON WHICH RUNG ALONG OUR CLIMB UP THE EVOLUTIONARY LADDER-
FROM HERE-
TO HERE-
Homo-sapien.
DID WE ACQUIRE THIS?

In the begin■ God created heavens and the earth.

And God sa Let us make man in our image, after our likeness

let them have dominion

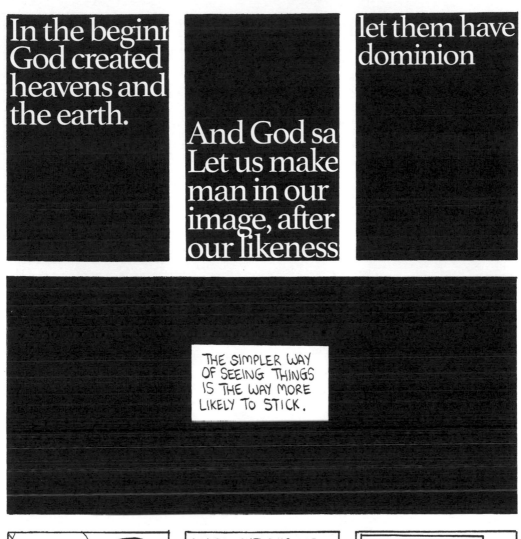

THE SIMPLER WAY OF SEEING THINGS IS THE WAY MORE LIKELY TO STICK.

CHICKIN'!!

HI CHICKEN!!

MY DAUGHTER IS OLD ENOUGH TO HAVE ASKED ME WHY IT'S OKAY FOR US TO EAT ANIMALS.

CAREFUL THEY DON'T PECK YOU!

AND I'VE TRIED TO EXPLAIN TO HER WHAT I THINK MAY BE TRUE:

THAT IT MIGHT **NOT** BE ALRIGHT.

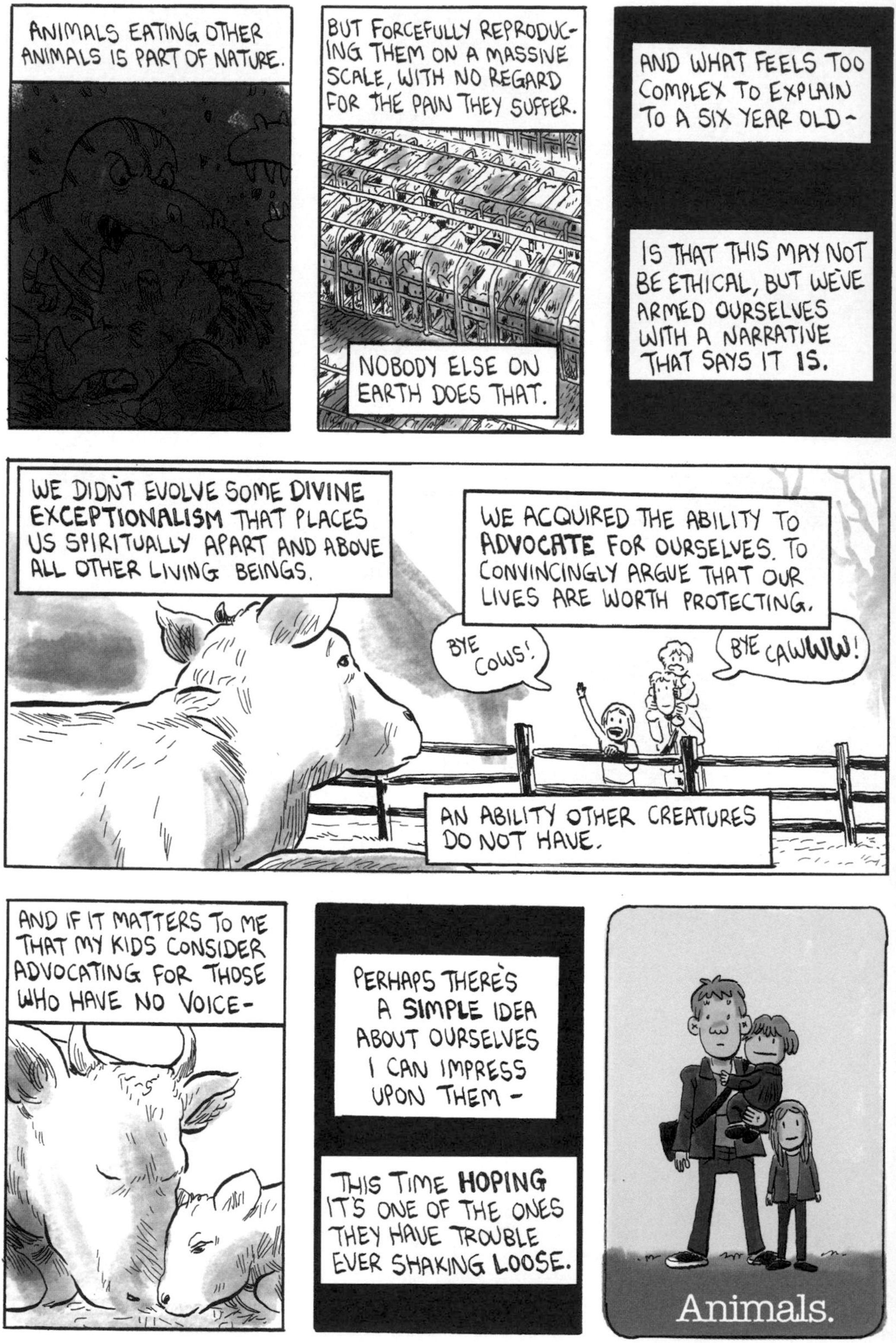
ANIMALS EATING OTHER ANIMALS IS PART OF NATURE.
BUT FORCEFULLY REPRODUCING THEM ON A MASSIVE SCALE, WITH NO REGARD FOR THE PAIN THEY SUFFER.
NOBODY ELSE ON EARTH DOES THAT.
AND WHAT FEELS TOO COMPLEX TO EXPLAIN TO A SIX YEAR OLD-
IS THAT THIS MAY NOT BE ETHICAL, BUT WE'VE ARMED OURSELVES WITH A NARRATIVE THAT SAYS IT **IS**.
WE DIDN'T EVOLVE SOME **DIVINE EXCEPTIONALISM** THAT PLACES US SPIRITUALLY APART AND ABOVE ALL OTHER LIVING BEINGS.
WE ACQUIRED THE ABILITY TO **ADVOCATE** FOR OURSELVES. TO CONVINCINGLY ARGUE THAT OUR LIVES ARE WORTH PROTECTING.
BYE COWS!
BYE CAWWW!
AN ABILITY OTHER CREATURES DO NOT HAVE.
AND IF IT MATTERS TO ME THAT MY KIDS CONSIDER ADVOCATING FOR THOSE WHO HAVE NO VOICE-
PERHAPS THERE'S A **SIMPLE** IDEA ABOUT OURSELVES I CAN IMPRESS UPON THEM-
THIS TIME **HOPING** IT'S ONE OF THE ONES THEY HAVE TROUBLE EVER SHAKING **LOOSE**.
Animals.

SUNDAY AUGUST 30TH 2015: MY SON ALWAYS WAKES UP FIRST AND THEN WAKES EVERYONE ELSE UP. MY DAUGHTER HAS BEEN GOING TO BED LATE AT NIGHT, SO SHE'S ALWAYS TIRED. THE KIDS ARE CRANKY - I CAN'T WAIT FOR SCHOOL TO START.

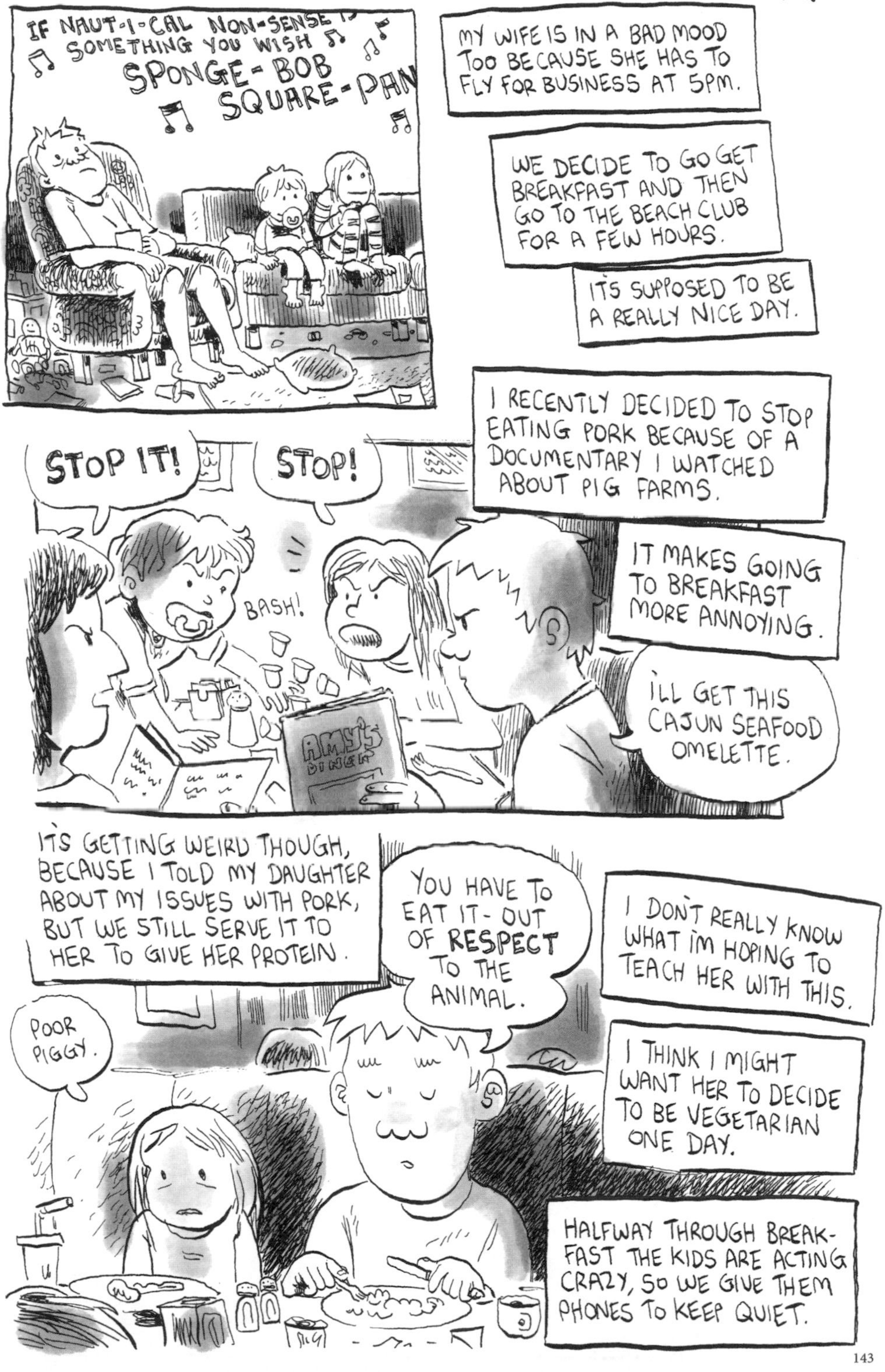

IF NAUT-I-CAL NON-SENSE IS SOMETHING YOU WISH
SPONGE-BOB SQUARE-PAN
MY WIFE IS IN A BAD MOOD TOO BECAUSE SHE HAS TO FLY FOR BUSINESS AT 5PM.
WE DECIDE TO GO GET BREAKFAST AND THEN GO TO THE BEACH CLUB FOR A FEW HOURS.
IT'S SUPPOSED TO BE A REALLY NICE DAY.
I RECENTLY DECIDED TO STOP EATING PORK BECAUSE OF A DOCUMENTARY I WATCHED ABOUT PIG FARMS.
STOP IT!
STOP!
IT MAKES GOING TO BREAKFAST MORE ANNOYING.
BASH!
I'LL GET THIS CAJUN SEAFOOD OMELETTE.
AMY'S DINER
IT'S GETTING WEIRD THOUGH, BECAUSE I TOLD MY DAUGHTER ABOUT MY ISSUES WITH PORK, BUT WE STILL SERVE IT TO HER TO GIVE HER PROTEIN.
YOU HAVE TO EAT IT - OUT OF RESPECT TO THE ANIMAL.
I DON'T REALLY KNOW WHAT I'M HOPING TO TEACH HER WITH THIS.
POOR PIGGY.
I THINK I MIGHT WANT HER TO DECIDE TO BE VEGETARIAN ONE DAY.
HALFWAY THROUGH BREAK-FAST THE KIDS ARE ACTING CRAZY, SO WE GIVE THEM PHONES TO KEEP QUIET.

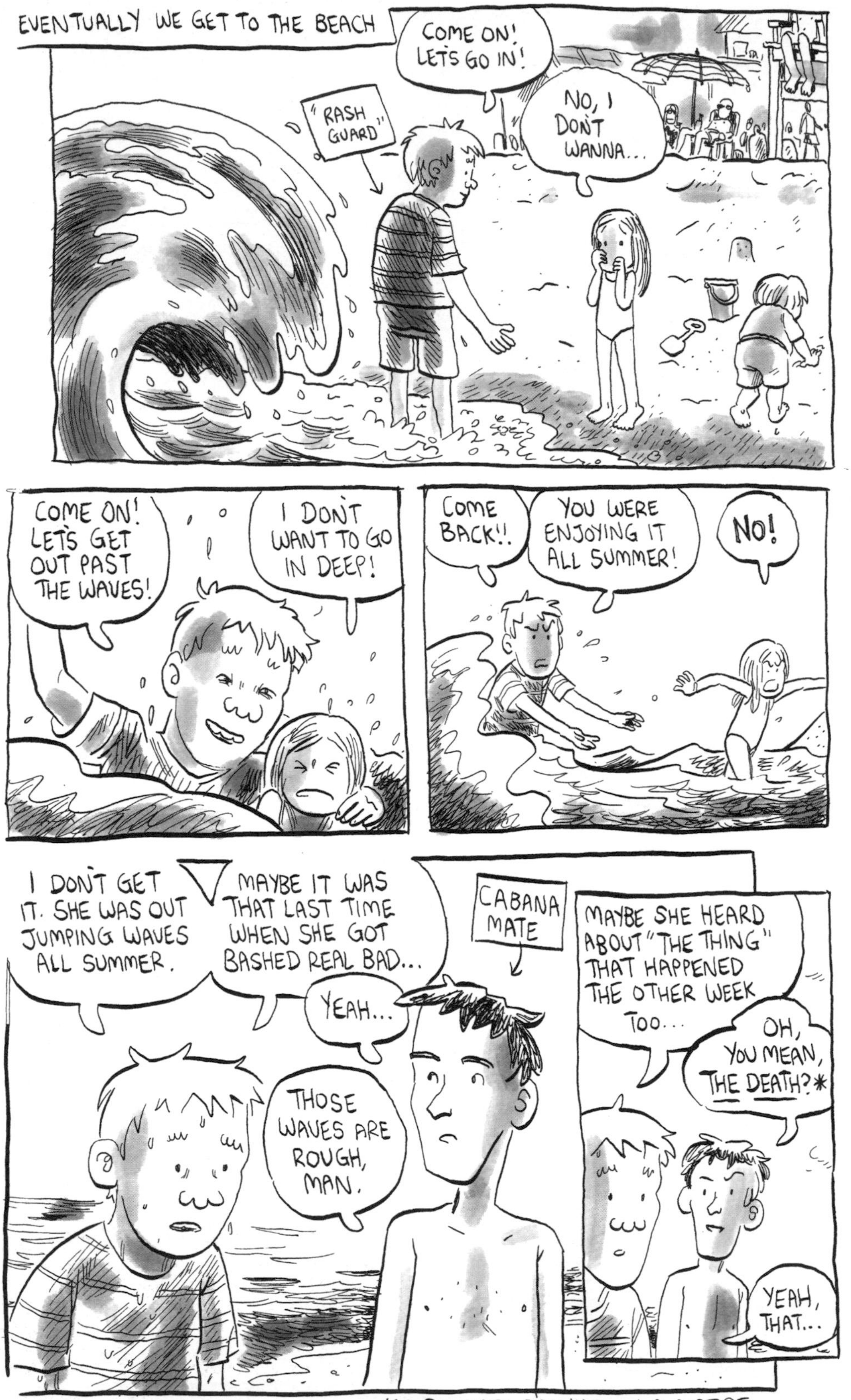
EVENTUALLY WE GET TO THE BEACH
COME ON! LET'S GO IN!
NO, I DON'T WANNA...
"RASH GUARD"
COME ON! LET'S GET OUT PAST THE WAVES!
I DON'T WANT TO GO IN DEEP!
COME BACK!!
YOU WERE ENJOYING IT ALL SUMMER!
NO!
I DON'T GET IT. SHE WAS OUT JUMPING WAVES ALL SUMMER.
MAYBE IT WAS THAT LAST TIME WHEN SHE GOT BASHED REAL BAD...
YEAH...
CABANA MATE
THOSE WAVES ARE ROUGH, MAN.
MAYBE SHE HEARD ABOUT "THE THING" THAT HAPPENED THE OTHER WEEK TOO...
OH, YOU MEAN, THE DEATH?*
YEAH, THAT...
*A SWIMMER DROWNED IN A RIPTIDE

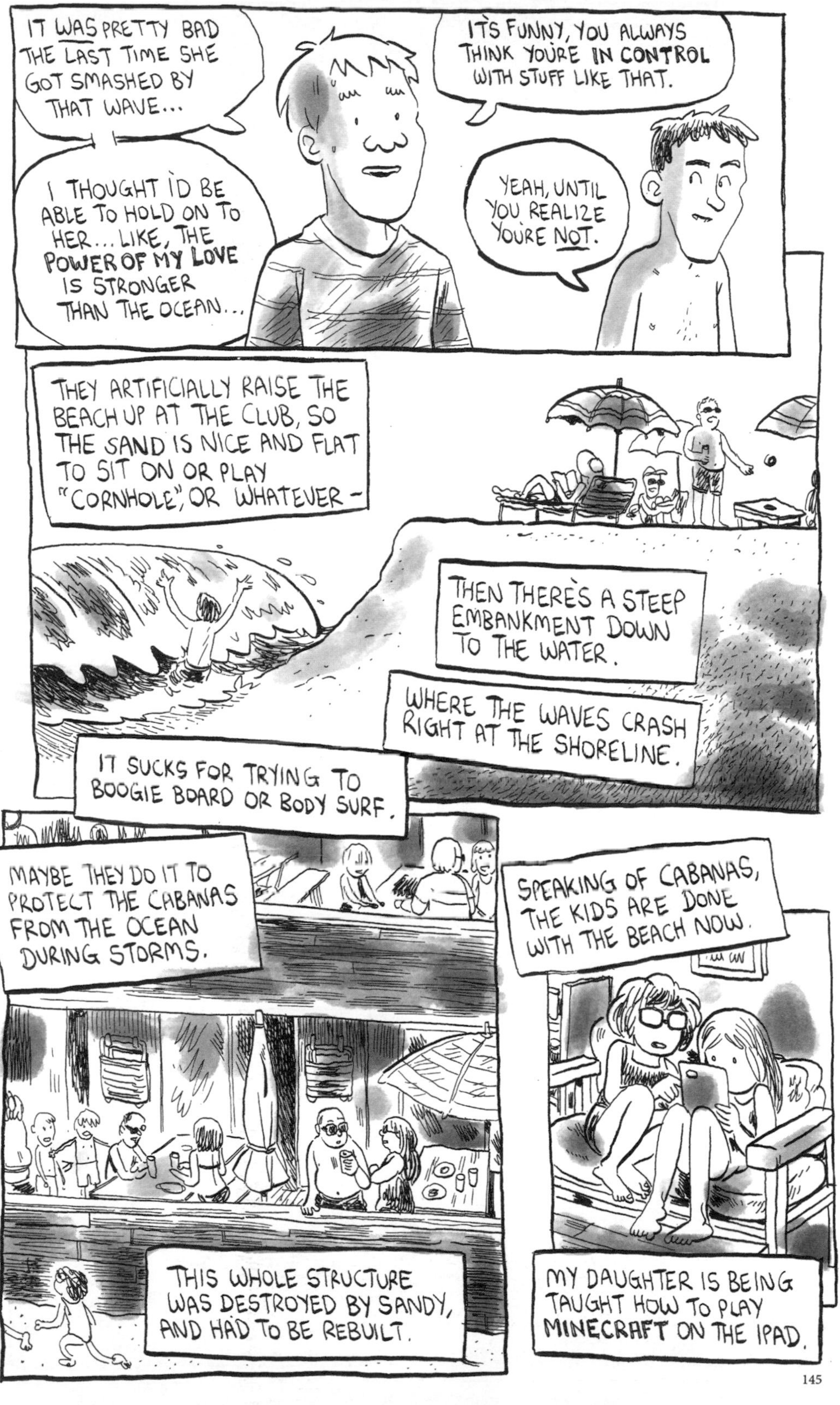
IT WAS PRETTY BAD THE LAST TIME SHE GOT SMASHED BY THAT WAVE...
I THOUGHT I'D BE ABLE TO HOLD ON TO HER... LIKE, THE POWER OF MY LOVE IS STRONGER THAN THE OCEAN...
IT'S FUNNY, YOU ALWAYS THINK YOU'RE IN CONTROL WITH STUFF LIKE THAT.
YEAH, UNTIL YOU REALIZE YOU'RE NOT.
THEY ARTIFICIALLY RAISE THE BEACH UP AT THE CLUB, SO THE SAND IS NICE AND FLAT TO SIT ON OR PLAY "CORNHOLE", OR WHATEVER -
THEN THERE'S A STEEP EMBANKMENT DOWN TO THE WATER.
WHERE THE WAVES CRASH RIGHT AT THE SHORELINE.
IT SUCKS FOR TRYING TO BOOGIE BOARD OR BODY SURF.
MAYBE THEY DO IT TO PROTECT THE CABANAS FROM THE OCEAN DURING STORMS.
THIS WHOLE STRUCTURE WAS DESTROYED BY SANDY, AND HAD TO BE REBUILT.
SPEAKING OF CABANAS, THE KIDS ARE DONE WITH THE BEACH NOW.
MY DAUGHTER IS BEING TAUGHT HOW TO PLAY MINECRAFT ON THE IPAD.

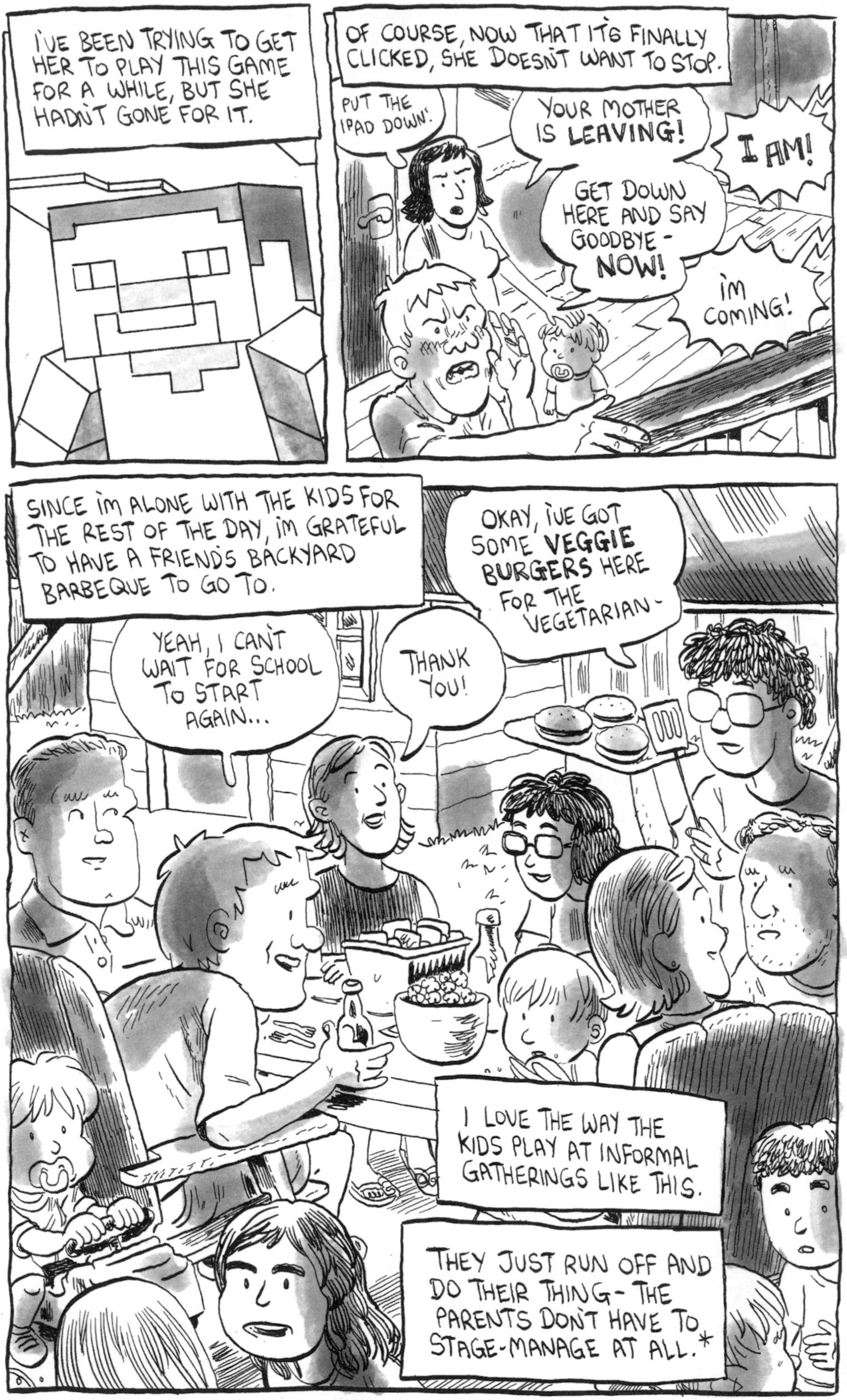
I'VE BEEN TRYING TO GET HER TO PLAY THIS GAME FOR A WHILE, BUT SHE HADN'T GONE FOR IT.
OF COURSE, NOW THAT IT'S FINALLY CLICKED, SHE DOESN'T WANT TO STOP.
PUT THE IPAD DOWN!
YOUR MOTHER IS LEAVING!
I AM!
GET DOWN HERE AND SAY GOODBYE - NOW!
I'M COMING!
SINCE I'M ALONE WITH THE KIDS FOR THE REST OF THE DAY, I'M GRATEFUL TO HAVE A FRIEND'S BACKYARD BARBEQUE TO GO TO.
OKAY, I'VE GOT SOME VEGGIE BURGERS HERE FOR THE VEGETARIAN -
YEAH, I CAN'T WAIT FOR SCHOOL TO START AGAIN...
THANK YOU!
I LOVE THE WAY THE KIDS PLAY AT INFORMAL GATHERINGS LIKE THIS.
THEY JUST RUN OFF AND DO THEIR THING - THE PARENTS DON'T HAVE TO STAGE-MANAGE AT ALL.*

*WELL, EXCEPT WHEN SOMEONE IS "TELLING"

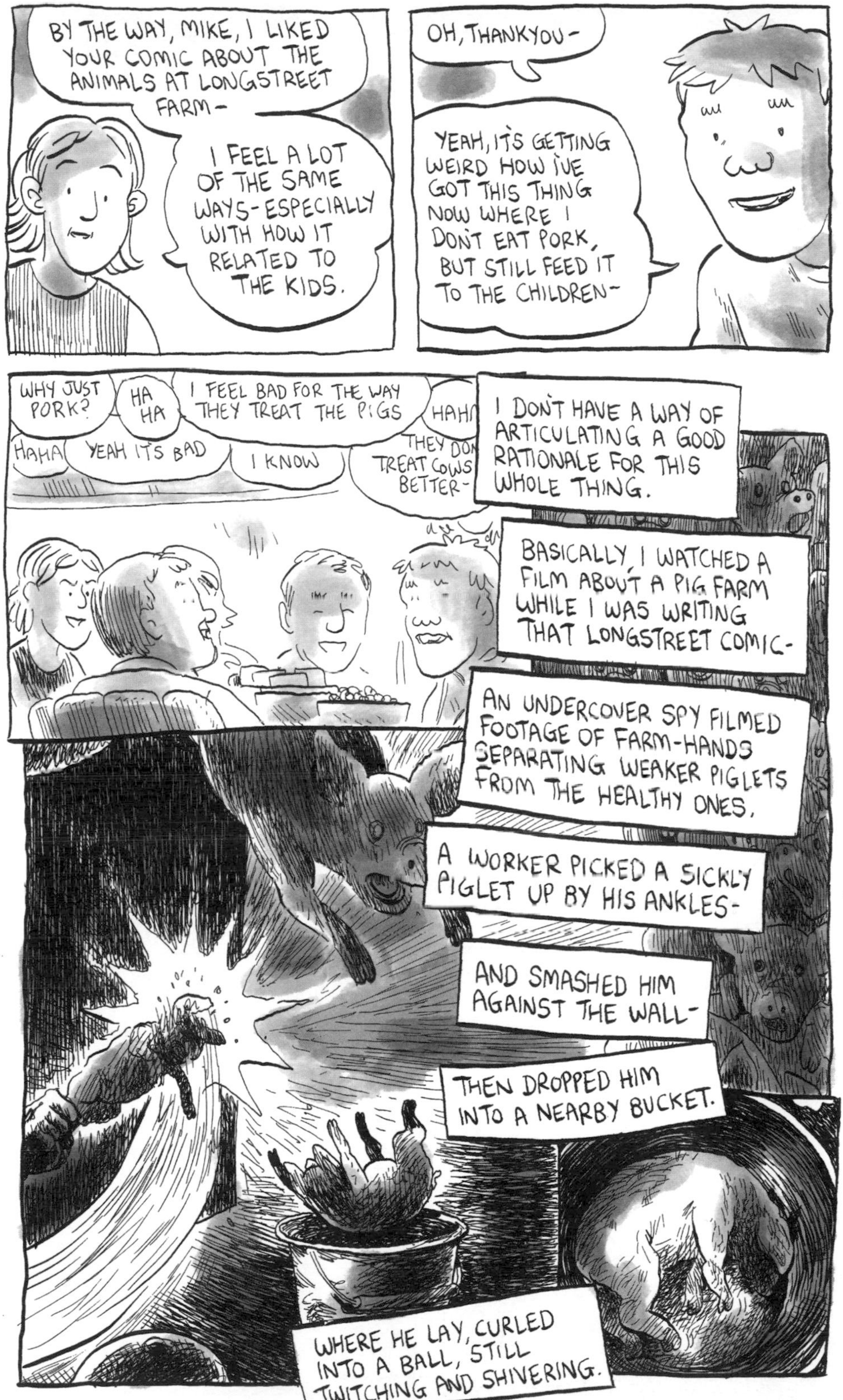
BY THE WAY, MIKE, I LIKED YOUR COMIC ABOUT THE ANIMALS AT LONGSTREET FARM-
I FEEL A LOT OF THE SAME WAYS- ESPECIALLY WITH HOW IT RELATED TO THE KIDS.
OH, THANKYOU-
YEAH, IT'S GETTING WEIRD HOW I'VE GOT THIS THING NOW WHERE I DON'T EAT PORK, BUT STILL FEED IT TO THE CHILDREN-
WHY JUST PORK?
HA HA
I FEEL BAD FOR THE WAY THEY TREAT THE PIGS
HAHA
YEAH IT'S BAD
I KNOW
THEY DON'T TREAT COWS BETTER-
I DON'T HAVE A WAY OF ARTICULATING A GOOD RATIONALE FOR THIS WHOLE THING.
BASICALLY, I WATCHED A FILM ABOUT A PIG FARM WHILE I WAS WRITING THAT LONGSTREET COMIC-
AN UNDERCOVER SPY FILMED FOOTAGE OF FARM-HANDS SEPARATING WEAKER PIGLETS FROM THE HEALTHY ONES.
A WORKER PICKED A SICKLY PIGLET UP BY HIS ANKLES-
AND SMASHED HIM AGAINST THE WALL-
THEN DROPPED HIM INTO A NEARBY BUCKET.
WHERE HE LAY, CURLED INTO A BALL, STILL TWITCHING AND SHIVERING.

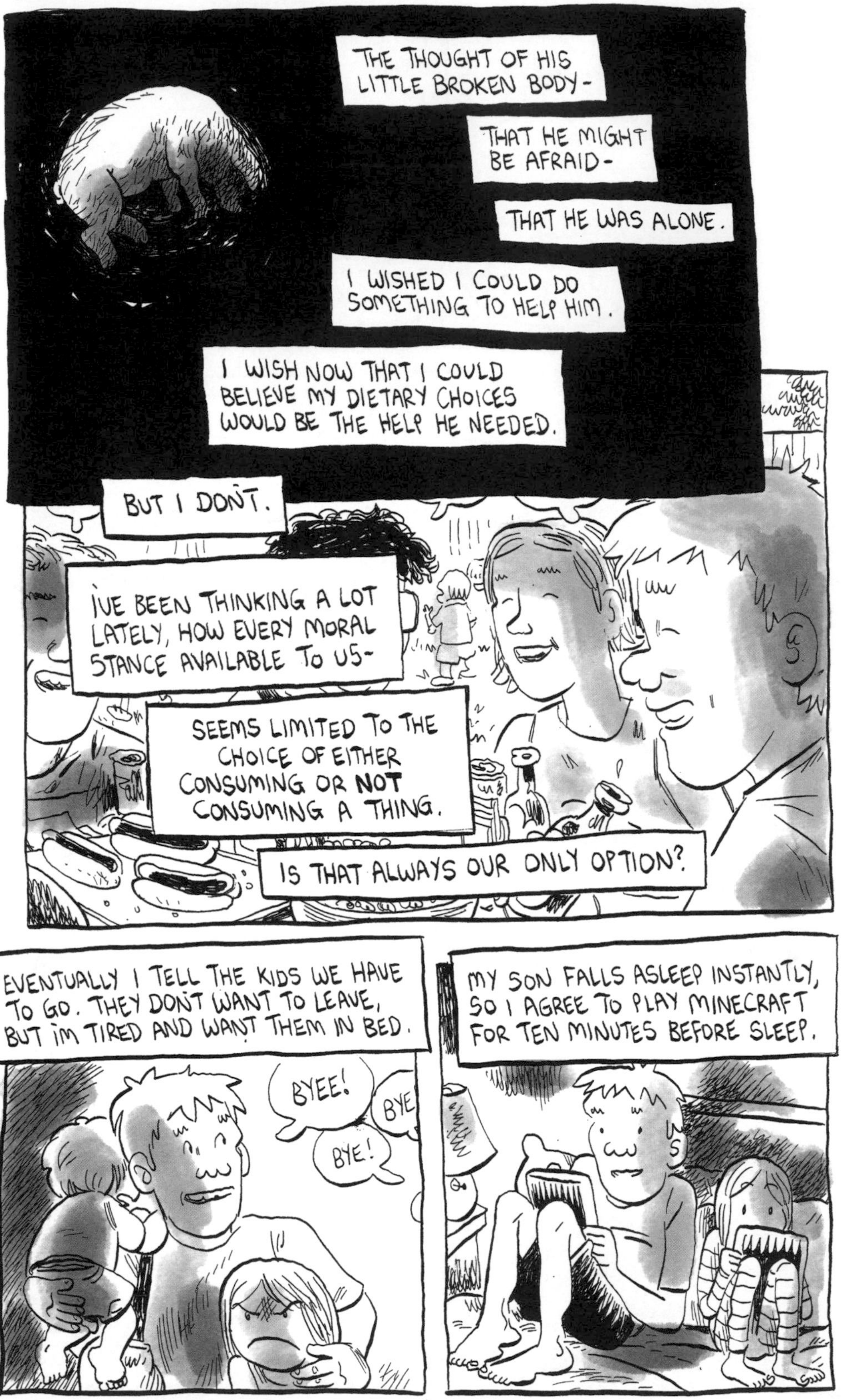
THE THOUGHT OF HIS LITTLE BROKEN BODY-
THAT HE MIGHT BE AFRAID-
THAT HE WAS ALONE.
I WISHED I COULD DO SOMETHING TO HELP HIM.
I WISH NOW THAT I COULD BELIEVE MY DIETARY CHOICES WOULD BE THE HELP HE NEEDED.
BUT I DON'T.
I'VE BEEN THINKING A LOT LATELY, HOW EVERY MORAL STANCE AVAILABLE TO US-
SEEMS LIMITED TO THE CHOICE OF EITHER CONSUMING OR **NOT** CONSUMING A THING.
IS THAT ALWAYS OUR ONLY OPTION?
EVENTUALLY I TELL THE KIDS WE HAVE TO GO. THEY DON'T WANT TO LEAVE, BUT I'M TIRED AND WANT THEM IN BED.
BYEE!
BYE
BYE!
MY SON FALLS ASLEEP INSTANTLY, SO I AGREE TO PLAY MINECRAFT FOR TEN MINUTES BEFORE SLEEP.

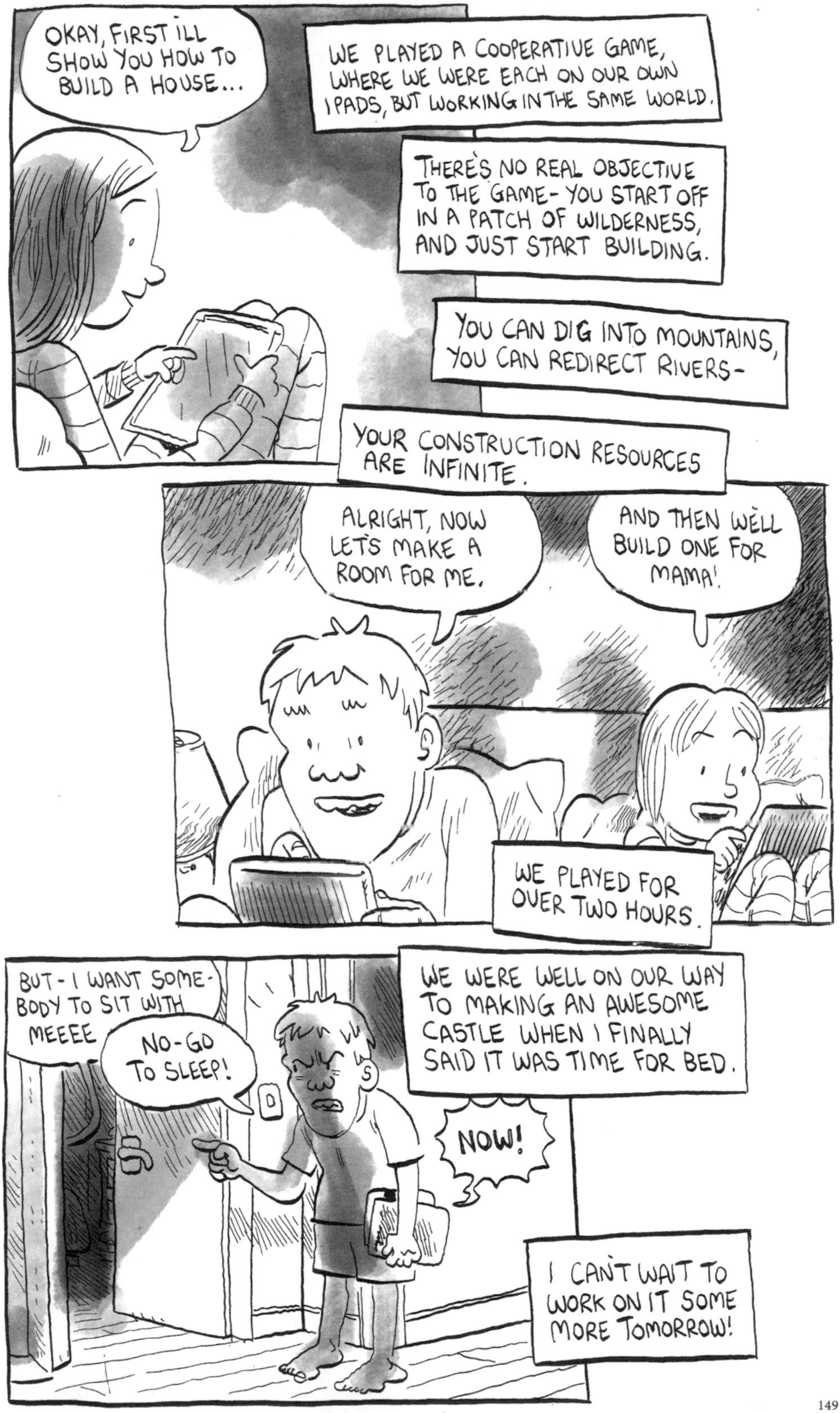

OKAY, FIRST ILL SHOW YOU HOW TO BUILD A HOUSE...
WE PLAYED A COOPERATIVE GAME, WHERE WE WERE EACH ON OUR OWN IPADS, BUT WORKING IN THE SAME WORLD.
THERE'S NO REAL OBJECTIVE TO THE GAME- YOU START OFF IN A PATCH OF WILDERNESS, AND JUST START BUILDING.
YOU CAN DIG INTO MOUNTAINS, YOU CAN REDIRECT RIVERS-
YOUR CONSTRUCTION RESOURCES ARE INFINITE.
ALRIGHT, NOW LET'S MAKE A ROOM FOR ME.
AND THEN WE'LL BUILD ONE FOR MAMA!
WE PLAYED FOR OVER TWO HOURS.
WE WERE WELL ON OUR WAY TO MAKING AN AWESOME CASTLE WHEN I FINALLY SAID IT WAS TIME FOR BED.
BUT- I WANT SOME-BODY TO SIT WITH MEEEE
NO- GO TO SLEEP!
NOW!
I CAN'T WAIT TO WORK ON IT SOME MORE TOMORROW!

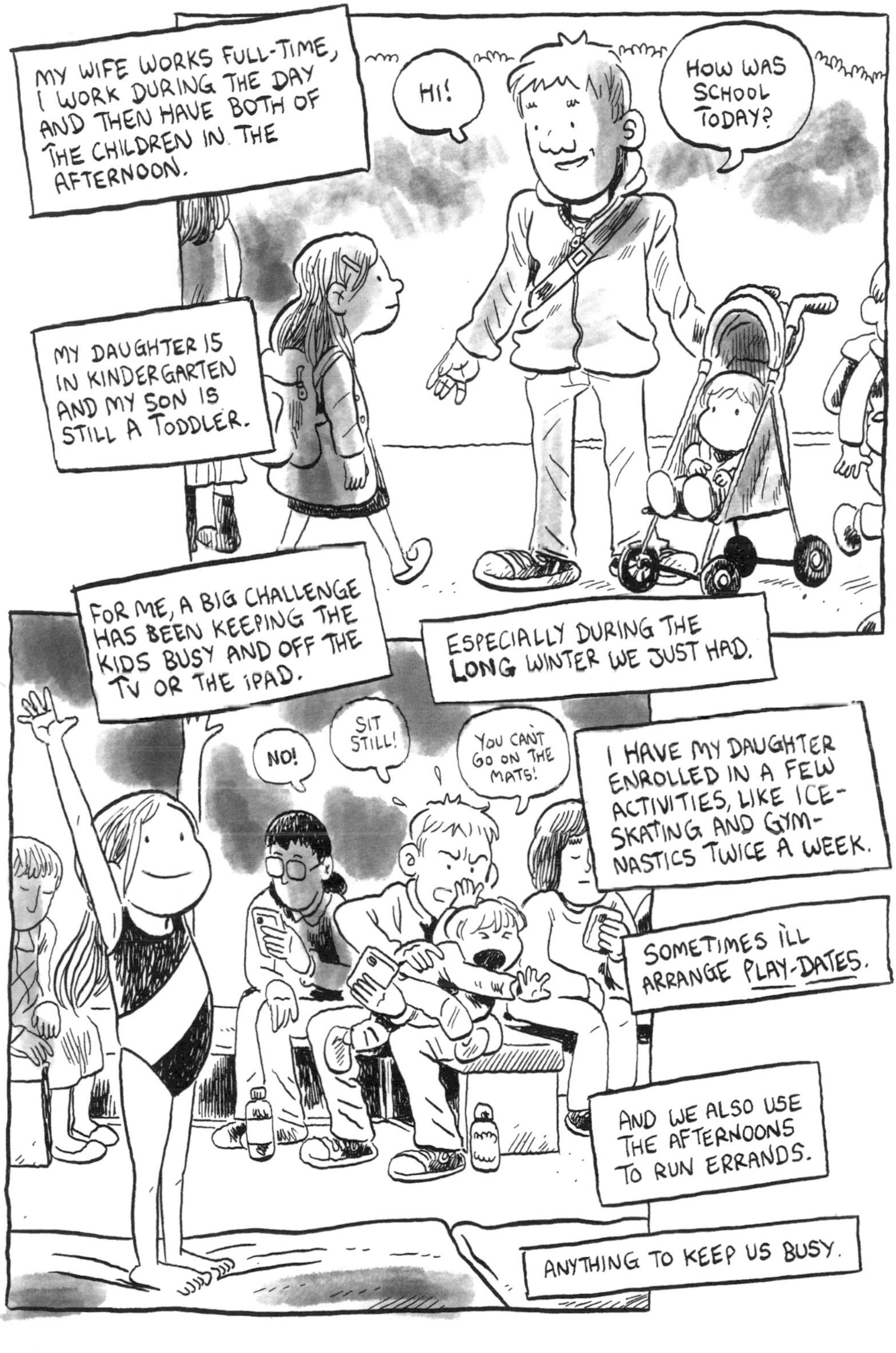
MY WIFE WORKS FULL-TIME, I WORK DURING THE DAY AND THEN HAVE BOTH OF THE CHILDREN IN THE AFTERNOON.
HI!
HOW WAS SCHOOL TODAY?
MY DAUGHTER IS IN KINDERGARTEN AND MY SON IS STILL A TODDLER.
FOR ME, A BIG CHALLENGE HAS BEEN KEEPING THE KIDS BUSY AND OFF THE TV OR THE iPAD.
ESPECIALLY DURING THE LONG WINTER WE JUST HAD.
NO!
SIT STILL!
YOU CAN'T GO ON THE MATS!
I HAVE MY DAUGHTER ENROLLED IN A FEW ACTIVITIES, LIKE ICE-SKATING AND GYM-NASTICS TWICE A WEEK.
SOMETIMES I'LL ARRANGE PLAY-DATES.
AND WE ALSO USE THE AFTERNOONS TO RUN ERRANDS.
ANYTHING TO KEEP US BUSY.

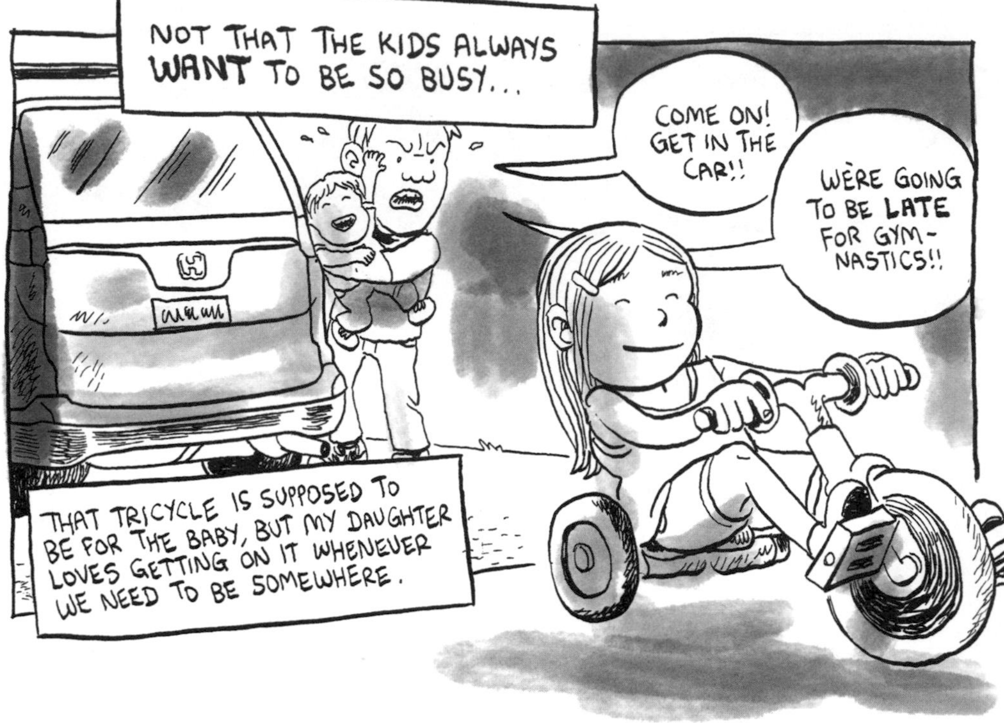
NOT THAT THE KIDS ALWAYS **WANT** TO BE SO BUSY...
COME ON! GET IN THE CAR!!
WE'RE GOING TO BE **LATE** FOR GYM-NASTICS!!
THAT TRICYCLE IS SUPPOSED TO BE FOR THE BABY, BUT MY DAUGHTER LOVES GETTING ON IT WHENEVER WE NEED TO BE SOMEWHERE.

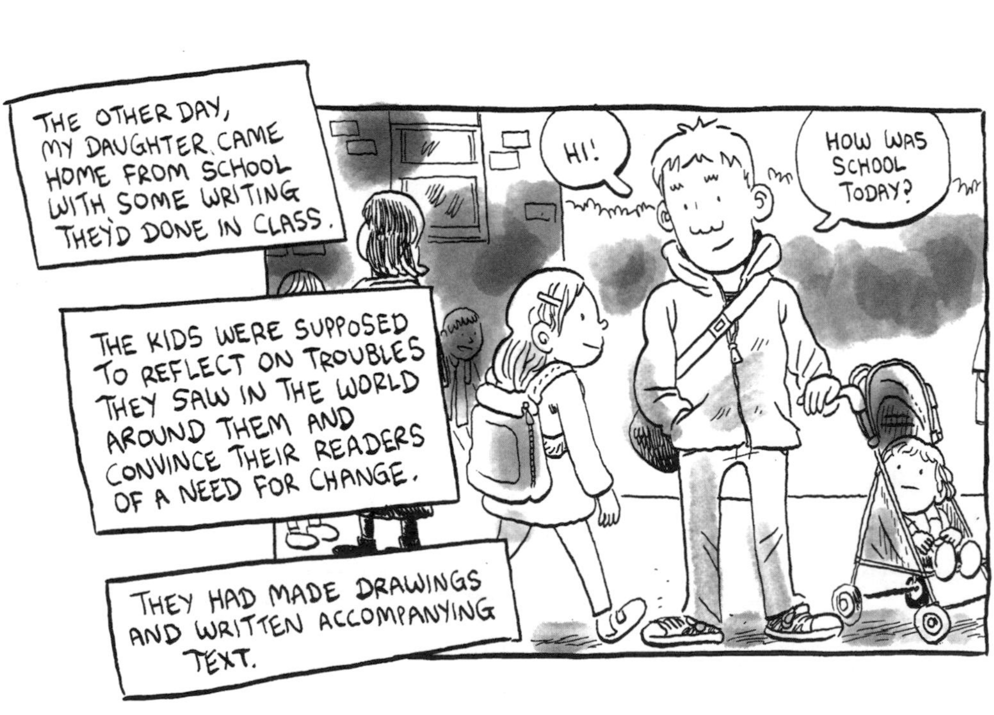
THE OTHER DAY, MY DAUGHTER CAME HOME FROM SCHOOL WITH SOME WRITING THEY'D DONE IN CLASS.
HI!
HOW WAS SCHOOL TODAY?
THE KIDS WERE SUPPOSED TO REFLECT ON TROUBLES THEY SAW IN THE WORLD AROUND THEM AND CONVINCE THEIR READERS OF A NEED FOR CHANGE.
THEY HAD MADE DRAWINGS AND WRITTEN ACCOMPANYING TEXT.

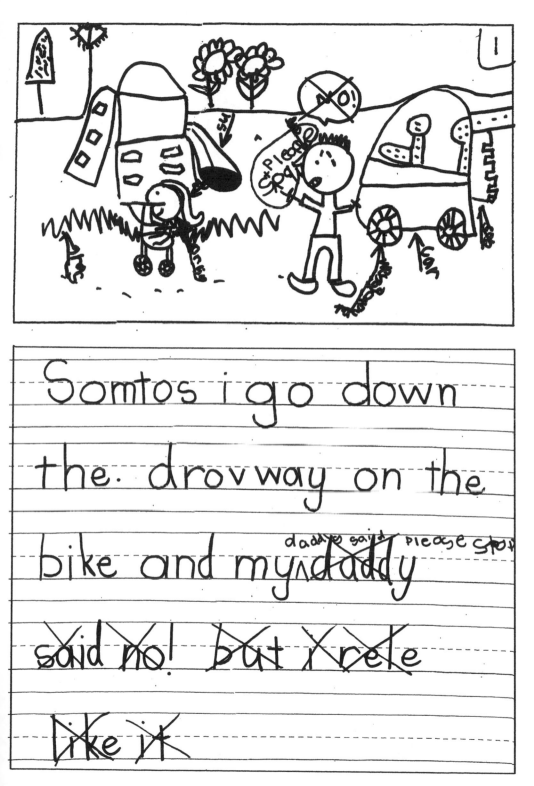

Somtos i go down
the. drovway on the
bike and my daddy daddy said please stop
said no! but i rele
like it

then he gets
me off because
we ned to go somwar
and somtoms he
sais no! but he
rele sh say
please stop

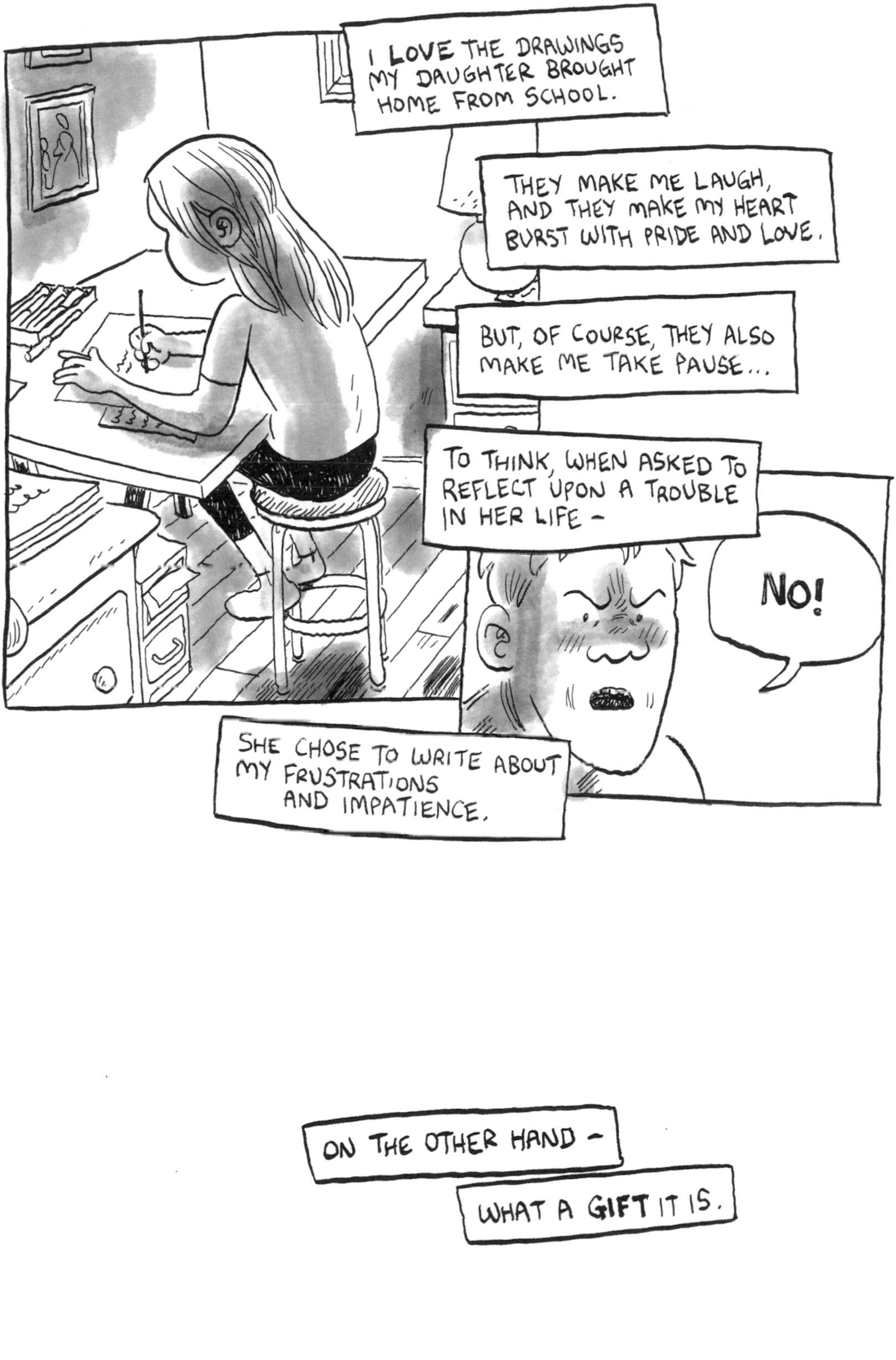
I LOVE THE DRAWINGS MY DAUGHTER BROUGHT HOME FROM SCHOOL.
THEY MAKE ME LAUGH, AND THEY MAKE MY HEART BURST WITH PRIDE AND LOVE.
BUT, OF COURSE, THEY ALSO MAKE ME TAKE PAUSE...
TO THINK, WHEN ASKED TO REFLECT UPON A TROUBLE IN HER LIFE -
NO!
SHE CHOSE TO WRITE ABOUT MY FRUSTRATIONS AND IMPATIENCE.
ON THE OTHER HAND -
WHAT A GIFT IT IS.

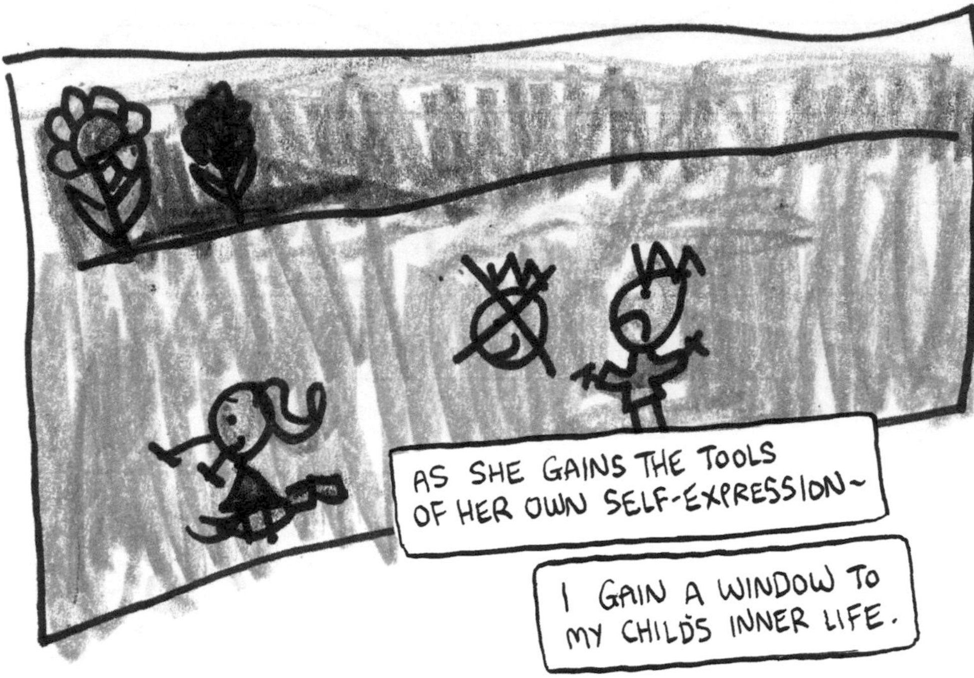
AS SHE GAINS THE TOOLS OF HER OWN SELF-EXPRESSION~
I GAIN A WINDOW TO MY CHILD'S INNER LIFE.

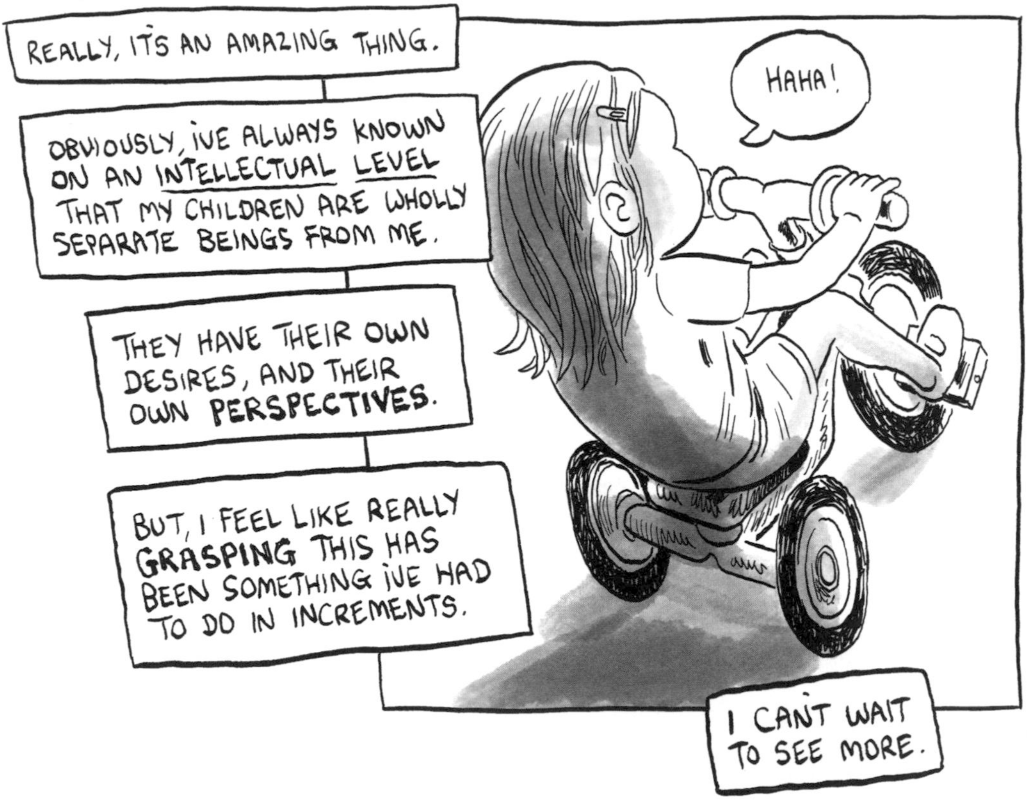
REALLY, IT'S AN AMAZING THING.
OBVIOUSLY, I'VE ALWAYS KNOWN ON AN INTELLECTUAL LEVEL THAT MY CHILDREN ARE WHOLLY SEPARATE BEINGS FROM ME.
THEY HAVE THEIR OWN DESIRES, AND THEIR OWN PERSPECTIVES.
BUT, I FEEL LIKE REALLY GRASPING THIS HAS BEEN SOMETHING I'VE HAD TO DO IN INCREMENTS.
HAHA!
I CAN'T WAIT TO SEE MORE.

AM I GOOD?

For Aliza, without whom there'd be none of this.

....

Thank you to my family, Alex R. Tony C. Josh C. Brendan L. Gary, Rob, Ted, Kym, Jennifer, Michael, Jess, Kal, Chrissy, Eric and Bree.

....

Special thanks and gratitude to Matt Bors, Eleri Harris, Dan Kois, Allison Benedikt, Tom Kaczynski, Serge Ewenczyk, Jordan Shiveley, Jamie Tanner, Heidi MacDonald, Keith Knight, Lisa Hanawalt, Julia Wertz, my fellow Olds, and everybody who supported the production of this project through Kickstarter.

....

Love to Orli and Ewan.

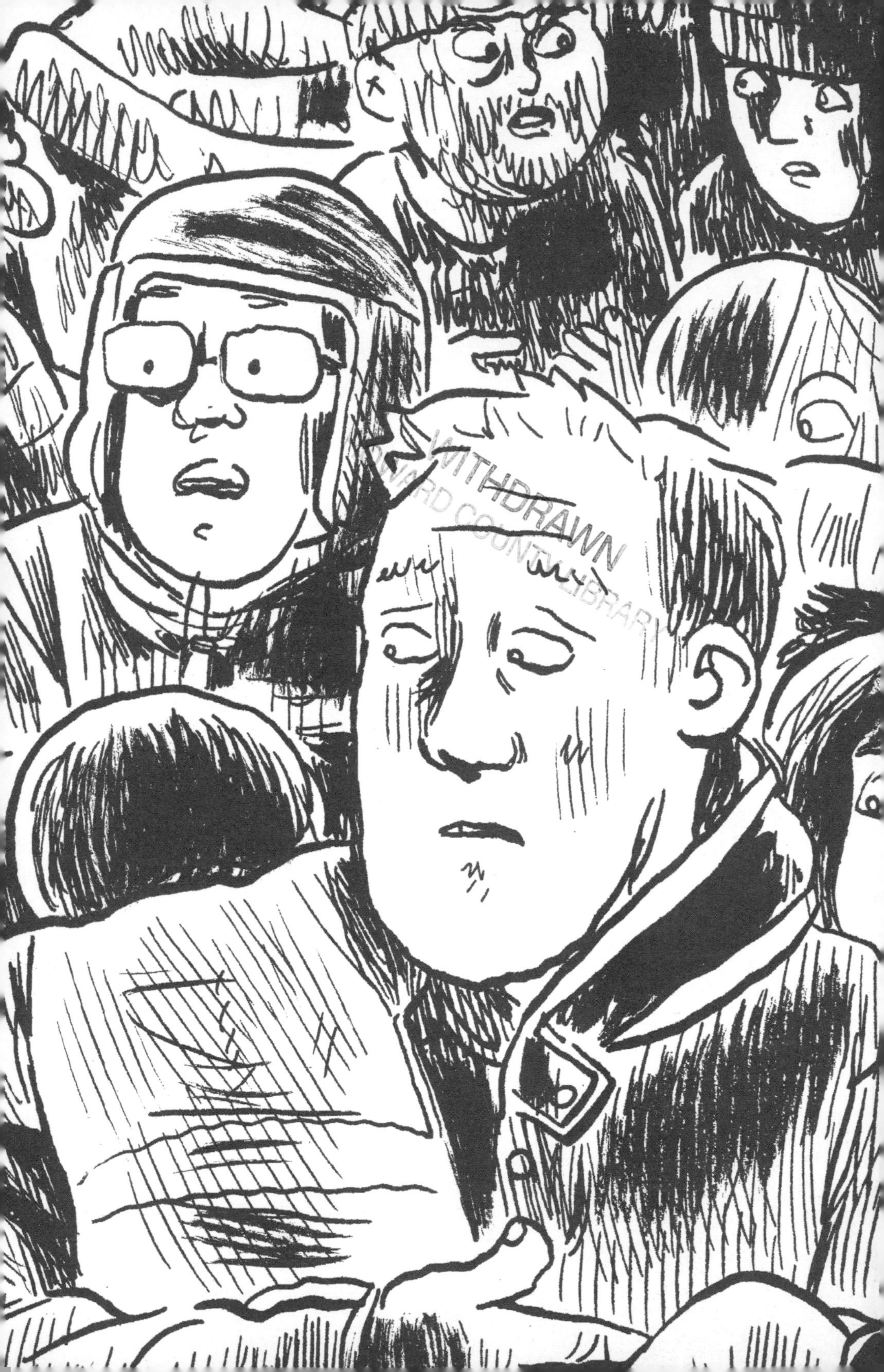